"If We Had the Word"
Ingeborg Bachmann. Views and Reviews

Studies in Austrian Literature, Culture and Thought

General Editors:

Jorun B. Johns
Richard H. Lawson

"If We Had the Word"
Ingeborg Bachmann. Views and Reviews

Edited by Gisela Brinker-Gabler
and Markus Zisselsberger

ARIADNE PRESS
Riverside, California

Ariadne Press would like to express its appreciation to the Deutsche Akademische Austauschdienst (DAAD) for assistance in publishing this book.

Library of Congress Cataloging-in-Publication Data

If we had the word : Ingeborg Bachmann, views and reviews / edited by Gisela Brinker-Gabler and Markus Zisselsberger.
     p.   cm. -- (Studies in Austrian literature, culture and thought)
Includes bibliographical references and index.
ISBN 1-57241-130-9
   1. Bachmann, Ingeborg, 1926-1973--Criticism and interpretation. I. Brinker-Gabler, Gisela. II. Zisselsberger, Markus. III. Series.

PT2603.A147Z6487 2004
838'.91409--dc22

2004057445

Cover Design:
Art Director, Designer: George McGinnis
Photograph courtesy of Dr. Heinz Bachmann

Copyright ©2004
by Ariadne Press
270 Goins Court
Riverside, CA 92507

All rights reserved.
No part of this publication may be reproduced or transmitted in any form or by any means without formal permission.
Printed in the United States of America.
ISBN 1-57241-130-9 (original trade paperback)

Contents

"If We Had the Word":
Inventing Language for the Memories Within
Foreword by *Gisela Brinker-Gabler*   1

Ingeborg Bachmann: To Die for Berlin
Translated by *Lilian Friedberg*   7

Part I. On Lyrics and Language

1 / The Music of the Unspoken
Peter Filkins   18

2 / Bachmann's Allegorical Lyrics and the
Subversion of History
Frederick Garber   33

3 / "Pont Mirabeau ... Waterloo Bridge ...":
A Contrastive Reading of Apollinaire's "Le Pont
Mirabeau" and Ingeborg Bachmann's "Die Brücken"
Sabine Gölz   47

4 / To Live with an Instinctive Resistance to
Language: Bachmann on Wittgenstein
Barbara Agnese   93

Part II. *Todesarten*

5 / Ingeborg Bachmann's "Eyes to Wonder":
Towards a Structural Interpretation
Robert Pichl   115

6 / "A man, a woman . . .":
Narrative Perspective and Gender Discourse in
Ingeborg Bachmann's *Malina*
Monika Albrecht 127

7 / *Senza Pedale*: Metaphors of Female Silence in *Malina*
Karen Achberger 150

8 / "It was murder": Who Framed *Malina*?
Ingeborg Majer-O'Sickey 170

9 / Living and Lost in Language: Translation and
Interpretation in Ingeborg Bachmann's "Simultan"
Gisela Brinker-Gabler 187

10 / The Woman Who Rode Away:
Postcoloniality and Gender in "Three Paths to the Lake"
Sara Lennox 208

Part III. Remembrance and History

11 / The Significance of Remembrance as a
Motif and Structural Dimension in the Work of
Ingeborg Bachmann
Andrea Stoll 221

12 / "Beneath the Rubble":
Correspondences in the Writing of
Ingeborg Bachmann and Inge Müller
Karen Remmler 241

13 / "Every name in history is I":
Bachmann's Anti-Archive
Michael Eng   262

Contributors   285

Index   287

Acknowledgments

The idea for this anthology grew out of a symposium on the occasion of the 70th birthday of the poet, philosopher and writer Ingeborg Bachmann. Organized by Gisela Brinker-Gabler at Binghamton University, the symposium brought together scholars from Europe and the United States to explore the transnational actuality, historical dimensions and contexts of Bachmann's work; it provided an inspiring forum for debate and exchange among the growing community of international Bachmann scholars, critics and translators about her work, the vitality and centrality of the issues addressed in her writings, and it has stimulated networking as well as collaborative projects on the work of this major modern Austrian writer.

The symposium was made possible through generous grants from the DAAD, New York (German Academic Exchange Service) and the ACI, New York (Austrian Culture Institute). Special thanks go to Heidrun Suhr, then Deputy Director of the DAAD, and to Peter Mikl, then Deputy Director of the ACI, for their encouragement and unqualified commitment to support the symposium. Thanks go also to their conscientious staff, especially to Barbara Motyka, Senior Program Officer of the DAAD, New York. Gratefully acknowledged is also the support by the Research Foundation of Binghamton University, the Harper's College Distinguished Speaker Fund, and by the Provost and Vice President of Academic Affairs at Binghamton University, Mary Ann Swain. For their commitment, kindness, and contributions to the event, we extend our gratitude to many respected colleagues and faculty members at Binghamton University. Special thanks for support in preparing and managing the symposium go to the student assistants Amy Burtner, Jutta Gsöls, Joseph Lewandowski, and Amy Wieber, also to Carol Less and Nancy Rounds of the Department of Comparative Literature, to William McClure and Debbie Collett-O'Brien of the Continuing Education and Summer Program, and to Kai Brinker for his assistance and steadfast good spirit during the conference.

We extend our special gratitude to Jorun Johns, the editor of Ariadne Press, who responded eagerly to the idea of this collection of Bachmann essays in English and provided immense encouragement throughout the production process. We also like to convey our appreciation to the readers of the manuscript for their assiduous attention. And we owe thanks to the DAAD for its continuous support of this project by granting a publication subsidy. A word of grateful acknowledgement belongs to the students of three graduate seminars on Ingeborg Bachmann at Binghamton University, who with their earnest curiosity, responsiveness and superb work provided continuous support and the incentive to building bridges between cultures with the work of Ingeborg Bachmann. And last but not least we truly are indebted to all the contributors to our anthology for their enthusiasm, cooperation and patience with this project.

Permissions

"To Die for Berlin" was originally published in German [Sterben für Berlin] in: Ingeborg Bachmann, *Todesarten-Projekt*, vol. 1, ed. Robert Pichl, Monika Albrecht und Dirk Göttsche, copyright Piper Verlag, München 1995, translated and published with permission; an earlier version of chapter 12, "Beneath the Rubble": Correspondences in the Writing of Ingeborg Bachmann and Inge Müller," appeared in German in *"Über die Zeit schreiben." Literatur- und kulturwissenschaftliche Essays zu Ingeborg Bachmanns 'Todesarten'-Projekt*, ed. Monika Albrecht und Dirk Göttsche, copyright Königshausen & Neumann, Würzburg 1998, with permission.

"If We Had the Word":
Inventing Language for the Memories Within

Foreword by Gisela Brinker-Gabler

In a famous poem by Silvia Plath "Lady Lazarus" proclaims, "Dying / Is an art. Like everything else / I do it exceptionally well." It is not surprising that these lines come to mind when one thinks about the art and craft of Ingeborg Bachmann today. Oppressive silence, on an individual or collective level, is a way of dying. Searching for "living words" that burst open unbearable silence carries the risk of dying and failure, too. Bachmann believed in the attendance to silence. For her it meant searching for words radiant of despair and redemption. Such words hold the power of flashing revelations of some kind of truth, the potential of genuine care.

Bachmann, the Austrian poet and one of the greatest writers of the 20th century, became famous in the 1950s, when she was celebrated as young poetess, a unique voice, her striking face appearing on the title page of *Der Spiegel* in 1954, Germany's number-one newsmagazine, a space reserved every week for public men. She drew attention to herself everywhere she went, although she was not a "performer" but more of a shy person. One of the remarkable events in her early career, and already a true acknowledgment of her grandeur, was Theodor W. Adorno's invitation in 1959 for her to be the first poet presenting the newly launched "Frankfurt Lectures on Poetry" in Germany. The images of this event, which was filmed for television in black and white, specifically live strongly in my mind, although there is much more film material of her available. During her lifetime, she may well have been the most photographed and filmed woman poet in German-speaking Europe. Comparable to the intensity of the images from the Frankfurt Lecture to me are only the images of a television documentary by Gerda Haller produced in Rome in June 1973, the year Ingeborg Bachmann was to die in October because of a fire in her Rome apartment. There was much speculation about her death, as there was earlier about her life, and, most sadly, there were cynical remarks. In this last TV production Ingeborg Bachmann is often seen strolling through the streets of Rome, the place where she settled for good later in her life. The persuasive power of these images seems to me their promise to provide a glimpse of something that is essential about her and her life.

Ingeborg Bachmann belongs to the modern poet wanderers, to use a phrase by George Steiner, who are unhoused in language, and as I would like to add, unhoused otherwise, because of gender, trauma and fascism. Her estrangement manifests itself lucidly in a poem she wrote in 1957 entitled "Exile." What at a first glance evokes an exilic situation based on language, reveals other facets when we notice that the reference is precisely to the *German* language as a cloud surrounding the exile's head, and that the lyric not yet allows her to replace the commonly gender neutral "he" with a gender specific "she." Already here the stage is set, so to speak, the stage for risking, who one is and for the arts of dying.

Born in Klagenfurt in 1926, Ingeborg Bachmann had the traumatic experience of German Nazi troops marching through this Austrian city in the year of the *Anschluss* in 1938, and of years of life under fascistic rule. Later, after studying philosophy at the University of Vienna and receiving her Doctor of Philosophy degree in 1949 with her dissertation on "The Critical Reception of the Existential Philosophy of Martin Heidegger," and subsequent work at a Vienna radio station she left Austria for good in 1953. She lived first in Rome, Italy, and various other places, traveled widely, and finally settled in Rome in 1965.

Two poetry collections, published in 1953, *Die Gestundete Zeit (Borrowed Time)*, and in 1956, *Anrufung des Grossen Bären (Invocation of the Great Bear)*, established Bachmann's aura. Her poems give voice to a specific mode of cautious "embarking" in the early postwar years, and then, only a few years later, with the intensity of a final reminder, her poems alert the reader to the "high noon" of the cold war and of the task to come to terms with the past. After loosing her trust in lyrical poetry, a move she announced in one of her later poems entitled "No Delicacies" [Keine Delikatessen] Bachmann published her first short-story collection in 1961, *The Thirtieth Year (Das dreißigste Jahr)*. Her stories evoke the experiences of her generation, most of all the enormity of the burden to live after the Holocaust and the permanence of silence affecting every aspect of life and all relationships. The critical reception of this prose collection was at best mixed. Apparently, critics and audience alike were not ready for these provocative flashes of the obvious and to let go of the "poet Bachmann." That was even more true when in 1971 Bachmann's first novel *Malina* was published, which in fact is the overture to a planned cycle to be entitled *Ways of Dying* (Todesarten). Two other parts of this cycle *The Book of Franza* (*Das Buch Franza*) and *Requiem for Fanny Goldmann* (*Requiem für Fanny Goldmann*), which Bachmann left unfinished, were published after her death in a collection of her works edited by her two Rome friends Christine Koschel and Inge von Weidenbaum, and also Clemens Münster. The cycle of *Ways of Dying* (Todesarten) with one finished novel and two novel fragments is to be distinguished from the *Todesarten-Projekt*, a four volume edition which was published in 1995 by Monika Albrecht, Dirk Göttsche and Robert Pichl with critical commentary. This edition brings together many of Bachmann's published and unpublished prose texts and drafts, even going back to the early fifties, and including also the five stories of her final publication *Three Paths to the Lake* (German title: *Simultan)* in 1972. All these texts are centered, as the editors argue, on the one problematic of *Todesarten* as a longstanding work in progress, a huge fragment of Bachmann's work.

With the *Todesarten-Projekt* Ingeborg Bachmann created a multi-faceted palimpsest that both reflects the presence of violence and fascism in society and subverts it with fragmentary remembering. In 1968 she had written a short draft, unpublished during her lifetime, on Sylvia Plath's *The Bell Jar* [Die Glasglocke], which had appeared in German translation the same year.[1] Bachmann had known Plath's work for some time. Her library had a copy, signed by Ted Hughes in 1966, of the English edition of *Ariel*, a collection of Plath's poems published by Hughes two years after her death in 1965. In the essay draft on Plath's *Bell Jar*, Bachmann states that this work must be defined as an "autobiographical novel," not in the sense that someone presents her private matters to an audience hungry for excitement, but autobiographical in a sense that there is a focus on an imaginary figure of a thoughtful, disintegrating, smashed and devastated creature. There is an illness, Bachmann later continues, that is as such horrific, something with a deadly ending. With these illuminating thoughts in mind, we can speak of Bachmann's *Todesarten-Projekt* as "*her* history," as a work that is singular and personal and at the same time political and historical. To write such a work one must dig deep into one's own memories and those of others, and what is most indispensable is one's imagination. A work of this kind is, to use a phrase by Tony Morrison, "literary archeology." It attends to the voices that come forth from the very deep, bearing cultural truth. We must ask, how can they be articulated? What for example could be living words of the deep-seated truth that Bachmann evoked in a statement in June 1973, four months before her death: "I thought about it already earlier [before writing the second chapter of *Malina*, "The Third Man," GBG], where does fascism begin. It does not begin with the first bombs that are launched, it does not begin with the terror, about which one can write in every newspaper. It begins in the relationship between people. Fascism is the first thing in the relationship between a man and a woman, and I tried to express in this chapter that here in this society there is always war. There is no war and peace, there is only war."[2]

Bachmann's *Todesarten-Projekt* is a profoundly opaque and cryptic work about a horrendous history, the hidden crimes in society, the ongoing fascism in human relations, revealed notably in the war between men and women, and most of all about the difficulty to write about all of this today. Her work problematizes both the very act of reconstructing history and the assumption of the transparency of language. Bachmann was familiar with the philosophy of Ludwig Wittgenstein since her study at the University of Vienna. The question of language in her case is that of a particular sensibility of embracing language at the same time when there is ambivalence based on the distortion and wounds words can cause. When Wittgenstein at the end of his *Tractacus logico-philosophicus* acknowledges, "[t]here is indeed the inexpressible. This *shows* itself; it is the mystical,"[3] he formulates for her the double task of the poet to give voice to the unsaid and to articulate silences otherwise. What has been noticed as the fatalism and passivity of Bachmann's female characters is closely linked with an understanding of linguistic duplicity, the awareness of how words define and extend our worlds, and of how words also hurt, abuse, and perpetuate patriarchal ideology. To remember the past, the personal, the national, and patriarchal therefore is a project that requires speech and silences, fact and fictions, stories, gestures, dreams and gaps.

Language is not transparent, neither is history. The opaqueness of both pushes the writer to new forms of writing. The *Todesarten-Projekt* and within it the novel cycle *Malina, Franza,* and *Requiem for Fanny Goldmann* are Bachmann's historiofictional memoir that questions profoundly our understanding of memory and amnesia, truth and lies, silence and speech. Undermining logocentric certitude, its mode of writing is fragmentary and elliptical, poetic and reflective, somber and sometimes ironic. As an alternative to confessional political writing her work is literary, historical and theoretical at once. Her idea of "true sentences" is linked to what Walter Benjamin defined as the "now of recognizability" [Jetzt der Erkennbarkeit]. A true image of the past is not to be gained with past-mindedness. The making present of the past is inseparably intertwined with the innermost image of the present. Only their simultaneity will produce the burst of telling. What Bachmann described as that *something*, which is present in every great work of art, the "withered, and weather-beaten," can be called forth only by shattered imagery, broken fables, and silent echoes. Clearly, in the attentiveness required for reading Bachmann, to follow always and again even deeper into the deepest, lies the irresistible beauty of her writing.

This collection of essays on Ingeborg Bachmann gives an assessment and reappraisal of her literary presence today. They explore her work from a variety of perspectives, and try to open different entries into her poetry, fiction and critical essays.[4] They focus on her poetry, her understanding of the lyrical and language. They present overviews of critical approaches to her prose work, which have been various and controversial, and they reveal with different focus the complexities inherent in Bachmann's landscapes of memory. They connect Bachmann's work with recent discussions on postcoloniality, translation, war-trauma, and the question of historicity. Ingeborg Bachmann invented a fragmentary language of disaster and actual remembrance. There is no evidence so far to allow ourselves not to remain haunted by it.

NOTES

1. Ingeborg Bachmann, "Das Tremendum—Sylvia Plath: 'Die Glasglocke.' Entwurf," *Werke*, ed. Christine Koschel, Inge von Weidenbaum, Clemens Münster, vol. 4: Essays, Reden, Vermischte Schriften, Anhang (München, Zürich: R. Piper Verlag, 1978), 358-360. On this draft see critical remarks in Monika Albrecht, Dirk Göttsche, ed. *"Über die Zeit schreiben."* 2. *Literatur-und kulturwissenschaftliche Essays zum Werk Ingeborg Bachmanns* (Würzburg: Königshausen & Neumann 2000), 209. See also in the same volume an essay by Leslie Morries on "The Ladies Lazarus: Sylvia Plath und Ingeborg Bachmann – Versuch einer vergleichenden Lektüre," 75-91.

2. Ingeborg Bachmann, *Wir müssen wahre Sätze finden. Gespräche und Interviews* (München: Piper, 1991), 144 [my translation].

3. Ludwig Wittgenstein, *Tractatus Logico-Philosophicus*, ed. and trans. C. K. Ogden (London and New York: Routledge, 1996), 187.

4. Some essays, and in some cases earlier versions of the essays, were presented as conference papers at the Bachmann-Symposium, organized by Gisela Brinker-Gabler, in 1996 at Binghamton University (Achberger, Albrecht, Brinker-Gabler, Filkins, Garber, Majer-O'Sickey, Pichl, Remmler, Stoll).

To Die for Berlin[1]

by Ingeborg Bachmann[2]
translated from the German by Lilian Friedberg

He arrived at Berlin's Tempelhof airport with the soccer fans he'd been with since they changed planes in Frankfurt. At least he knew now that the international championships were being held at this time tomorrow. For years, he'd feigned interest in soccer, later he feigned interest in wines, and, he in fact did have *some* interest in wines and soccer and stocks and casino slots. But right now he'd just had his tonsils removed and, since his attempts to shut off the air conditioning in the plane failed, he'd wrapped his scarf three times around his neck. He wasn't thinking about his lecture tomorrow or the upcoming soccer match, but was concerned instead with his tonsils and the stabbing near his heart on the left side of his chest; then it occurred to him that he would have to speak German and would soon be hearing nothing but German. Of course he'd almost always spoken German, but in recent years had seldom heard it spoken because his wife was French and he'd given up trying to improve her accent and sometimes, when they weren't speaking their everyday French they spoke English in order to express things that were difficult to say, and there were some sentences he always said in English— "it is so trying, absolutely trying," for example. And here he was about to face something that was "absolutely trying," too, but he couldn't quite get the sentence out. The soccer fans gathered in groups on the concourse, pushing him aside until he finally circled around them to the left, following the signs pointing to the exit. Two gentlemen approached him and they all shook hands; he didn't know them – just their names from the correspondence that precipitated their meeting. He had a carry-on bag with him, and, as they exited the building, a photographer snapped two quick shots without using the flash in the foggy winter light, then handed his colleague a pink slip.

In the taxi, he said, "I've been here before, it was about —wait a second—ah, it doesn't matter anyway." Back then he'd been alone in the taxi and the chauffeur spent the entire ride explaining what had been where before, but all he could remember from what was said was where the Roman Cafe had stood, replaced now by two wooden shacks and a taxi service advertising cars for hire.

But even that probably wasn't the same anymore, and now he at least recognized the Gedächtniskirche which had since been adorned by a drab silo towering behind it, after that, he didn't see anything familiar, only the weather reminded him, the dreary light, the icy wind that again targeted his neck, this time through the cracks around the window frame. To die for Berlin, the refrain kept going through his mind, more precisely, he thought it first in French with a question mark, recalling something he'd read in the newsmagazine *Express*: *Mourir pour Berlin?* and he asked Herr Herbert Schüddekamp who was seated beside him, "There was fog on the way into Berlin, that is, it was foggy until we reached Berlin, but the machine handled itself so well, no turbulence, no nothing."

Herr Schüddekamp asked, "What would you like to see?"

"I don't know yet, I have to catch up on my sleep first," he said.

In the hotel lobby, they got acquainted, made each other laugh. The soccer enthusiasts, about thirty Swiss guys, stood with their luggage in the lobby filling out registration forms. The German gentleman laughed and excused himself; then he laughed again, too, saying there was really no need to apologize, and proceeded to tell a story about the boxers, both English and German, he'd once ended up with in a hotel in D.[3] and how he'd much rather have been in a hotel with the soccer players themselves, not with these people who, unfortunately, were only fans—still, he preferred even these fans over the usual tight-lipped hotel guests you normally encounter slipping through the half-lit corridors to the bathroom or waiting for the elevator with you, silently and discretely staring into space.

The German gentleman said goodbye and wished him a good rest. Once in his room, he closed the curtains. He unpacked his toiletries and, without washing, lay down on the bed.

He was in Berlin. A sharp recurring ache in his ear. Headaches set in, but he barely took note of them, if only because he was too preoccupied with the pain in his neck and ears. He slept until evening.

The German's secretary called to ask if he'd slept well, if he needed tickets to the opera or would perhaps prefer the theater. No, he said, but wondered if she wouldn't care to go out for a drink—the secretary was silent at the other end of the line, and he said, "Are you too old or too ugly or too boring, or why is it you don't want to have a drink with me?" The woman laughed and said, it was very possible that she was all of the above, but that she would join him anyway.

She was neither particularly old nor particularly ugly and was perhaps only boring because he was so bored himself. She knew a bar where they often went. (They, who were they?)

At the bar, he danced with her once, then said, "If you don't mind, I'd rather we just have a few drinks. I believe I'm a bit behind the times—these weird flailing movements they make with their arms—I can't do that, and I wouldn't want to embarrass you." She gave him a discerning look of approval, clinging to his every word.

"You would be wise not to be so utterly approving," he told her, "you don't even know what I'm thinking."

"Well, what are you thinking?" the woman asked.

"That I don't want to see anything in Berlin," he said.

Defiantly, the woman carped back: "I'd presumed you to be a bit more original, kind sir. There are those who come wanting to see it all and those who come wanting to see nothing at all. So, that's not very original."

At midnight, he took her home in a taxi and started to think it had been pretty inappropriate for him to have invited her out—Herbert would likely consider it rather odd: he'd have to confess to it first thing in the morning. Then he went back to the bar since he didn't feel like sleeping. When he got to the bar, there was a strobe light flashing and a house band blaring. He squeezed himself in to a table where a couple of young Germans sat with their girlfriends and coke bottles and rum on the table. A man with a microphone <>

"No one's probably going to fly out of here today," the desk clerk said, "because of the fog."[4] He was sitting in the hotel lobby with the Swedes and the Swiss, the conquerors and the conquered who'd all but forgotten victory and defeat and spoke in collectively choreographed monotones, drinking beer and rye, guzzling down Steinhager brandies. The newspapers reported that, under the cover of fog, seven people had succeeded in crossing the border between West and East Berlin. It made him think of the phrase "under cover of night."

Under cover of night.

When his call came, it was very dark outside. *Chérie, disait-il, c'est à cause de la brume, que je serai en retard. Ne "t'en préoccupe pas," non, ne t'en fais pas.* He laughed into the phone. *Il riait. Peut-être je ne rentre plus, pensait-il, mais il ne le prononçait pas, il disait: je t'embrasse. Je te téléphone demain matin.*

Tear-gas on both sides. He kept reading. Two students approached. He listened to what they had to say; one of them said that M. wanted to meet him over on the other side—he could cross over at the Friedrichstraße. Why? he thought, then they placed a phone call before they left, and he left, too, and—while he didn't actually want to meet M.—he did it anyway, continuing on foot without looking too closely at the wall—you couldn't make out much of it in the fog anyway, so he "crossed over" under the cover of fog. He climbed into the car and shook hands with M. They drove along without seeing much through the fog. I'm not curious, he thought, despairingly, I'm not the least bit curious! I can't bring myself to so much as look out the window. Here I am talking to M., but what *are* we really saying, we lacquered little animals, finely finished crocodiles encased in the condensation of our greenhouses.

He joined M. and his wife, Mrs. M., in their apartment, she was a charming woman who immediately served them tea. I thought you might not be able to make it or wouldn't want to come . . .

I suppose those literati just wanted to hoard you hide and hair to themselves. No, that's not it, he explained about the soccer fans and everyone was relieved, they chuckled, three to two for Switzerland, to play for Berlin, to speak for Berlin, to sleep for Berlin, to drink for Berlin.

Is there something special about this place, he heard himself ask suddenly. No, some precocious little student said, no, there is nothing special about this place. So this fine gentleman of a student was pretty clever then—at least you could carry on a conversation with him. That's going a bit far back for the likes of us, he said to M., we're glad not to have your worries, even though we, of course, nonetheless have them—yours over here and theirs over there (he gestured toward the wall in what he thought was the approximate direction of West Berlin).

And what are we supposed to think about having them nonetheless, M. asked, hesitantly.

Merde, you think to yourself. I really wouldn't know what else to tell you, either; I hate to disappoint you, but everyone's so disappointed, so it's best to talk about the fog. Under cover of night, you know?

M. cracked the cake and he crumbled the cake, the student wouldn't touch the cake and the woman was lying in a plush upholstered chair, up to her ears in contemplation. They were all up to their ears in contemplation of so little consequence.
Do you really believe so?
Think about it.
What do you think.
And of course mistakes are made all over the place.
Mistakes.
Miscalculations.
Misconstrued sentences.
Misconstructions.
Under cover of night.

He drove back under cover of night, walked back with the student who left under cover of night, leaving him blanketed by the folds of night closing in. In the end, he wanted to give M. a hug, a man to whom he had no ties, someone who didn't concern him in the least, with whom he'd spoken about nothing of import, but he left him behind under cover of night, without an embrace, nor did he hug anyone else here, he bumped his head against an advertising post in the fog and said Mercy as he rubbed his head.

The next day, he went to the zoo again. It looks as though I've come to Berlin to see the animals. And [he] wondered if he'd have enough time to get to the fish. It certainly wasn't a very good place for people watching. Had he ever looked (the others) in the face, M. or Schüddekamp, or Fräulein Helga? Even the student.

The next day, after he'd placed a call, *c'est toujours la brume, chérie*, he went to the zoo again.

This time he didn't go to see the big animals, the pythons, iguanas, crocodiles, but wound up with the small ones instead.

Two toads had died—he tapped against the glass wall with his finger, but there was nothing save an empty form, frozen, encrusted, a death, and the school kids passed by, as children tend to do, with insatiable eyes, but he carried on a conversation with the two dead, contorted toads and the turgid eye of the chameleon, the fleas and the smallest of the frogs.

He deciphered their language as he had been unable to do with the language of others, break into the language, crack it open, he said, and the orange-colored frog imported from the most distant country held him captive, placing its existence on display with its eyes, eyes that had nothing to do with him, eyes which, in their oblivion, mirrored their own obliterated existence, the glass houses and greenhouses, their unconditional <>

That afternoon, at 5:45, his plane took off.

He walked once around the block where his hotel stood, the wind ripped and tore at his head, he went around the block a second time, this couldn't possibly make him hoarse, it was here that he fortified his health—in this raw, desolate wind.

In the back rooms, where you could sit and drink, he found a vacant corner, the men, soccer enthusiasts—speaking Swedish and *français fédéral*, Swiss German, just returning from the Kurfürstendamm, from the taverns, the restaurants—their sentences blended into a dense, boisterous batter of languages from which not a single word emerged discernable, not a single word inclined to belong to any given language. Again, they sat around in a semi-circle drinking beer, celebrating victory and defeat; they'd come to Berlin in such good spirits, in Frankfurt they'd been just as elated, he had seen the cheerful way they approached the stewardesses and counter clerks, the way they herded back and forth, inspecting everything, the souvenir shop and newspaper stand, the bar, the signs, the glass walls, the gates. Even in Berlin, they had retained their blithe demeanor, and now, though, they weren't happy anymore to be in Berlin, they ate and drank just to dull the pain of the hapless little wreck that Berlin had become now that the fight was over; glassy-eyed in their mutual incompatibility, so they set out one more time to celebrate.

After midnight, he found a tattered necktie in the corridor and, a few feet away, a wallet; he was so tired, the runner was overturned as though someone had stumbled over it or tackled it and thrown it off track—he was so tired that even these signs of devastation, of misfortune, didn't seem out of the ordinary. He just closed the door behind him a little less quietly than he might have at night in a hotel, thinking that wasn't likely to wake any of the drunken guests.

Herr Schüddekamp picked him up. In front of the hotel, a group of Swedes gathered, gesticulating, screaming. Two of them broke into a run—they were chasing after some Swiss guy. The hotel porter said: Now, if they get their hands on him. One of the Swedes picked up a rock. Herr Schüddekamp shoved him into the taxi saying, we'd best be on our way.

While giving his lecture, he suddenly thought he saw a dead man before him, that Swiss guy whom he'd only heard running away, but had barely seen running down there along the hotel.

He had skipped a sentence, he broke out in a sweat, then came to another sentence on the page, which he had to translate from the singular to the plural, he said to himself, just translate the damn thing, say, *we* went - - - and then <>

When Herr Schüddekamp brought him back to the hotel, the suitcases were standing, as they had been in the beginning, heaped in the hall; this time they were on their way out, the soccer enthusiasts, but they were still waiting to be herded out of there —drinking coffee or sitting around yawning in the hall. One of the men was draped pale in a chair and two others flanked him like angels about to transport him to the Last Judgment; one of the men spread out there bent over and smacked the one reclining in the face, then they both slapped him in the face. He and Herr Schüddekamp looked at each other: if he isn't dead already, that means he's still alive and someone should call a doctor, Herr Schüddekamp said. Suddenly, he grew queasy and was about to give Herr Schüddekamp an affirmative nod when the guy they'd mistaken for dead staggered up, supported by the two who had slapped him and they went out with the rest of them. They departed.

I don't know what it was, maybe it was the gecko that appeared on the glass wall, almost climbed up, almost climbed into my hand resting there.

When he then walked through the center of the city and the trees—something sort of like trees, cold trees with branches like antenna wires—the camels were suddenly standing there and the only thing separating him from the camels was a fence. The camels, one-humped and two-humped. One camel was standing and two were lying in the sand, on a sterile trapezoid box of Mark Brandenburg sand, a real hygienic playground for camels; a stretch of water, a half-yard wide, separated the camels' sandbox from a half-yard wide strip of green, then the green stripe dropped off into an unformed, untouched wilderness, and that is where the fog first set in, the gloaming root, pock-marked prairie, gray-brown. He got off the pedestrian path, slid in slippery shoes to the fence in order to get a better glimpse of the camels. They were very visible, to everyone. They were the representatives of this deforested enclosure and, in the same sense—though not here on the fine Mark Brandenburg sand, but nonetheless on some strip of sand set apart by a stretch of water and a strip of green—he, too, would be put on display, the animal that speaks a different language with an aching throat. But the llama gave him a look that could have been taken as a sign of mockery. He'd never known how much he liked observing animals; he watched the camels, imagined himself stepping in time with their muscles as they picked their way across the sandy enclosure. He imagined himself falling to his knees in this same strange way, stretching, living in the same breath as they; he was not the least bit removed from them, but they were separated from him—the camels, what the hell did they know about his fence and of <>

And the way it must feel to inhabit a body like that, the way its head rests on its rump, and the way it must feel to be him and how earnest he is, very much so when he's facing the camels, and the way he tried to comprehend the camel's system and the way it feels for them to be in *their* bodies. And one of them—that one had surely come straight from the desert, but the others were likely to have already been considered Berliners—he could sense even that and didn't forbid himself the feeling that he *could* sense what it felt like to be a desert animal and that it is possible to sense which people haven't yet become Berliners, Germans, Portuguese and Bulgarians, and the way they suffer on sacred grounds, and how they remember the places that hadn't yet become playgrounds to which they'd been assigned.

And he dropped a megaton of tenderness on the city, and no one could have escaped the dust of that tenderness, the ash of that tenderness—not even a crocodile, a little gecko, no Herr Willem or Herr Schüddekamp, not even Fräulein von Brücken—they wiped their eyes, bewildered, under cover of night.

The excitement here, in the beginning, you should have been here to see it.

Ach ja, he said.

Even now, they're crucifying each other left and right here, Fräulein Helga said, perhaps that makes you wonder.

Ach nein, he replied, in the same tone of voice.

Everyone is entitled to his own opinion.

About what? he asked.

I'm not sure you see what I'm getting at, she responded spitefully. About the circumstances. This is a situation you couldn't imagine existing anywhere else.

Can you imagine it even here? he retorted.

She stared at him and bit her tongue.

Just who do you think you are? she asked, you have no right!

I never claimed to be right, he said, I have absolutely no right to be right, none of us has a right.

Why did you seek me of all people out to talk to about it. It's something we talk about a lot.

Talk.

You have to be able to talk about it, she said, irritated. I'm sure you have your own opinion.

I do, he said. I've got my own take on it.

NOTES

1. Translator's note: the German original title, "Sterben für Berlin," alludes to an article by the US-American journalist Stewart Alsop, also printed in the November 15, 1961 issue of the German news magazine *Der Spiegel*. The title, posed there in the interrogative, "Sterben für Berlin?" refers to the question facing the Western world at the time this story was written, in the midst of the "Berlin crisis."

2. Originally published as a fragment under the title "Sterben für Berlin" in Ingeborg Bachmann, *Todesarten-Projekt*, vol. 1, ed. Monika Albrecht and Dirk Göttsche (München: Piper, 1995), 70-80. Editors' note: the sign <>, reproduced in the translation, is used by the editors of the *Todesarten-Projekt* to indicate interruptions or omissions in the original text.

3. Translator's note: probably Dortmund or Düsseldorf.

4. Translator's note: possible allusion to a *Spiegel* (June, 1961) article about Tempelhof Airport in which East German Walter Ulbricht, when asked whether the agreement over the free city of Berlin would result in closing the airport, responded by saying, "Maybe it will shut itself down on its own." ("Vielleicht schließt er sich von selbst.")

1 / The Music of the Unspoken

Peter Filkins

> Das Unsägliche geht, leise gesagt, übers Land:
> schon ist Mittag.
>
> (The unspeakable passes, barely spoken, over the
> land: already it's noon.)
> —Ingeborg Bachmann, "Früher Mittag"

The last line of "Früher Mittag," or "Early Noon,"[1] represents a touchstone to Bachmann's poetry in its effort to speak to the horrific and the ineffable contained within "Das Unsägliche." It is the epitome of what Bachmann pursued throughout her career. To evoke "Das Unsägliche," to elicit the unspoken, the unspeakable, that which cannot be said, this remained Bachmann's unwavering aim in a career that saw numerous changes of direction, serious work in no less than six different genres, early meteoric success, a life of chosen exile followed by a decade of semi-neglect, and finally a late resurgence cut short by a tragic early death.

Bachmann's "Das Unsägliche" touches on a border, namely that quality or state which exists between two states—between the immediate and the unknown, between the present and the past, between life and death itself. Indeed, borders are important for this writer, for Bachmann's was a life spent living on borders, a life hypersensitive to the paradox of their simultaneous sense of limitation and possibility from the very beginning. "I spent my childhood in Carinthia, in the South," she tells us in the well-known commentary on her birthplace found among her papers after her death. There she reflects on how she grew up

> on the border, in a valley that has two names—one German and the other Slovenian. And the house in which for generations my ancestors had lived—both Austrians and Wends—still bears a name that sounds foreign. Hence, near the border there is still another border: the border of speech—and on

either side I was accustomed to stories of good and bad spirits from two or three lands: for an hour away, over the mountains, there also lay Italy.[2]

From the start, "the border of speech" was Bachmann's "native land," a realm that lay both within and beyond the multilingual state of that actual border, and that actual house, which in itself represents a microcosm of the "house" of Austria and its past.[3] In this manner, "the border of speech" for Bachmann remained a metaphysical realm manifested within the physical, while the immediacy of the physical, the actual, and the historical would always contain a sense of limitation threatening the passage beyond or through "the border of speech" into the realm of "Das Unsägliche." As Bachmann states in her poem "Of a Land, a River and Lakes" ("Von einem Land, einem Fluß und den Seen"), "borders pass through every word" (*Songs*, 125). Throughout her poems, and throughout her writing life, her determination remained singular, namely "to speak across borders," to fuse "Wort" ("word") with "Ort" ("place") in order that we stand in "accord" with and through the border of each "word."

But what precisely is "Das Unsägliche," or better yet, of what does it consist? How is it made manifest in the work of Bachmann, and what are the mechanisms by which she evokes it? If "Das Unsägliche" is elicited or "leise gesagt" by Bachmann's poems, stories, novels, even her essays and libretti and radio plays, is it something different for each, or is there a single shared goal that spans the entire career? Given the array of genres in which she wrote, "borders" also pass through the work of Bachmann; yet how does her work "speak across" the "borders" set up by the numerous turns she took in her work, and which we now know occurred often side by side? Finally, how do we as critics and scholars, even as translators, speak across those same borders in order to make sense of such a complicated career and a writer as complex as Bachmann?

To explore some possible answers to these questions, I would like to look at a couple of Bachmann's poems, specifically a very early and a very late one, in order to consider the nature of "Das Unsägliche" in Bachmann's lyric poetry, and then to offer a possible new model for how we might think of Bachmann's entire multi-faceted career, as well as the place and nature of "Das Unsägliche" within it. First, however, let us begin where Bachmann begins, namely with poetry and "the music of the unspoken" inherent in her lyric voice.

In a very early poem, "[Abends frag ich meine Mutter]" ("[On Many Nights I Ask My Mother])," written in 1948, Bachmann paints a portrait of a mother and daughter sitting together at night, listening to a clock chime:

> Abends frag ich meine Mutter
> heimlich nach dem Glockenläuten,
> wie ich mir die Tage deuten
> und die Nacht bereiten soll.
>
> Tief im Grund verlang ich immer
> alles restlos zu erzählen,
> in Akkorden auszuwählen,
> was an Klängen mich umspielt.
>
> Leise lauschen wir zusammen:
> meine Mutter träumt mich wieder,
> und sie trifft, wie alte Lieder,
> meines Wesens Dur und Moll.

> On many nights I ask my mother
> furtively after the hours chime,
> how I should learn to tell the time
> and ready myself for the night.
>
> In my inner depths, I always demand
> that all be made completely clear,
> picking out from the chords I hear
> what confuses me within their strains.
>
> Quietly we sit and listen together:
> my mother dreams what I will be,
> arranging, like any old melody,
> my essential notes, major and minor.[4]

Clearly the daughter wonders how she will make her way in life, though at the same time she struggles against pressure from the mother to be a certain way, or at least the ease with which the mother arranges, "like any old melody," her "essential notes, major and minor." The link between the roles offered by the mother and the music of "meines Wesens" causes the daughter to think about her life as an arrangement of "major and minor" notes, just as, earlier in the poem, she struggles to pick out "from the chords I hear / what confuses me within their strains" ("auszuwählen, / was an Klängen mich umspielt."). Hence, on the surface, the poem depicts a young girl trying to find her way in life while struggling with and against the available roles offered and arranged by her mother, a struggle common between many mothers and daughters.

However, how much more interesting the poem becomes if one argues that the "mother" presented here is not an actual mother at all, but rather "Die Muttersprache," language itself being the essence that arranges the poet's "essential notes." Read this way, the poem reveals that Bachmann, as a young poet, feels the strain of having her "major and minor" notes controlled for her by the tradition she has been handed, and as early as 1948, she is determined to press against those constraints. Unlike Paul Celan, who felt empowered to step outside those constraints and literally rewrite the German language on his own terms, Bachmann knows that she is born into the tradition against which she presses, much like the way that she is born into that "house" where "there is still another border, the border of speech." Hence the poem's rhyme scheme and meter: a traditional tetrameter line or "melody" arranged in formal quatrains, but with the slight oddity of a rhyming couplet bracketed by unrhymed first and last lines in each stanza. The result is a music that on the surface *sounds* traditional, but cuts against its own grain in subversive fashion. Furthermore, the final flatness or heaviness of "Moll" in the German underscores the poet's urge to violate the tuneful "melody" of "wieder" and "Lieder" that has been handed to her. On top of the dissonance created by that final sound of "Moll," there is also a slight irony in the fact that it picks up a rhyme from the last line of the first stanza, "und die Nacht bereiten soll," where the girl ponders how she should "ready myself for the night." The sub-theme of the poem's musical score is that the note she will go on to strike, unlike those struck by the chimes or the mother, can be heard in the slant rhyme of "soll/Moll."[5] Indeed, in order to get that rhyme, we have to cross the "border" of the poem's traditional structure, i.e. to cut against its own "major" notes in order to hear the "minor," yet more truthful note, for it is a note that remains unspoken in terms of the formal arrangement the poem promises us at the beginning.

The notes, then, "should be minor." This is the answer that Bachmann discovers for herself in asking "Die Muttersprache" "wie ich mir die Tage deuten / . . . soll." Indeed, if the poet is to find a way to work within and against "alte Lieder" or "die Muttersprache," both of which seek to arrange her notes for her, she will have to re-write the score by allowing the unspoken "minor notes" to be "leise gesagt," barely spoken, if not barely heard, in the face of the tradition's more major notes. This would remain Bachmann's pursuit throughout her career, for even as late as *Malina*, the struggle is still the same. As Marjorie Perloff has pointed out, the prosaic flatness of the novel's final sentence, "Es war Mord" ("It was murder"), can be seen as a counter music to that of Ivan who represents "the traditional poem, . . . the maker of meters, of rhythmic regularity, even as Malina regularly speaks the 'plain truth' of prose."[6]

Yet can one feel secure that reading the "mother" of "[Abends frag ich meine Mutter]" as "Die Muttersprache" is a viable interpretation, or does Bachmann's later work, given its own intense focus on gender, call for a gender-based reading of the earlier poem? In addition, what precisely is the relationship between Bachmann's early concern with "the border of speech" and the more pointed issues of gender politics in the later prose? Are they distinct, sequential stages in Bachmann's career, or are they concerns that occur simultaneously throughout her career and remain interrelated all along?

To answer these questions, let me turn to a late poem, "Exil," written in 1957, though slightly revised when it appeared in its final version in 1964. Here is the poem in its entirety:

Exil

Ein Toter bin ich der verwandelt
gemeldet nirgends mehr
unbekannt im Reich des Präfekten
überzählig in den goldenen Städten
und im grünenden Land

abgetan lange schon
und mit nichts bedacht

Nur mit Wind mit Zeit und mit Klang

der ich unter Menschen nicht leben kann

Ich mit der deutschen Sprache
dieser Wolke um mich
die ich halte als Haus
treibe durch alle Sprachen

O wie sie sich verfinstert
die dunklen die Regentöne
nur die wenigen fallen

In hellere Zonen trägt dann sie den Toten hinauf

Exile

I am a dead man who wanders
registered nowhere
unknown in the prefect's realm
unaccounted for in the golden cities
and the greening land

long since given up
and provided with nothing

> Only with wind with time and with sound
>
> I who cannot live among humans
>
> I with the German language
> this cloud around me
> which I keep as a house
> press through all languages
>
> Oh how it grows dark
> those muted those rain tones
> only a few fall
>
> Into brighter zones it will lift the dead man up

In considering this remarkable and complex poem, I wish to focus on only a few key points for my purposes here. By 1957, and certainly by 1964 after her move to Rome, Bachmann is indeed an exile who carries the "house" of "the German language" with her. Poems, however, are not the same as biography, and Bachmann's opening statement that "I am a dead man" serves as a reminder that the poem is not merely about her move to Italy. Rather, though the German of "Ein Toter bin ich" holds the possibility of being read as a neuter entity, such as "I am a dead person" or perhaps even "I am a corpse," Bachmann's well known use of a male voice in her later fiction supports the reading that the poem is spoken by a male voice. Again, I place my emphasis on *later* fiction, for the way in which the *later* Bachmann helps us to read the *early* Bachmann is not only similar to how a key point is evoked in "Exil," but also how "Exil" helps us to read, if not re-read, the much earlier "[Abends frag ich meine Mutter]."

For it is in the last line of "Exil" that a key "unspoken" event of the poem occurs, namely the pronoun "sie" and the difficulty of finding its referent. As we read that "In hellere Zonen trägt dann sie den Toten hinauf," Bachmann forces us to go back through the poem in search of the pronoun's source. At first we might be tempted to stop at "Regentöne" as a source for "sie," though we quickly realize it is a plural noun and thus will not work with the singular. The next possibility is the "alle Sprachen" at the end of the fifth stanza, but again this is plural. Only with "dieser Wolke" in the second line of the fifth stanza do we find the first feminine singular noun that can possibly connect with the "sie trägt" of the last line, a separation of some six lines existing between noun and pronoun within the poem. This gulf, however, is immediately widened, for though "dieser Wolke" works in connection with "sie," we immediately "press through" to discover the true source of what it refers to as a metaphor, and what in fact is the *only* source of that which "Into brighter zones" can "lift the dead man up"— namely "*Die* deutsche Sprache" of the fifth stanza's first line, despite the manner in which the word's feminine gender is masked by the dative "der" of "Ich mit der deutschen Sprache."

Much in the same way that Bachmann asks us to cross the "border" of the traditional music she presents "[Abends frag ich meine Mutter]" in order to hear the unspoken "minor" rhyme of "soll/Moll," her shrewd play upon the *gender* of the pronouns inherent in the language of "Exil" demands that we arrive at the poem's last line only to return to its first. However, this does not occur in a traditionally cyclical manner, but rather by carefully reading our way *back through* the poem. Put another way, the only way to eventually understand "Exil" is to read it backwards, as well as forewards, "mit dem scharfen Gehör" or "the ear sharply tuned" as Bachmann notes at the end of "Große Landschaft bei Wien" ("Great Landscape Near Vienna") (*Songs*, 70-71). In fact, it is this same sensitivity to gender embedded within language, and most importantly, the "unspoken" emphasis Bachmann places on the feminine gender of "Die deutsche Sprache" in "Exil," which allows us to read the "mother" of the earlier poem as a stand-in for "Die Muttersprache" itself. Hence, in reading "Exil," not only do we have to re-read it in order to comprehend it fully, but such a re-reading also leads to a re-reading of "[Abends frag ich meine Mutter]."

How this re-reading occurs speaks to the dialogue between the issues of gender and language that exists within, and *between*, each poem. Leaping beyond the worldly gender of the "mother" in "[Abends frag ich meine Mutter]," we arrive at a question of language. Focusing on the language of "Exil," however, we arrive at a gender-sensitive reading tied to the feminine nature of "Die deut-

deutsche Sprache" in counterpoint to the historically exiled "dead man." Hence, in the first poem, gender gives way to language, while in the second the opposite occurs. What's important to add is that it is the initial language-sensitive reading of the later "Exil" that helps reveal the deeper reading of the earlier "[Abends frag ich meine Mutter]." Thus, not only are language and gender issues at work in each poem, but in an important sense, each poem "reads" the other.

It is not unusual, of course, to read a writer's early work in terms of major work that occurs later on. In the case of Bachmann's poems, Hans Höller has made a very convincing argument that the early and late uncollected poems are best read in tandem, for in this manner they function as a commentary on the development of Bachmann's thinking.[7] Even the way that the poet of "[Abends frag ich meine Mutter]" strikes a "minor" note in order to subvert the "major" notes, corresponds with Bachmann's continued use of music as a symbol of the inexpressible pursuit of the utopian, as Karen Achberger points out in regards to the role of music in *Malina*.[8]

Yet the relationship between Bachmann's early and late work is a particularly complicated one, perhaps one that requires a different model or different way of thinking about the meaning and development of this writer's career. We know very well the ambivalent, if not negative, reception accorded Bachmann's turn to prose with the publication of *Das dreißigste Jahr* in 1961. Only towards the end of Bachmann's life, and certainly just after her death, was her prose as valued and studied as her poetry, the prevailing myth being that she had "failed" as a poet, or at the very best had made an outright and unfortunate refusal to write the kind of poems that had brought her early fame. Later, critics would discover that Bachmann's "turn" to prose was not a turn at all, for she had been working seriously within it since the 1950s. So much, in fact, did the emphasis shift from the poetry to her prose, particularly with the critical focus directed towards *Malina, Der Fall Franza*, and now the entire *"Todesarten"-Projekt* itself, that Bachmann's early success as a poet came to be seen as, at best, more of a springboard to the serious venture of her later prose, or at worst, a failed aestheticism from which she had to turn away in order to engage more immediate political concerns in her prose.

However, as Bachmann's poem "Alle Tage," or "Every Day," reminds us, "Der Krieg wird nicht mehr erklärt, / sondern fortgesetzt" ("War is no longer declared, / but rather continued") (*Songs*, 40-1). In much the same manner, the "war" that Bachmann launched against the "crimes" of the everyday in her later prose is one *continuous with* the one she carried out in her poems. Given the shared concern with the limits of language, as well as the direct urge to elicit "Das Unsägliche," both the poetry and the prose share obvious and repeated connections. However, there exists another possible, if not necessary approach to Bachmann's work, other than that of merely seeing the connections *between* her poetry and prose, and that is to see her entire oeuvre as a *connected* whole, one that values the poems, or libretti, or essays, or prose, not so much as separate stages or different "turns" in her development, but rather as essential components or acts in the same composition.

Bachmann's notion of writing as a process of "composition" supports the way in which any of her works can be looked at as a musical scoring of the various allusions and echoes contained within it. However, what might be even more useful is to think of Bachmann's entire career as a single musical composition, one in which all of the genres in which she worked stand side by side within a contemporaneous whole, rather than a linear progression. For in the same way that a major strategy of the poetry is its use of fragments and allusions organized into mosaic patterns by the silence between them, one can think of Bachmann's entire output as a series of movements that continually repeat themes and motifs, but in altogether different settings and arrangements.[9] "Like a symphony," one might be tempted to say, but that seems too grand or "major." "Perhaps then an opera," though again that would risk the problem of a "major" production that would threaten to swallow up the "minor" notes of its own composition. Nonetheless, why not a "word opera," perhaps the very one that Bachmann threatens to "annihilate" in her last published poem "Keine Delikatessen" ("No Delicacies"). Indeed, in the last poem she wrote, "Bohemia Lies by the Sea," her pursuit remains utopian, her will undiminished in the fact that she can say, "I still border on a word and on another land, / I border, like little else, on everything more and more, . . ." (*Songs*, 313).

The advantage of considering Bachmann's career as a single work is that it also allows us to "border . . . on everything more and more" (*Songs*, 313), rather than divide her career with borders that compartmentalize and limit it. Taken thus, the issue then becomes not only to trace the various themes and motifs, but to see *how* those motifs thread their way through different means and materials is as much a part of the "unspoken" quality they wish to elicit as any one expression of the "unspoken" by any one particular work. In "[Abends frag ich meine Mutter]," for instance, "Das Unsägliche" is precisely that, "unspoken," for it requires an interpretive leap, whereas in "Exil" the grammar speaks it for us if we listen closely. What both poems share, however, is a concern with and performance of the unspoken, one that cuts against the grain of their separate linear progressions down the page, the earlier working against the formal structure of its meter and rhyme, the later against the gender oppositions woven into its own grammar.

The concern then is the same; it is the medium and the approach that differ. *How* they differ, however, represents a dialogic struggle that runs throughout all of Bachmann's writing. As Karen Achberger has said of the struggle between the narrator's inability to express herself versus Malina's power to express her, "One can view the narrator-Malina-problem specifically as the absence of the female in the male world . . . Or one can view it, in accordance with the philosophy of Ludwig Wittgenstein, as a more general problem, namely, as the experience of the inexpressibility of human existence in rational discourse."[10] However, given Bachmann's own urge "that no thread [be] lost" in the writing of *Malina*, and her feeling that "Such a story is, after all, a woven fabric,"[11] I would argue that the same can be said for all of Bachmann's writing, as well as for how we might read it. Neither a gender-based reading nor one that focuses on linguistic inexpressibility needs to predominate at the exclusion of the other. Rather, they exist side by side, representing different, but deeply connected motifs in Bachmann's approach, much in the same way that a careful reading of "Exil" calls attention to Bachmann's play on linguistic gender, as well as the gender of her speaker, only to lead us to a structural, indeed philosophically "unspoken" re-reading of "[Abends frag ich meine Mutter]."

As Bachmann herself reminds us in "Of a Land, a River and

Lakes," "To stay together, each must feel separation" ("Daß uns nichts trennt, muß jeder Trennung fühlen") (*Songs*, 124-5), the gulf between being the very same as that which we must cross in relation to both language and gender in "Exil," or symbolically and figuratively in "[Abends frag ich meine Mutter]." The result is that borders no longer pass through their "every word," when we recognize that their separate approaches speak to, allow, and in an "unspoken" manner, help "read" or interpret each other. Similarly, in our own critical focus on the variations with which Bachmann strikes the same theme, we come to better appreciate how each poem stands "in accord" with the same overall pursuit, though each maintains its separate identity through the means by which it approaches and crosses "the border of speech."

What such an approach can offer is not only a plurality of themes in the various projects completed and commenced by Bachmann, but also the challenge to think of those themes as united in a cohesive, though nonetheless fragmentary whole. Such consistency is of itself of no particular value, nor would one wish to force readings that try to make tidy sense of a very complicated career. But if a reading of a later poem can inspire a re-reading of an earlier one, perhaps the same can occur between the later prose, which is more gender-based in its concerns, and the earlier poems, which clearly hold Wittgenstein's famous dictum that "the limits of my language are the limits of my world," as their touchstone and inspiration. Nonetheless, the connections made between the early and late Bachmann should not be made for the sake of the connections themselves, or simply to establish a linear sense of Bachmann's development, but rather to better appreciate the *connectedness* of the shared manner with which each strikes its own "minor" note in the larger composition.[12]

Only then, it seems to me, will the import of Ingeborg Bachmann's life and writing be truly retrieved and appreciated. Failed poet? Poetic novelist? Prisoner behind the "border of speech"? Victim of the imprisonments of gender politics? Each of these is too reductive, and thus deadly, in terms of Bachmann's subtlety and complexity, as well as the nature of "Das Unsägliche." Let me instead suggest that we consider her for what she was—a writer who speaks in several different voices at once; a poetic novelist, and a novel poet; a philosopher of the mystical limits of language as well as the realistic confines of historical contingencies. In short, a consciousness: fleeting, fragmentary, yet consistent and pervasive. Finally, the composer of, in all she wrote, a multi-toned "border" music—the music of the unspoken.

NOTES

1. Unless otherwise indicated, all translations are taken from my translation, *Songs in Flight: The Collected Poems of Ingeborg Bachmann* (New York: Marsilio, 1994). Here: 38-39. Hereafter cited as *Songs*.

2. Ingeborg Bachmann, *Werke*, 4 vols, ed. Christine Koschel, Inge von Weidenbaum, and Clemens Münster (München: Piper, 1978), 4:301 (my translation).

3. See Mark Anderson, "Death Arias in Vienna," afterword to *Malina*, by Ingeborg Bachman, trans. Philip Boehm (New York: Holmes & Meier, 1990), 230. Anderson reads the novel as a "fictional microcosm of the House of Austria," a point I feel can be applied to the "house" in which Bachmann is born, as well as to all of her work.

4. *Songs*, 244-5. In translating this poem, I was unable to achieve the rhyme of "soll" and "Moll" in the fourth and twelfth lines. Instead, I chose to create the rhyme of "together" and "minor" in the first and last lines of the final stanza in order to violate the previous rhyme scheme of the poem in a fashion similar to the way that the "soll/"Moll" rhyme violates the formal argument of the poem, as well as to call more attention to the word "minor" by turning it into a "major," but formally dissonant rhyme.

5. My colleague at Simon's Rock College of Bard, Colette van Kerckvoorde, informs me that the "ll" sound of "Moll" is known as the "dark *ll*" in linguistic pronunciation, whereas that of "soll" is known as the "clear" or "bright." In English the equivalent would be the difference between the "ll" sound of "fill" and "full," the latter being the "dark" or more guttural sound. Hence, a further "musical" reading of the poem reveals that Bachmann moves from a "bright" sound in the first stanza, where the clocks chime, to a darker, more mercurial sound in the last stanza which more fittingly corresponds with the "night" she readies herself for in the first.

6. Marjorie Perloff, *Wittgenstein's Ladder* (Chicago: University of Chicago Press, 1996), 176.

7. See Hans Höller, *Ingeborg Bachmann: Das Werk—Von den frühesten Gedichten bis zum "Todesarten"-Zyklus* (Frankfurt: Athenäum, 1987), 170-190.

8. Karen R. Achberger, *Understanding Ingeborg Bachmann* (Columbia: University of South Carolina Press, 1995), 113.
9. See my introduction to *Songs in Flight,* xxviii. Also see Wolfgang Bender, "Ingeborg Bachmann," *Deutsche Literatur der Gegenwart,* ed. Dietrich Weber (Stuttgart: Kröner, 1976), 585.
10. Achberger, 118.
11. Ingeborg Bachmann, *Wir müssen wahre Sätze finden: Gespräche und Interviews* (München: Piper, 1983), 114. Cited and translated by Achberger in *Understanding Ingeborg Bachmann,* 120.
12. See Sabine I. Gölz, "Reading in the Twilight: Canonization, Gender, the Limits of Language—and a Poem by Ingeborg Bachmann," *New German Critique* 47 (1989): 45. The way in which Prof. Gölz speaks to how Bachmann "uses the remembrance of the past not to make it return in the same shape but repeats it in order to make something new appear" also seems a useful mechanism for reading Bachmann's earlier work, i.e. not to simply reaffirm its early reception, or to argue how it compares to the later prose, but "to make something new appear."

2 / Bachmann's Allegorical Lyrics and the Subversions of History

Frederick Garber

Ingeborg Bachmann begins her second collection of poems, *Anrufung des Großen Bären* (*Invocation of the Great Bear*),[1] with a poem addressed to a brother ("The Game is Over," *Songs*, 110-3). The speaker pleads for rescue from an unspecified situation, the mode of recovery modeled on snippets of fairy tales she examines as though thumbing through some well-worn children's book. Though she is tied to a stake, her brother will ride out of the valley of death and carry her away. Though their feet are sore from many, many stones, "a children's king" ("Kinderkönig") (*Songs*, 112/113), perhaps a king out of children's tales, will fetch them and they will sing. Echoing popular readings of the ethos of fairy tales, she says that those who fall have wings; that the winding sheets of the poor will be hemmed with red foxglove from which digitalis comes, promising resurrection; that, whatever may happen to her brother, his bud is sunk in her seal, all that potential preserved forever. Yet it is in just such suggestions, in the seal that locks up life, forever only potential (as in Keats's Grecian urn), that intimations of a more complex ethos emerge. If the siblings should build a raft to sail down the sky, she foresees their excess weight; the burden of their bodies will sink them with the raft. When they sketch a map with countries and railroad tracks, she knows that the tracks will be lined with mines. Watch out for the tricky raven, the sticky spider, the feather in the bush: they can fool you, entice you, trap you. Bachmann's poem recalls alternative readings of fairy-tale-ethos, suggesting a potential for aporia no nostalgia can resolve. Recognizing the warning, the narrating child is wise enough to know when "das Spiel ist aus," "the game is over" (*Songs*, 112/113). That trope names this introductory text, setting a texture and a tonality for the poems that are to follow, promoting a set of instructions for reading which, like all such, should be accepted with the utmost care.

At the end of the poem, she notes how their white nightshirts puff out, perhaps the source of the nightly haunting their parents tell them about. Maybe ghostliness originates in what they wear and do, their terror emerging from actions of their own. The subversion of popular readings of fairy-tale-ethos echoes in the self-subversion with which the poem ends. None of that escapes the precociously wise child whose voice begins the book.

How then are we to understand the long poem that follows? "The Game is Over" played with generic expectations, instructions for reading cultural history; but if we were warned not to be fooled by the lures of spider and raven, Bachmann's cool play with readings of fairy tale suggests the need for equivalent caution with the indicators of genre and mode, their patent solicitations, their ways of catering to the libido of, in particular, the informed reader. Thus, as though to test our alertness after the business of the played-out game, the title of the next poem, "Of a Land, a River and Lakes" ("Von einem Land, einem Fluß und den Seen"), precisely echoes the title of one of Grimm's fairy tales. Clearly the old concerns continue, suggesting a dialogue among these introductory poems, a speaking of poem to poem. In fact there is that and more, not only expectations of genre but textual play among them in a game that seems just to begin. Tucked into the echo from Grimm, linked to and picking up from it, come the cooler, covert sounds of an epic's introduction:

> Von einem, der das Fürchten lernen wollte
> und fortging aus dem Land, von Fluß und Seen,
> zähl ich die Spuren und des Atems Wolken,
> denn, so Gott will, wird sie der Wind verwehn!
>
> (Left behind by one who wished to learn of dread
> in leaving the land of his birth, a river and lakes,
> it's footprints that I count, a breath's own cloud,
> which later, as God wills, the wind will take!)
> *(Songs,* 114/115)

Epic cadences and components—a heroic traveler, a landscape, a narrator at work recording epic gestures, the hope for divine attention—all these emerge from this fairy tale allusion. To confirm such interweaving, Bachmann speaks in line six of "the odysseys"("Die Odysseen," *Songs,* 114, my translation), matching the title of one of

Grimm's texts with the title of one of Homer's. In a move Borges would understand, Bachmann begins a catalogue.

However, she stops it as soon as it was begun, in the midst of uttering Homer, confronted by an oddity that seems inherent in such travels. All those tracks she had been counting bear the traces of previous journeys as well as this particular one. The "footprints" ("Spuren") to which she refers are imprints, indices, that which is left behind to indicate that which has gone before. Metonyms for a past presence, these antique inscribings speak now of the absence of all but themselves; yet it turns out that what is inscribed marks not only the journey the poet planned to trace, but the traces of many others that went on before: this hero's "Spuren" will look like other traces because destinies resemble each other, all are Odysseys ("sie werden vielen gleichen. / Die Lose ähneln sich, die Odysseen" ["finding they're much the same. / Each journey has its twin, as well as each destiny"], *Songs*, 114/115). The poet stops in mid-counting as she sees what the hero learned early. In the wave of his own journey, Grimm's adventurer finds his story always-already-written, inscribed in the wave even before the wave took him away ("Er fühlte seine Welle ausgeschrieben, / eh sie ihn wegtrug und ihm Leid geschah" ["In waves he felt his destiny was written / before it pulled him out into sorrow's lake"], *Songs*, 114/115). Yet what is inscribed in his wave is not only his own story-to-be, but also the imprinted story of previous travelers: the waves swing his cradle with the same ironic rocking that Moses' cradle knew on its own trip down the river. This fairy tale turned epic, this quest-romance that seeks out the lineaments of dread, is spoken in multiple voicings. In fact it is so ubiquitous that any genre can speak the tale. The plethora of literary kinds that marks the beginning of Bachmann's book argues the broad presence of this radical narrative.

As if to put that claim to the test, the poem's introduction ends with the disappearance of the hero of the quest, the poet marking the vanishing by speaking in old, comfortable discourse about the faith that leads us home. At that point, once more conscious of the mortgaged time we live in, she is moved by the memory of a forgotten narrative, a tale that takes in the history of the race as well as certain newer histories, from ancient ice caves to recent days of slaughter. Her poem narrates that tale. At the end, in a scene in a stable, the brother who appeared in "The Game is Over" returns as one more traveler about to leave his native land. He asks the poet to sing, their dialogue a perfect echo, in these pastoral surroundings, of the rhetoric of classical pastoral, phrased, at the song's beginning, in classical stichomythia:

> "O Schwester sing, so sing von fernen Tagen!"
> "Bald sing ich, bald, an einem schönren Ort."
> "O sing und web den Teppich aus den Liedern
> und flieg auf ihm mit mir noch heute fort!
>
> Halt mit mir Rast, wo Bienen uns bewirten,
> Mich Engelschön im Engelhut besucht . . ."
> "Bald sing ich – doch im Turm beginnt's zu schwirren,
> schlaf ein! Es ist die Zeit der Eulenflucht."
>
> ("O sister sing, O sing of the days to come!"
> "Soon I will sing; soon in a lovelier place."
> "O sing and weave together the carpet of song,
> and together on it today, come, let us race!
>
> The rest with me, where bees will entertain us,
> myself an angelic beauty whom angels attend. . . ."
> Soon I will sing – yet in the tower there rustles
> a bird – so sleep, for the owl will soon ascend.")
> (*Songs*, 132/133)

At the end, then, there is lyric and the close of the growing cycle. The poem goes out in autumnal tones, birds heading for the south, the brother stacking up corn, the siblings standing silently as garlands are torn from their hair. At the end, having run through a thesaurus of poetic kinds, the poem turns to lyric as appropriate for the season, allegorical lyric for this time of mortgaged time.

If our time is "mortgaged" ("gestundet"), that means we have not yet paid for it. Mortgaged time is time for which we are still in debt, not yet redeemed. Bachmann makes much of the endemic play of meaning in terms like "mortgaged" and "redeemed." She seems especially taken by their echo of the suggestion that "guilt" and "debt" are metaphors for each other, metaphors in the system that defines our worldly condition. The play that appears in "gestundet" also appears in "Schuld" ("guilt") and "schuldig" ("guilty"), terms she uses meticulously. To be guilty is to borrow, to be guilty is to owe. The time we have mortgaged is not our own: that fundamental possession is the property of another until we have paid it off. Bachmann also makes much of the antiquity of this play, its place in an antique discourse that in one form or another, to varying degrees of belief, has worked its way down to our time. The question of Bachmann's belief is less pertinent at this point than the suggestions of continuity and the use she makes of it. When she posits, in the poem that names her first collection of poems, that the time we mortgaged is due and soon will show on the horizon ("Borrowed Time," *Songs*, 22-3), she taps into antique discourse that still remains in play and speaks of the same issues. When the epic hero she tracks disappears one night, in doubt, she picks up that play of language again, addressing our mortgaged time, confirmed as mortgaged when the hero vanishes.

Of course, this argues for a radical thematic constellation, a sense of pervasive guilt, original or newly minted, ancient but brought to a pitch even the ancients never knew. Yet it suggests much else that clearly took Bachmann's attention, not only the thematic constellation and its attendant metonyms but its ongoing history as well. Time that is mortgaged, borrowed on, is separate from other time, different in mode because unfinished. It is, in that sense, fractured, fundamentally disjunct, broken off from the ongoing time it hopes to join with when redeemed. Though it looks like other time, it has an "aura" of its own that makes it, in Benjamin's sense of aura, present among us but separate, here but unique in its kind. But when Bachmann speaks of such time in the rhetoric of ancient discourse, as she often does, she finds for fractured time a place in an ongoing history. By tapping into ancient rhetoric, her language seeks a site within an interrupted sequence, as though the tropes such history speaks can overcome temporal fracture by being invoked in "borrowed time." When we describe our temporal fractures in immemorial tropes, fundamental to Western culture, we seem to be claiming that such connections indicate a place of tying in to the perennial, suggesting an aesthetics of the lyric of decadence, a genre separate from history, a version of "la poésie pure."

Karen Achberger is correct in showing the insufficiency of any reading of Bachmann's poems in terms of their pure beauty[2], and she suggests Bachmann's rejection of such an approach in the late poem "No Delicacies."[3] Bachmann, she argues, is too aware of recent history to accept the claims for absolute beauty that took over much of the lyric from Poe's time to some of the higher reaches of modernism. Still, as I shall indicate in the further course of this essay, Bachmann works on and with a reading of history that thinks of it in terms of temporality as well as of a set of events in recent German history. On the crucial question of genre she uses the matter of lyric (in her case the most pertinent genre) as a model instance of the phenomenology of genre and how it works with history. These distinctions are crucial to any attempt to specify the tone and tenor of Bachmann's work. It is not only our personal histories that temporality subverts, but also the histories of the generic instruments with which we encounter history.

The functions of the history of genre had been a fundamental matter in romantic-modernist practice, obsessive in figures as different as Baudelaire, Rilke and Stevens. Obsessive in Bachmann too, it is essential to her poetics, and her sense of how allusion seeks to link language and form to history. "Of a Land, a River and Lakes" reads like a position paper on the subject. This time she links guilt-as-debt to old literary forms. Beginning with a fairy tale, the poem morphs to echoes of epic, "Odysseen." At the end, as though to frame the poem with claims about history, she invokes not only pastoral but the patterns of lyric as well, recalling its grounding in music and the sounds of a singular voice. In so forming her poem, she argues for the claim that we can access continuity by accessing genres and modes that have long histories. Bachmann's poem seeks connections between tropes and temporality. It links history and guilt and poetics and redemption in ways fundamental to the functioning of her work.

That makes a poem like "Psalm," near the end of Bachmann's first collection of poems (*Songs*, 56-9), an index to her reading of issues of genre. The title puts the question of genre plainly enough, too plainly, perhaps, for the caution a reader of Bachmann must always exercise. Those links of poetics and history also make "Psalm" an occasion to ponder *when* and *what* a genre is. Like all psalms, Bachmann's poem is phrased in direct address, the speaking-to of relation; but perhaps we should put that point as in fact enacting the hope for such an address (compare similar situations in

Hölderlin). Bachmann uses direct address as it has to be used in fractured time, something akin to sympathetic magic, seeking to bring an effect into being by performing the ancient gestures that signal the presence of the effect. Long before the ending of "Of a Land, a River and Lakes," Bachmann turned to traditional lyric, its blend of melos and voice, turning each into a model lyric for a mortgaged time. Of course the psalm is a special mode of lyric that is openly a song. It holds the sounds of a singular voice that speaks not only the sounds of a David, wielder of sling shots and harp strings, but also those of the community that speaks in and through his voice. His is the singing of an "I" that is always also a "we." And that is precisely the problem in this song for "mortgaged time." The poem sings its direct address, but it sings also of butchers with gloves, fastidiously clean as they close off the breath of the naked. It sings then (therefore) of the moon that breaks into "pieces" ("Scherben") (*Songs*, 56/57), and therefore of final rites never finalized, of a sacrament that cannot be accomplished. That moon is as fractured as the linkage the sacrament requires. But if the sacrament cannot be completed, how can this lyric be addressed? Putting it in other terms: since we can always attempt to address, how then can this lyric, this psalm, complete the addressing it needs in order to be what a psalm, fully, generically, should be? History, it seems, may be the enemy of genre. The time in which one seeks to realize the psalm may subvert the psalm's fulfillment. Maybe what one needs is a temporal poetics, aware of the potential for subversion that history holds and could produce at any time. How then can we speak of genre, considering our desire to speak of lyric in ways that speak of it always? How can we speak of lyric in ways that do not give in to the pressures of history?

Most poems in Bachmann's two books, as well as poems outside those books, ponder precisely such questions, meditate on and enact them in an obsessive, continuous quest. Several, like "Psalm," face these issues openly, probing the omnipresent potential for subversion, watching in fascination as the potential enacts itself. In some of her finest poems she turns this potential against herself, drawing her own acts and convictions into the circle of bitter ironies surrounding the making of poems in this time of mortgaged time.

Take, for example, the poems succeeding "Psalm." Bachmann follows "Psalm" with "In the Storm of Roses" ("Im Gewitter der

Rosen") (*Songs*, 62-5)—dark, ponderous, stormy, quasi-gothic—then follows that romantic holdover with "Salt and Bread" ("Salz und Brot") (*Songs*, 60-1). The series of titles suggests that Bachmann wants to do in these poems what she does in other poems with the rhetoric of salvation and the examination of genre: tie the acts of a fragmented time to the ongoing continuities of a venerable discourse. In "Salt and Bread," Bachmann taps into archetype, drawing once again on the trope of the journey. Its significance had been signaled from the beginning of her first book, because she began *Borrowed Time* with the brilliant instance of "Journey Out" ("Ausfahrt") (*Songs*, 4-7), an ornate voyage out whose gestures and tonalities echo through the rest of her poems. To think in archetypes is to think in repeatable history. Drawing on archetypes is another way of taking up the mending of temporal fractures. This time she journeys in ships like "slow trains," "in langsamen Zügen" ("Salt and Bread," *Songs*, 62/3) that take her to new islands; but those islands, it turns out, offer only more of the same, a Nietzschean eternal return. We succeed only in switching one intimacy for another. Still captives to the continent, we shall slip back into its illnesses, the waves of truth rare as ever. The trip to the new islands turns out to be one more journey whose contours are always-already-written. History repeats itself, as it does with the fairy tale hero, locked into intertext, who finds that his journey echoes every other text. Bachmann gets a renewal but not of precisely the sort she had hoped for: archetypes, it seems, may behave like prisons.

Much the same conditions appear in "Salt and Bread," which shows Bachmann seeking still another discourse to which she can bond her needs. The results hold bitter ironies because she does bond with the discourse but only to enact it in its lowest, most frustrating form, another round of the same. What seems to be a voyage turns out to be only a trip within a circular hall of mirrors where we see no more than ourselves and the images we repeat, where Bachmann sees herself at work merely reiterating tropes. She does in "Salt and Bread" what she did in "Journey Out" and "Of a Land, a River and Lakes," namely echo the archetype, partly in order to show herself helplessly echoing the archetype. In one sense she acts like a painter painting an image of herself painting. Yet, unable to control that image, what she shows herself performing is only an ironic *Reigen*, a round dance that puts her back where she began.

What she hoped would turn out to be an ingathering of the exiles turns out to be only another formulation of exile.

In a plea directly addressed to an apparently intimate "You" ("Du"—or is the utterance of "Du" only more sympathetic magic, a trick for fostering intimacy by using the terms of intimacy?), she asks a figure in feverish vestments to tear a thorn from the flesh of the cactus (it too was ironically crowned). Tempted, she cannot resist one more Nietzschean remark: the thorn is a "Zeichen" ("sign") (*Songs*, 62-3, translation modified) of that impotence to which we, ourselves impotent, bow helplessly, without will. The thorn stuck in the flesh, the weak that bow to the weak—these confirm the self-direction of her manifold ironies. Sardonic, self-subverting, her action unmasks the archetype's contemporary condition, revealing it as torn and corrupted, fundamentally rotten. Archetypes are as fractured as every other holdover in this time of mortgaged time.

What, then, of the salt and bread that name this lyric allegory? Taken separately or together they make up tropes of ingathering, emblems of community. The salt, taken alone, echoes the Hebrew Bible's salt of the covenant, the sign of the Hebrews' agreement with Yahweh that there will be linkage between them. The covenant indicates a direction to which they can post their addresses. The bread, taken alone, is that of Christian communion, a sharing not only among the communicants, but also with the direction of their intention. Salt and bread, taken together, make one more symbol of unity: sitting down to salt and bread is an ancient gesture of friendship.

At the end, then, in the final two stanzas, the ironies culminate in a scene of salt-and-bread amity. Overcome by the sea, the speaker draws from the water the salt of the covenant and places it on her threshold in a gesture of hospitality. Then, in a richly emblematic scene, they (the "I" becomes a communal "we") share with the rain a bread, a "debt" ("Schuld") and a house (*Songs*, 64-5). "Psalm" told that the sacrament cannot now be completed; the requisite links are fractured beyond immediate repair. In "Salt and Bread," all that the immediate has now is the salt and bread of amity, communion only with the rain; hardly the grand communality Bachmann has heard of indirectly. As the sacrament is fractured so does the archetype of the quest end up uncompleted, turning into yet another dull, entrapping round that undoes all the multivalent significance of the trope, leaving it, too, incomplete. The wholeness of the total journey, the journey to the truly new, is now beyond their grasp. The wholeness of the total communion, the absolute community to which all journeys should lead, can only be for the future, the time beyond "borrowed" or "mortgaged time."

That is another way of putting what we have already put by questioning Bachmann on genre. If history subverts genre, turns out psalms that, in our time, cannot be realized, it also subverts those tropes to which Bachmann turns in the hope of establishing continuities. Genre and thematic constellation run into the same hindrances, act out the same frustrations. Genre and thematic constellation are in no sense to be treated as separable items for they turn out, in Bachmann's poems, to be two ways of speaking of the same radical issues, those confrontations with history that appear at every point in her productions of lyric poems. Genre and thematic are surely the same element seen from different points of view; they are different ways of reading her allegorical lyrics.

And it is precisely the question of lyric that indicates not only their indissolubility, but also the reason why genre and thematic constellation are so vulnerable to history, its fissures and fragmentations. Bachmann's poems continue issues associated with the romantic-modernist lyric, bringing to brilliant fruition its late modernist possibilities, suggesting the conditions that were to turn it postmodern. In particular, she continues the romantic-modernist emphasis on voice, a characteristic of lyric from at least the time of Sappho, a characteristic of poetry from at least Herder and Poe, when we routinely began to identify poetry and the lyric. To give primacy to voice is not only to make prominent the sounds of subjectivity, it is also to emphasize the making of subjectivity, the naming of the self. Whether or not we identify the "I" that speaks in the poem with the speaker of the poem, whether or not we identify that "I" with the name subscribed to the poem, the act of presenting and naming the self characterizes the lyric voice. Bachmann's attraction to the lyric surely stems in part from its ancient relation to melos; its grounding in song must have been enticing to one so passionate for music. The voice that sings in *melos*, the central voice in lyric, sings itself into being, its fundamental need the finding of a name for itself. Whatever else her allegorical lyrics take as thematic, they are always, fundamentally, allegories of naming.

To put it another way: most romantic-modernist lyrics dwell on centrality, even as—perhaps because—they sense the numbering of its days. The naming of that centrality is an obsessive act of the time, an act of poems that define the time, like Rilke's *Dinggedichte* or the later work of Stevens. Bachmann does the same in her own defining poems; awareness of naming inhabits her poems throughout. She learned early what Hölderlin learned as his mind lost all contour: the threats to centrality seen in the difficulties of self-naming. In the early poem "How Shall I Name Myself?" ("Wie soll ich mich nennen?") (*Songs*, 264-5), Bachmann raises those points, not only *what* to name myself, but (given identity's shiftiness) *how* to name myself. Once she had been a tree, bound; then a bird that slipped away, free; then, chained in a ditch, deliverer of a dirty egg. She is the thorn shot into the deer as well as the deer that flees. She is a dove, a rolling stone, evading the arrow of the "guilt" that goes on in its own "round dance" ("Reigen"). Surely this is consistent but it is the consistency of a voice that is constantly shifting species, never the same kind in its ongoing flight from guilt. The only consistency lies in the consistent undoing of the centrality of kind, of what we fundamentally *are*. "Only one word is lacking!" ("Ein Wort nur fehlt!") (*Songs*, 265, translation modified), she says, a word that remains the same, a stable, authenticating noun. But "How shall I name myself," she ends, "without living in another language?"

How indeed can language make possible the naming of self if words must work in history? If tropes are subject to history's insidious undoings, if genres cannot hold under the subversions of history, how then can self be one single thing and persist as that single thing whatever history's pressures and fissures? Many of Bachmann's poems state openly that it cannot, that naming cannot be fulfilled and therefore lyric cannot be fulfilled. Lyric, as we have known it from Sappho to Poe and beyond, seems to have met its nemesis in this age in which we query the very writing of poems. One answer, of course, is that names *must* be asserted and poems *must* be written in this of all ages. One must write durable, "lasting" ("haltbar") sentences, she says in her late poem to Anna Akhmatova (*Songs*, 308-9), sentences that hold against the storms of history. One lasting sentence will suffice, one structure that holds on throughout the ding-dong of words. Yet in the final sentence of her poem to Akhmatova, she cautions through negatives ("no one" ["keiner"], "not" ["nicht"]) that "No one writes this sentence who does not sign her name" (*Songs*, 309). The efficacy of the sentence depends on the efficacy of the name and the self it indicates. The sentence calls for a self so good at being a self that it can sign its name underneath with the fullest confidence that the act is meaningful, the undersigning valid for more than the moment of its making.

The poem to Akhmatova, ironically called "Truly" ("Wahrlich"), does not tell us how to do this, only that it must be done. The question still remains: "how shall I name myself?" No answer comes forth, only a compulsion to go on with words, to refuse dusty old images, "dying words," the words of dying ("Sterbenswort,") ("You Words," *Songs*, 304/305). If the world, finally tired of language's incompletion, insists that language is "alwaysalready-spoken" ("schon gesagt sein," *Songs*, 302/303, my translation), she urges refusal of its demands. Words will only pull other words after them just as sentences pull sentences, so let us acknowledge and follow their lack of finality. We have learned from history not only that history will not stay put, but that it will not permit us to do so, will make definitive signing impossible for most if not all. In "No Delicacies" (*Songs*, 320-3), at the end of her poetic career, Bachmann says she will get by but has to go on living through the problematic self-naming whose insistence drives her lyrics. At the end of the poem, naming is posed once again. Frustrated by writer's cramp, she will sweep away the word-operas she has already plotted. In that gesture, she will annihilate all the grammatical shifters we use to point to our identity, "I you and he she it / we you . . . " (*Songs*, 323), her nearly exhaustive litany of our positionings in grammar. The poem ends—poems end—with the hollow sounds of shifters, pronouns that can stand for anyone at all. They stand for us temporarily as we take a grammatical position within a sentence. Then they shift into standing for others as those others take positions, become the "I," the "she," the "we" for as long as their own sentence runs. Shifters are namings for the moment, identities for the occasion. In the world of shifters the self is just as much a text, a weaving for the moment, as the poems in which it takes part. In the world of shifters the self is a grammatical function, subject, therefore, to erasure when we wipe away our words. At the end of Bachmann's career as a poet, self-naming remains a fundamental problem because, at the end as at the beginning, its stability seems only a matter for the moment, a point in borrowed time. Bachmann turned to allegorical lyrics because she guessed, as Walter Benjamin did, that modern readings of allegory would show it steeped in history, able to handle history's fractures. Yet the allegory she practiced in her poems was patently not in itself enough to sustain the lyric voice as Bachmann understood it, nor did the work of others set up sufficient models. Many postmodern poets—one thinks for example of the Language Poets, their work later than hers but fully aware of the issues—support and sardonically build upon the fracturing of genre, of archetype, of voice, characteristic elements of the late modernist lyric. Some call postmodern poetry post-lyric or anti-lyric because it seeks to build upon the demise of just those qualities, the struggle with which made the substance of the romantic-modernist lyric. Bachmann's poems could have taken a corresponding turn, figuring the contours of a post-lyricism that sought to turn its back on a genre whose history Bachmann had mastered; but she chose to put poems aside rather than take that particular tack. What she left were shards of an exemplary struggle.

NOTES

1. Two collections of poems were published during Bachmann's lifetime: *Die gestundete Zeit* (*Borrowed Time*), 1953, and *Anrufung des Großen Bären* (*Invocation of the Great Bear*), 1956. Quotations from both the German text and the English translation of Bachmann's poems that appear in this essay are taken from *Songs in Flight: The Collected Poems of Ingeborg Bachmann*, trans. Peter Filkins (New York: Marsilio, 1994). Hereafter cited as *Songs*.

2. Karen Achberger, *Understanding Ingeborg Bachmann*, (Columbia: University of South Carolina Press, 1995). T. S. Eliot's *From Poe to Valéry* remains a classic comment from within modernism (New York: Harcourt Brace, 1948), 15-6.

3. Ibid., 22.

3 / "Pont Mirabeau... Waterloo Bridge...": A Contrastive Reading of Apollinaire's "Le Pont Mirabeau" and Ingeborg Bachmann's "Die Brücken"

Sabine I. Gölz

Prefatory Remarks

The essay before you offers a contrastive reading of two poems whose central figure is that of bridges and bridging.[1] That figure turns out to go far beyond being a simple metaphor. Both poems—Guillaume Apollinaire's "Le Pont Mirabeau" ("Mirabeau Bridge") and Ingeborg Bachmann's "Die Brücken" ("The Bridges")—invoke concrete, identifiable and named bridges in Paris and London. Yet both also play strategically and performatively on a historically evolving poetic language. In Apollinaire's poem, this complex play of metaphorical, intertextual, inter-sensual (visual and aural) and even interlingual bridgings serves to construct and buttress a specific poetic subject-position. In Bachmann's poem, similar strategies are employed to reframe the space constructed by Apollinaire, and to re-read it from a larger and expanding horizon in such a way as to deconstruct its founding and constitutive exclusions, and ultimately to undo the very "bridge" Apollinaire constructs. Bachmann's title "Die Brücken" refers no longer to any architectural construct as much as precisely to the type of poetic subject constructed by Apollinaire's text. What emerges most strikingly in the end, then, is the contrast between two distinctly different poetic subject-positions organizing these poems, with one of them functioning as the deconstruction of the other.

In Apollinaire's poem we observe a poetic subject that places itself in both a literary tradition and in a given historical, geographic and linguistic space. Apollinaire, who came to France as a person of somewhat uncertain nationality and parentage, situates himself in Paris, at the center of things French. He strives to define his position (and assure its permanence) (from) within that given literary and cultural history, and he negotiates the support of this order through the appeal to a profound asymmetry inherent in that poetic and representational order that is based on the gender difference. Such support is available to the poem in the very moment of composition in the form of a *gradient*, of the specific statistical *inclination* of a readership to read in one way rather than another, and to reproduce the metaphoric structures already in circulation. To establish a place for himself in the existing canon the poet relies, in other words, on the continuation and permanence of that very canon in a readership which reproduces and thus amplifies the rhetorical moves of the literary language which it (be)speaks. Such a supportive readership is the metaphoric heaven into which such poets desire for their works to blossom, where the crucial dissemination must take place, and where they can hope to "live on." Tradition, when it is considered as a way of reading that is *in circulation,* creates a space-time in which the direction of a reversed gravity makes that ascent what one could call a "downhill battle" for a poet who knows how to play the existing field of tropes. The ironies of that mechanism become visible only from a different perspective—that of the expanding (and thus ultimately *open*) frame of a general economy of literature. We will observe in Apollinaire's poem(s) the effort to both use and deny that general economy, and thus to restrict and negotiate it by means of a combination of rhetorical turns, a series of spatial and temporal displacements. By cutting, displacing, and re-framing textual fragments, by separating out discrete contexts, Apollinaire's text feeds on and reinforces the canon's underlying "broken symmetry." It creates limits and differentiates spaces that align him with a long tradition of similarly constructed poetic subjects.

The construction of the poetic subject is strikingly different in the case of Bachmann's poem. Rather than placing itself in a given and named cultural space—as Apollinaire's text did—her poetic subject relies on an expanding relativistic frame that no longer banks on historical probabilities, and that dissolves the power of language to name. The only gradient of literary spacetime acknowledged by this poetic subject is precisely the one which Apollinaire's text denies. In Bachmann's poem, the only incline is the "slope of transitoriness," that is spanned by "no dream" ("Doch übers Gefälle des Vergänglichen/ wölbt uns kein Traum").[2] Supplying the "missing" element that restores the symmetry that was broken by excluding her, her poem supplements and exceeds Apollinaire's in every direction, articulating a scenario that is precisely complementary to Apollinaire's. Thus her text also becomes a reading of his poem and of the restricted frame within which it operates. The poetic subject in Bachmann's text can no longer be considered a "speaking subject" in the restrictive (namely: gendered) sense which characterizes the maneuvers in "Le Pont Mirabeau." Nor is her poetic subject any longer a "feminine" subject, since, in order to be able to discern the place of femininity in that old and restrictive economy, she has to let go of the attempt to determine the "gender" of her text through the appeal (observable in Apollinaire's poem) to a specifically gendered readership. Everything in Apollinaire's poem—its point of departure, its rhetoric, its intertextual and interlinguistic relations, and above all its hopes for the future—hinges on a hidden gender asymmetry that becomes untenable if seen from the horizon over which "she" has disappeared.

What emerges as a crucial notion for the analysis is the effect of "superposition": a doubling (or multiplication) of contexts, which is the mark of the irreducible *complexity* of language.[3] Both continuity and difference, and ultimately *sense*, is always produced by a doubling of text by reading, of past by present; it appears as a *relation*. This notion of complexity is related to, but also to be distinguished from the "undecidability" of deconstruction, because the latter tends to neglect the element (and possibility) of *decision* inherent in that moment. The same applies to the notion of the "play of the signifier." The only seemingly uncontrolled dissemination over time and in space is precisely that which provides the (dissimulated) discursive framework that supports Apollinaire's project. For what is undecidable and "random" in every specific case, can nevertheless produce macroscopically describable and predictable probabilities, distributions, pressures, and "currents," and it is precisely the type of currency which is already in circulation which validates some coins and devalues others. The limits enforced by this flowing frame are what Bachmann's poem brings out. She aims at invalidating that circulating frame itself—rather than any specific crystallization of it.[4]

It is possible, then, if not to hear "Bachmann's voice," so at least to discern in the contrastive figuration that appears when her text is read against and allowed to read a text (such as Apollinaire's) that exemplifies what she is leaving behind. The result is "comparative literature": the emergence of readability out of the superposition of (at least) two texts.

Once this complexity of language/literature—the making of sense at the juncture between *and* disjunction of two heterogeneous contexts/poems/languages—has been perceived, the invocation of the subject's transitoriness can no longer operate as a prohibition against the production of specific (comparative, relative, complex) readings. It then becomes clear that sense is made only in translation, comparison, in the relative shifting of positions, and that we can perhaps read a text *only* if we succeed in ceasing to speak its language.

Guillaume Apollinaire's "Le Pont Mirabeau"

From the start we are dealing in this poem with a superposition of voices and perspectives. More specifically, we perceive a layering of geographic "reality" and poetic "memory," the superimposition of a metaphorical reading over a river in Paris. That superimposed reading will become recognizable as the return of something that was purposefully lost before. And its return we will recognize as one of the many circlings, displacements and sense-crossings in a continuous differential play that selects, admits, invokes, and excludes, and that ultimately serves to construct and empower the very specific location assumed by Apollinaire's poetic subject.

Apollinaire's poem has four stanzas, each of which is followed by the recurring refrain-like insertion of two lines:

Le Pont Mirabeau

Sous le pont Mirabeau coule la Seine
    Et nos amours
  Faut-il qu'il m'en souvienne
La joie venait toujours après la peine

    Vienne la nuit sonne l'heure
    Les jours s'en vont je demeure

Les mains dans les mains restons face à face
Tandis que sous
Le pont de nos bras passe
Des éternels regards l'onde si lasse

    Vienne la nuit sonne l'heure
    Les jours s'en vont je demeure

L'amour s'en va comme cette eau courante
L'amour s'en va
Comme la vie est lente
Et comme l'Espérance est violente

    Vienne la nuit sonne l'heure
    Les jours s'en vont je demeure

Passent les jours et passent les semaines
Ni temps passé
Ni les amours reviennent
Sous le pont Mirabeau coule la Seine

    Vienne la nuit sonne l'heure
    Les jours s'en vont je demeure[5]

(*Mirabeau Bridge*

Under Mirabeau Bridge flows the Seine
And our loves
Do I need to be reminded
The joy came always after the pain

    May night arrive the hour strike
    The days they go I remain

Hands in hands we stand face to face
All the while underneath
The bridge of our arms passes
Of eternal gazes the wave so slow

> May night arrive the hour strike
> The days they go I remain
>
> Love departs like that water running
> Love departs
> How slow is life
> And how violent is Hope
>
> May night arrive the hour strike
> The days they go I remain
>
> The days they pass the weeks they pass
> Neither times that have passed
> Nor the loves return
> Under Mirabeau Bridge flows the Seine
>
> May night arrive the hour strike
> The days they go I remain)[6]

What will interest us here is the way in which this poem moves: each of the stanzas gives its trajectory a particular turn, with the recurrence of the refrain, too, serving a very specific function.

In order to understand the function of the refrain, we have to leave the text for a different, earlier text from which these two lines are borrowed, and to which they in a sense take us back every time they recur. That earlier text was written by Apollinaire while he was imprisoned under the suspicion of (no less!) having been involved in the disappearance of the *Mona Lisa* from the Louvre:

> Dans une fosse comme un ours
> Chaque matin je me promène
> Tournons, tournons, tournons toujours
> Quand donc finira la semaine
> Quand donc finiront les amours
> Vienne la nuit sonne l'heure
> Les jours s'en vont et je demeure[7]
>
> (In a ditch just like a bear
> Every morning I go strolling

We turn and turn and turn all days
Oh when will the week be done
Oh when will the loves be done
May night arrive the hour strike
The days they go and I remain)

The creature who is here forced to act like a bear is the poet himself. He is imprisoned in a circular movement without beginning or end, and this un-articulated circularity threatens to translate him out of language and history and back into a state in which he becomes indistinguishable from an animal. The danger of lapsing into unproductively uniform repetition thus marks one of the poles the poet needs to avoid. In order to counteract it, Apollinaire resorts to an interesting type of articulation: he leaves the "prison" text unpublished, cuts it up, and distributes its fragments over various other later poems. The reappearance of the earlier text's last two lines as the refrain of "Le Pont Mirabeau" is thus no exception: all the lines of the prison text eventually find their way into one of Apollinaire's poems.[8] All, that is, but one: the line which runs "Quand donc finiront les amours" ("Oh when will the loves be gone") is "lost"—and through that very loss acquires a particular significance.

The invocational refrain of "Le Pont Mirabeau" can now be recognized as a bridge or, if you will, as a shuttle connecting two radically different situations: imprisonment, stagnation in empty repetition on the one hand, and loss without return on the other hand. Both the enclosure in a circular rut ("fosse"), or, inversely, the complete lack of structure in a scenario of generalized flux threaten the desirable mean, where openness and closure are available in turn, where change is tempered by continuity.

The lines in the refrain that invoke the coming of the night and the sounding of the hour ("Vienne la nuit sonne l'heure / Les jours s'en vont je demeure"—"May night arrive the hour strike / The days go by I remain"), precisely due to the circularity of their return in a different context, create a point of indeterminacy between two contexts, a suspension or bridge "between" the two dangerous scenarios: "Le Pont Mirabeau" re-frames the lines from prison by transporting them into a scenario of "loss," thus superimposing a new reading on them. It makes a big difference whether one says "I remain" ("je demeure") in prison and captivity, or while looking at the icon of eternal changeability and loss—water passing under a bridge. In the refrain, then, an opposition is both produced (put to use) and immediately suspended for/by the poet. Rather than translating him into any definite state, the re-framing of these lines creates a superposition of both states/readings on which he can stand as on a "bridge"—now able to negotiate between the two conditions of imprisonment and flux without being trapped in or lost to either.

But while he has an interest in being neither confined nor lost, the poet also needs to be sure that the difference between these two possibilities remains stable. For only if both states are clearly defined is the undecidability *between them* sufficiently specific to be profitable. The question therefore becomes: who or what keeps the difference in place while the poet enjoys its suspension? And since the difference is only produced by the shifting of frames or readings (in this case by the introduction of the "scenario of loss"), it is evident that it is precisely the lamented loss which maintains it. The issue for the poet thus will be to keep the river going, to keep losing something, so that the river, through its hidden opposition to the prison (elsewhere in space and time), keeps producing that liberating ambiguity in the "je demeure" ("I remain"). Our question thus has been rephrased to "Who or what keeps the river in place?"

If we take seriously the fundamental relativity which has become an irreducible feature of a 20th century view of the world, then, in the absence of an absolute point of reference, both imprisonment and loss can only be relative terms. Imprisonment is only perceptible in terms of an "outside" where one would be "free." The scenario of loss provides that outside. But loss also is a relative term, for if it were not defined in relation to something that remains, it would not be loss but undirected chaos. It is thus the *prison* that transforms the chaos of undirected flux into a *channeled* flow, while, inversely, the staged *loss* of the loves provides the stabilizing outside against which the imprisonment in circular repetition can be properly appreciated as stability and permanence. The two define and inscribe each other. However, they do not deconstruct, but rather sustain each other. The undecidability is *useful* and desirable, and it is the whole point of the machine to create and stabilize it.

The difference between the two frames can itself be maintained only through an ongoing exchange between them. Imprisonment and freedom, permanence and loss must at any moment each have an object. In other words: there must always be at least one complementary element that occupies the other position while the poet occupies the one. Our inquiry thus takes the form of the search for one (or more) elements that are similar enough to the poet to be able to stand in for him and be exchanged for him, and different enough from the poet not to be confused with him.

We are looking for a particle that goes in the other direction when the poet goes into one, that makes the whole "creation" conform to the law of the conservation of energy. We are looking for a place of absence elsewhere that corresponds to his presence here, creating a web of relations which would add up to zero if there were anybody around to do the adding.

Poets, just like everybody else, including God, create out of nothing. In empty space, the only way to build up momentum is to push something in the direction opposite to the one in which one wants to go. The sum of his creation is zero, and therefore he must make sure that it not be drawn. Mistakes must be made, numbers lost, positions overlooked, if the "work" is to prevail. And for Apollinaire (insofar as he is writing poetry) to lament the loss of his loves is equivalent to a rocket's lamenting the loss of the firestream that propels it. Within the gravitational field of a historically accumulated mass, things are, however, easier: the water flows downhill "all by itself."

The project thus is to locate what is missing, to observe the mechanics of the methodical loss we have postulated. In this effort we will eventually have to return to our first question and ask: what specific turn does the poem take in each of the four stanzas? Before we do so, however, we will have to make another preparatory excursion into yet another text by Apollinaire. This additional text will help clarify some of the implications of the postulate that there must be a second element involved in this creation which "conserves energy."

The poem that incorporates the largest part of the pre-text which we have just examined, and the only one that remains a "prison-poem" (and thus exactly complementary to "Le Pont Mirabeau") is the third in a cycle of six poems entitled "A la Santé."

(The *Santé* prison in Paris having been the one where Apollinaire was detained for about a week.) The first stanza of this poem is:

> Dans une fosse comme un ours
> Chaque matin je me promène
> Tournons tournons tournons toujours
> Le ciel est bleu comme une chaîne
> Dans une fosse comme un ours
> Chaque matin je me promène[9]

> (In a ditch just like a bear
> Every morning I go strolling
> We turn and turn and turn all days
> The sky is blue just like a chain
> In a ditch just like a bear
> Every morning I go strolling)[10]

Here occurs the double return of the passage concerned with the threat of a loss of language in empty repetition. But the stanza does more than merely repeat the same. A new line has appeared, and with it a new element: the prisoner looks up, seeking escape in the third dimension, and sees a sky, "blue like a chain." The sky is blue and thus presumably open to the view of the speaker. It is therefore all the more surprising that this openness is, via the analogy introduced through the word "comme," immediately transposed into what appears as another instrument of imprisonment: the chain. The figure of the chain is further remarkable insofar as it is characterized by the displaced repetition of the same circular element, and thus as a figure in which linear progression can be achieved without giving up the closure of the circle. It can also, therefore, be read as that chain of tropological substitutions, and of language itself. The latter, it turns out, provides a combination of play and slippage on the one hand, yet without surrendering as strong sense of constraint on the other hand. It has become possible to feel that one is going somewhere by going around in circles.

The look up into the sky thus opens the view onto and access into language through the daring analogical "similarity" posited by the simile "blue like a chain." Through this bold move, it would seem, the poet has pulled himself out of the prison-yard by his own bootstraps. And the move certainly seems to have been successful, for after this paradoxical—because already linguistic—leap into language, the self-haunting first two lines return once more, but this time without the third line. That absence indicates that the "toujours" ("always," or, etymologically, "all days") of the captive circular movement has indeed been broken. It has been displaced, we suspect, into precisely this blue and heavenly chain where repetition leads to linear progression rather than stagnation and muteness.

What is "lost" relative to the *Urtext* from prison, thus, is ultimately not just one line, but two:

    Tournons, tournons, tournons toujours

    (We turn and turn and turn all days)

and:

    Quand donc finiront les amours

    (Oh when will the loves be done)

The two lines—one concerning the eternal return of an as yet undefined "we," the other the desire for the end of "love"—thus enter into a relation through the mere fact of their loss. That relation is reinforced by the fact that the lines rhyme and that their rhyme echoes the danger that the poet is trying to counteract: *-ours* (bear). It seems, then, that there is a subterranean link between the fear not to be human, the end of love, and the fear that repetition be empty or: zero.

But the two lines also differ because they are lost at different "times around." The call for the end of the loves never returns on the surface, while the unproductive circling of the "we" is lost only after it has been repeated once. The two are also not lost in the same way. The "turning"-line is displaced into the sky, where the little circles begin to form a chain, and where perhaps from now on the constraint of the tropes will be located. By contrast, there seems no indication as to the path taken by the call to end the loves. But the second half of "À la Santé," III can provide a hint as to the whereabouts of that wish. For in comparison to the little *Urtext*, we now see a second prison-cell introduced in the latter half of the poem. The accommodations have doubled:

> Dans la cellule d'à côté
> On y fait couler la fontaine
> Avec les clefs qu'il fait tinter
> Que le geôlier aille et revienne
> Dans la cellule d'à côté
> On y fait couler la fontaine
>
> (In the cell next door to mine
> There one makes the fountain flow
> With the keys that he has tinkle
> So that the guard may leave and return
> In the cell right by my side
> There one makes the fountain flow)[11]

The "repetition" or doubling of the prison cell itself introduces a difference that allows the poet to negotiate his situation. Once displaced, the prison-cell no longer "frames" merely the poet, but also some unseen second element "next door."

Remarkable are the mysterious keys that seem to operate by their mere sound, rather than by a mechanical procedure of lock-and-key. Even more important seems the fact that the sound made by the keys would be quite indistinguishable from that made by a chain. The difference between chain and keys exists only visually, but not acoustically. This reveals one of the constructive principles at work here: operative in the ongoing construction we have been following is a separation of the realms of vision and hearing respectively. The result is that the subject, instead of being confronted by one closed prison wall and an unreachable and infinite sky, faces two semi-permeable limits. A superposition created by means of a metaphoric reading reverses the allocation of openness and closure through its alignment with two different senses of the perceiving subject. The partial closing of the sky in the appeal to its color provides access to (is made possible by) the controlled imprisonment in the desired chain of substitutions. It is compensated for by the partial (aural) opening of the wall that becomes permeable for sounds—but not colors—from next door.

The maneuver relies on the presence of the "wall" that is established by the move from one text to its repetition and variation, from the *Urtext* to "A la Santé," III. The doubling is figured in the second poem as the appearance of a neighboring cell. Walls are as unmanageable in their difference as the circling in the yard is in its sameness. Yet a suspension is effected, textually, by the simple means that the lines, in the move from the one poem to the other, remain to a considerable degree *the same*.

The suspension—the half-closure performed on the sky and the subsequent half-opening of the wall—is maintained by means of the partial blind- and deafness respectively, which results from (or finds its expression in) the two moves, as bold as they are limiting: the hallucinatory reading of the sky as a chain on the one hand, and the wishful naming of that which is not seen, but only heard next door as "keys." Likely enough, however, we have here two divergent readings of the same chain: two readings which now both seem (i.e. half look and half sound) promising to the poet. Language is that limitation of our senses that limits the infinity of the sky insofar as we "see" it as blue, and that in a second step provides the inspiring "key" which opens our prison—insofar as it makes us "hear" something we have never seen, something that perhaps cannot be seen.

What is behind the wall? "He" who makes the keys tinkle. We ought to be surprised to see the masculine gender awarded to that place where the poet so methodically *sees nothing*, and we may suspect that this attribution is somewhat wishfully determinate. Here, then, is the key that we have been looking for: everything that is "behind the wall" is accessible only via sound, not through vision. For a reading interested in undoing the prison house of language, it will be important to "hear" and to "see" things in funny places and at odd times, to perceive the walls separating one from the other, and the contexts and frames which bias the outcome by encouraging at any given point one reading over the other.

It thus appears that the "cellule d'à côté" is introduced in order to allow the negotiation between openness and closure. It adds a complementary space, similar yet different, a place to which something can disappear from view in order to be misheard, a place which is closed when the poet is free, and open when he is confined. Precisely the type of place, in other words, which had to be postulated for that other element which conserves energy, which is there to make the sum total of what is created remain zero, without thereby preventing that creation altogether. The question thus becomes whether we are not witnessing the production of a minimal pair in the coupling of "*ciel*" and "cell," a pair related through that ambiguous "chain" which links up to both and is neither. A pair also which, strangely, no longer relies on the differences within one language, but on the similarities between two different ones, and which takes this form only because we happen to be writing in English . . .

But there is something else we are told about that other cell: it is the locus of, lo and behold, a "fontaine," a fountain or a spring, perhaps even the wellspring of a river. This is, it would seem, a rather unlikely thing to be found in a prison cell. And so we cannot help but wonder how it got there, and what its purpose is. One also wonders who this anonymous, impersonal "on" is or are, that make(s) this spring flow, and whether this agent is in any way connected with the coming and going of the jailer, and thus, whether the "fontaine" flows intermittently or continuously. This, however, finally leads our speculations back to that chain in the sky, and we begin to wonder whether it may not in some way be connected to that mysterious "fontaine," and what would happen if somebody pulled on it. . . . Whether, in other words, the glorious ascent of the poet into the canonical heaven of poetic language might not have a rather mechanical and ignominious counterpart in the abject disappearance of something else out of sight and down the drain. If that were so, however, then it is indeed this cell next door where that other lost line returns unseen, and is lost again—not up into the sky, but down the Water-loo, not to be seen again until, much farther downstream, something resurfaces into the poet's consciousness as an unwelcome memory "out of the blue," over that river in Paris. Such is the poetic value of modern sanitation. And this, finally, takes us to the beginning of "Le Pont Mirabeau."

The poem begins with the pronouncement of a simple geographical fact about a bridge in Paris: "Sous le pont Mirabeau coule la Seine" ("Under Mirabeau Bridge flows the Seine"). This fact is, however, immediately supplemented with the addition "Et nos amours" ("And our loves"). One wonders whence this came, for it certainly does not follow from geography. It seems to come out of the blue indeed, intruding into the stanza as if spoken by a voice other than that of the speaker of the first line. A voice that speaks for more than one subject, for a collectivity united by the reference now not to a geographic fact, but rather to a common object of loss: *our* loves. For the poet is neither the only nor the first one to stand on that "bridge." The latter, rather, is positively crowded with precedents.

The beginning of the poem, it appears, starts with a moment at which the carefully established and artfully sorted out differences from "A la Santé," III, enter into a larger context and seem about to recollapse. A momentary reversal occurs when the reflection of the sky paints the river blue, when what was posited into the sky and what was lost down the drain becomes indistinguishable through a surface-effect, when ascension and abjection stage a common return and the glance into the river echoes as a voice. If any was needed, this sudden reappearance of the "amours" at this precise moment is the confirmation of our suspicion that the fontaine in the cell next door sprang indeed from the desire expressed in the line "Quand donc finiront les amours ("Oh, when will the loves be done")— the desire to lose in order to gain poetic momentum.

The third line reacts to this return with a rebuke directed at the source of that intrusive reminder, identified as "il" ("it" or "he"): "Faut-il qu'il m'en souvienne" ("Do I need to be reminded," or, more literally, "Does it/he have to remind me of that"). But who or what is the "il" which here functions grammatically as a subject? The pronoun could, of course, simply refer to the arrangement as a whole, bridge, sky, and river, to "it" which occasions the involuntary appearance of memory, a sudden conjunction of fact and voice. It also, however, has (once more) the effect of coloring this voice with the masculine gender. The "il" is furthermore linked not only to the neutral and impersonal "il" in *Faut-il*, but it also and secondly has a dark and invisible companion in the shapeless and sexless "en," that mere "it" or "that" which is the object of the memory as much as of the instantly repeated abjection (Kristeva's use of the term).[12] That the separation should be made along those or any lines is far from immediately obvious, for the problem in this joint return is, as we have just argued, precisely the fact that there is a fair amount of confusion as to whether this visual echo or aural reflection over the river consists of poetic sighs or of lost loves. This confusion is "cleared up" by the attribution (in the rebuke) of the male gender, however indefinitely, to the voice, and the repetition of the loss in the dismissive (and ungendered) "en." Which is a different way of saying that the threatened difference is re-established instantaneously by the defensive motion of the poet, which divides the intruding memory. A split effected through gender in the sense that it attributes the male gender to voice.

In this splitting we witness the "spontaneous" (that is: unpremeditated—precisely because so mechanically in keeping with the operation of the machine we are here analyzing) return of the prison-wall of difference. This moment also provides support for the hypothesis that the "loves" are such a useful complement for the poet because, on the one hand, insofar as they are "human," they can be exchanged for him, while on the other hand, at the slightest danger of confusion, an appeal to their "difference" quickly sends them off on their separate path again—not the path of the poet, but precisely that of his elusive complement. The beginning of "Le Pont Mirabeau" is characterized by the threat of such a confusion. The minimal pair which keeps inside and outside, loss and gain apart and thus delimits the space of play, is the couple, half of which is always on the other side of the wall . . .

The last line of the stanza finally shifts the tense into the past, thus distancing the "event" in time: "La joie venait toujours après la peine" ("The joy came always after the pain"). The voice which speaks this last line is no longer that of the "je" ("I") that is "experiencing" this threatening collapse of difference. It is a voice that proleptically reassures the poet that *after* this pain there is pleasure in store for him. It is a voice situated in the future. In other words: this move is comparable to the linguistic leap into language which we have observed in the previous poem ("Le ciel est bleu comme une chaîne," "The sky is blue like a chain") insofar as here a displacement of the voice in time makes the pain experienced into an always already past event. Time is introduced as a new dimension/element in the construction insofar as it (as tense, that is, as linguistically constructed temporality) allows the poet some pur-

chase on yet another "other" side—the future of the text in reading.
At this point I would like to embark on another digression. For there is the suspicion that the return of the "amours" is in fact not wholly abhorred, but also to a large degree purposefully solicited by the act of mentioning that conjunction of bridge and river "into the blue," out of which the supplementary response then so speedily descends. The response comes "out of the sky," and its force cannot sufficiently be explained (nor can its "origin" be identified) by the appeal to one or two other poems by Apollinaire or anybody else. Rather, the supplementary memory "and our loves" descends from a generalized, delocalized, and random-access poetic memory. These loves are part of a stream much larger than one "fontaine" out of a prison cell, a stream that has been fed out of many prisons of this type over a long time.[13] The contact between the celestial and the subterranean component of this "memory-pool" is brought about by the carefully selected reference to a poetically serviceable piece of "reality." The supplementary metaphoric reading is then felled out. Only the conjunction of the two, triggered by the floating piece of trivia, sets off the process of poetic production.

That the "origin" of the intrusion is to be found in the generalized circulation of metaphoric readings rather than in individual poems, however, does not make a critical consideration of Apollinaire's double appeal to the sky and the "fontaine" (as observed in "A la Santé," III) expendable. What we have to do, however, is to reinterpret these moves in order to accommodate the emphasis on the collectiveness and generalized character of the blue voice of memory. Such a reinterpretation would emphasize that, through the analogy of "bleu comme une chaîne" ("blue like a chain") as well as the more oblique reliance on the loss of the "amours," the poet logs into a metaphoric sky or strikes a sounding board belonging to an instrument with a much greater capacity than that of an individual poem or voice. The move triggers an *amplification* of the tiny difference he is about to set up into something solid and reliable by means of a richly repeated echo through centuries' worth of books and poems. Such amplification can empower the lone *comme* ("like") of a simile as well as the inconspicuous *d'à côté* ("at the side" or "next door") of metonymy sufficiently for them to be considered poetically "sound" and able to find the desired echo in the future.

Amplification is the result of repetition, of the multifarious echoes and mutual allusions set off for all practical purposes throughout the infinite number of works produced by crowds of poets who over time have repeated variants of the same metaphoric moves which we are here observing in Apollinaire, until it became impossible to look into a river without hearing the choral echo of all those sighs of poets who have stood on bridges since time immemorial, glancing at the always already metaphoric river, musing over their lost loves in anticipation of the "joie" of poetry. These sighs/these loves hover like a stationary wave of indeterminate frequency (is it "light," is it a radio wave? Are we to look at it, or could we not also tune in an amplifier at the receiving end, a machine that makes audible the frequencies that we cannot see?) over "the" river, as its indelible metaphorical reading, which cannot be erased, because it is no longer "written," but precisely placed there through a double loss. It is a worn-off inscription, it is the return of loss as profit, which Derrida terms *usure*.[14] At its most powerful it is *only* heard, out of nowhere, out of anybody's mouth, even one's own. It is everywhere and nowhere. It comes so naturally, that it takes us a long time to realize that it is no longer us who are speaking, but that what we hear is the memory of other voices and texts ringing back at us from any ordinary picture of reality, out of our own mouth.[15]

Let us continue with the less than casual way in which the poet deals with the reverberations that the re-connection of what was separated out in prison sets off in the watery foundations of his poetic edifice at the beginning of "Le Pont Mirabeau." After taking his leap into the future, the poet ends up on his "suspension-bridge": for the first time, he breaks into the refrain-like invocation:

> Vienne la nuit sonne l'heure
> Les jours s'en vont je demeure
>
> (May night arrive the hour strike
> The days they go I remain)

The cyclical recurrence of the refrain is not only (inter-textually) a place of suspension and connection, but also structurally (inner-textually) an element that dis-connects. It marks the fact that the stanza that preceded it is now "completed," and that the next one can make a new start.

The return of these two lines furthermore appeals to two other types of articulations. One of them is the periodic alternation between day and night that spaces the passage of time in a seemingly natural way through the presence or absence of light. We are permitted to suspect, however, that the coming of the night is at this point particularly welcome to the lyric subject insofar as it temporarily does away with that unfortunate reflection of the blue sky on the river. Secondly, there is the not visual but auditory, the not so much "natural" than decidedly "cultural" incision made by the sounding of the hour. And once more the suspicion is permitted that this hour tolls *for* someone—if only for the ghosts who according to convention are allotted one hour out of twenty four, who inhabit a little prison-cell in time and are obliged to disappear again when the next hour is full. In the absence of the sun, sound becomes a means of insisting on difference. Contrary to Hegel's dictum, then, it seems that not all cows are equally black during the blackout of the logos. The bells still tell them apart.

The negotiation thus once more involves a "cell" which it is the project to keep separate from the rest of the world, or, more precisely: the rest of the time, which thanks to the limitation imposed on that which inhabits "la cellule d'à côté" ("the cell next door to mine") becomes inhabitable in turn. That limit can take a variety of forms: it is that between the metaphoric and the "literal" or factual, between the world of the living and the world of the dead, or the past-ness of love and the future of the poet. In proceeding to the next stanza, we enter into this time-cell. It is the hour of the ghosts.

In stanza two of "Le Pont Mirabeau" the poet finds himself transported face to face with a spooky revenant(e), with an unidentifiable *Doppelgänger(in)*. He is locked into an uncanny encounter with an unidentified personage.

> Les mains dans les mains restons face à face
> Tandis que sous

> Le pont de nos bras passe
> Des éternels regards l'onde si lasse
>
> (Hands in hands we remain face to face
> All the while under
> The bridge of our arms passes
> The wave of the eternal gazes so slow)

Who has returned here, risen from the waters or descended from heaven, and taken up a position that exactly mirrors that of the poet himself? Is it *He*, or is it *She*, or is it one in the guise of the other, and thus once more a superposition, an ambiguous figure? What encounter is this?

That moment in the poem is usually read as a representation of "love": two lovers standing on a bridge holding hands. The "amours" that in the first stanza were so abruptly superimposed as a metaphoric reading onto the river "Seine"[16] have risen from the waters to join hands with the poet and speaker. But a more fruitful reading is the one that this is not any lover's hand, but that the poet has now taken the hand that was proleptically extended in his direction from the future, promising joy. The verb "restons" ("we remain") is in the present tense, the time is the timeless temporality of the text. Any such a textual present, however, has its counterpart in the Now of reading. The verb "restons" can further also be read as an invocation, a request: "let us remain," implying a desire to extend the textually prefigured moment into the future—the text's future, which once again is decided in the present moment of reading. And finally, the verb is in the first person plural, and in the coupling of that "we" the poet reaches out to include another person. Besides the hallucinated "lover," there is thus another candidate for the position of that undefined alter ego that so precisely mirrors the position of the poet. The spectral presence may well be none other than the reader—a reader who reads in identification with the poet, the poet himself, proleptically turned reader. The "hands" for which the poet reaches out are our own insofar as we consent to function as his alter ego. We are asked to become part of a symmetrical figuration, to mirror what the text prefigures for us:

Les mains dans les mains restons face à face

(Hands in hands we remain [or: let us remain] face to face)

This would explain why there is not so much a sense of eroticism and love about that moment than a sense of specular stability that once again borders on entrapment. The moment of identification and symmetry is not so much about "love" than about homosociality—the call on the reader to stop and identify, to stand in for the poet. There is a certain *rigor mortis* to that scene which is generated by that virtual crossing, and which Paul de Man analyzes in his essay on Prosopopeia.[17] The invitation extended by the text is not only designed to allow the poet to return and (virtually) walk again among the living as a *revenant*, but inversely also commits the reader to stand in for the (dead) poet. As the living thus imbue the text and the figure of the poet with their own life, they in exchange are struck with the latter's pallor, sharing in a joint half-life and half-death.

The text seems to offer that uncomfortable fixation as a passing moment of limited duration: it is a state which is assumed "while" ("Tandis que") something else is happening—while the wave of gazes passes under the "bridge of our arms." The short moment for which this arrangement is meant to last is the fleeting moment of reading. Yet that moment turns out to last an eternity, because time comes to a standstill in the virtuality of these interactions.

Tandis que sous
Le pont de nos bras passe
Des éternels regards l'onde si lasse

(While under
The bridge of our arms passes
Of eternal gazes the wave so slow)

The gazes that flow by in that river are significant strictly by virtue of statistics. To the poet's gaze responds a wave of immense inertia—the "slow" ("lasse") movement of a massive "normal distribution" (the curve of "l'onde") that rolls by through the ages and "sees" what the poet is saying. For the mode of reading to which Apollinaire appeals here is no news, but precisely the most likely outcome already. What the gazes see is, probably, once again "love." What it also sees is a "metaphor": the one absolutely classical metaphor in the whole poem—"The bridge of our arms" ("Le pont de nos bras").

In these flowing gazes, the stanza seems to offer a second textual site for reading to alight—one that supplies the scenario of loss corresponding to the stability of arrest we have just discussed. But insofar as that loss is actually needed to make the specular entrapment palatable as "stability," it does not offer a true opposition to it. The identification with the "gazes" is itself merely another reflection of the identification with the poet. Far from offering an alternative, that wave of gazes can be read as a portrait of the *effect* (and insofar as it is already the most likely mode of reading he is likely to encounter, the *source*) of the poet's success in coupling of the figure of the poet with an identificatory reading. That success is articulated over time on the landscape of reception. The slowing of the flow and the heaving rise of that statistical wave is the direct product of a textual tradition that has created a muted readership trapped in specular identification with the speaker and producer of discourse. The reader who identifies with the poet and joins him in that configuration is precisely the one whose significance is reduced to statistics, but who experiences the pull of that probability hump as the force of "truth," of readability and "reality." They inhabit a viscous prison cell of specular identification to which they cannot discover any alternative.

The poet and the readership responsive to his call are not only joined in the half-life of textual half-death described above, but also in a place of being half-read and half-reading, half-writing and half-written. Their cell is also that of a textualized world, much like the one theorized by deconstruction, which also famously knows no "outside."

To be stabilized, however, that "cell" calls once again for sites where the suspension characterizing it does not apply, where one either becomes a pure object of reading, without recourse to a supportive reader. Or, alternatively, where one is limited to a readerly position, and without purchase on representation, where one's reading is indeed washed away, because it does not participate in the fluid stability of the standing wave that answers to representation and makes it "true."

In order to gain access to that other "cell next door," therefore, we must, once again, shift registers from one sense to another and make audible how that moment, which *looks* like a moment of union in love, is also a moment where difference is asserted. In order to do so, let us make yet another excursion into yet another pre-text that has been linked to Apollinaire's poem.[18] Form and rhythm of "Le Pont Mirabeau," namely, are prefigured in and based on an anonymous women's work-song, dating from the 13th century and beginning with a scene where two sisters, Gaieté and Orior, "hand in hand [sic!] go to the spring to bathe" ("Main a main vont baignier a la fontaine"). At the spring, a young man takes Gaieté away with him to marry her, and Orior is told by her sister to go back home by herself. Orior goes away ("s'en va"), pale and sad, and laments the loss of her sister:

"Lasse!" fait Orior, "comme mar fui nee!
J'ai laissié ma seror en la valee; . . . "[19]

("Alas!" cried Orior, "how unlucky my birth!
I have lost my sister in the valley, . . .")

With Orior's complaint at the loss of her sister, with her "Lasse!" in our ear we return to Apollinaire's poem, where we read, once more:

Des éternels regards l'onde si *lasse*.

(Of eternal gazes the wave so slow)

At the moment that the rhyme is sounded, *we* now hear voices— much like the poet did in the first stanza. In the echo of the "passe" we no longer "see" the languid slowing of time ("lasse" = "slow") in the peak of probability, but rather the exclamation ("lasse" = "alas") which marks the swift loss of the link between sisters ("laissié" = "lost"). That loss significantly occurs "en la valee" ("in the valley")—in the depression of its own low probability as reading in a patriarchal literary tradition, crowded out by the

the "onde" or "wave" whose counterpart that valley is. What underlies the stability of the metaphoric "bridge of our arms" and the homosocial transfer it signifies, is thus the severing of the link between these two other participants. The severing of that link in the name of heterosexual coupling in "love" is precisely what creates the two missing complementary elements postulated above. The first is the figure of his "love," the figure of the lover as shadowy stand-in for the poet, easily evoked and easily dismissed go-between that is ultimately reduced to the mere membrane marking the difference between him here and him there, him then and him now. The second is the differing reader, the one who does not identify with the specular poetic subject, and whose voice is relegated to inaudibility by an order whose gaze is trapped in the image it takes for its own, and deaf to the world.

We have once again reached the end of the stanza, and once more the hour strikes that bids the ghost disappear and the refrain return. [20]

This whole stanza of "Le Pont Mirabeau" has taken place in an entirely virtual space, where nothing literal was left. It was indeed the hour of the spirits. The passing of this moment is announced by the return of the refrain.

In the next stanza we witness a re-translation of the scenario back into a non-metaphorical, "literal" space. The superimposed metaphoric reading evaporates. What runs after the bridge is, after all, only water:

> L'amour s'en va comme cette eau courante
> L'amour s'en va
> Comme la vie est lente
> Et comme l'Espérance est violente
>
> (Love departs like that water running
> Love departs
> How slow is life
> And how violent is Hope)

This translation is effected with the help of a "comme" which functions, unlike the similarity-(symmetry-)based metaphor, as a *disjunctive* bridge, a translator back into the only apparently simple language of reality, to the exclusion of all spooky doubling. An "amour," which now significantly stands in the singular, is sent away with "that water," the latter now stripped of all metaphoric overtones, with the exception of the anthropomorphism that sends it "running."

The first line is followed by a repetition of the assertion that (the) love is indeed going away, plus another "comme"-addition—which now, however, is very different from the preceding one in that it no longer performs any determinate translation of one thing into another (as in bridge-arms or love-water). Rather, it is a "generalized" exclamation directed "nowhere in particular"—a direction which we by now recognize as being aimed at a very specific place, namely the blue sky which now is once more separate from the "real," re-literalized water: "Comme la vie est lente" ("How slow is life") . . . We are witnessing the return of a phenomenon already observed in "A la Santé," III: difference is re-established as a difference of direction: *down* the drain versus *up* into the heaven of generalization and universalization.

But this difference is no longer the only one. The disappearance of "love" seems itself to occur in two steps. After the dismissal of the reader-sister (Orior "outside" of the text) in the previous stanza, it is now time for the "love" that was sent back into the river from whence she rose to return from this bath as an allegorical figure *in* the text. The moment he reaches for the right to speak for "life" in general is also the moment when she reaches a different type of generality: that of allegory, as a figure, which embodies and signifies his hopes.

Why is life "slow" all of a sudden? Could it be that the word "lente" is another instance where something heard from next door is misnamed in the interest of the speaking subject—this time not to open the wall (cf. *keys*), but to close it again through a translation which insists that there is nothing to be heard? Could it be that he reads the word "lasse" and takes it to mean languid, tired, slow-moving, in short "lente," and through this translation seals the wall which is to keep the love and the "alas" of her sister out of earshot?

But there it is once more, that intrusive metonymic "et" which we have last encountered in line two of the first stanza—"Et nos amours." It once more insists on adding another "telling" similarity of sound, a rhyme:

> *Et comme* l'Espérance est violente.
>
> (And how violent is Hope)

So there it is, the allegorical figure we have been anticipating. But she rises a bit too insistently from the water, the allegorical "Hope," and the completion of the deceptively incomplete "lente" adds once more the silenced second reading of "Lasse!" to remind us: "vio-lente." At the moment that his work is completed, and she has turned into a figure that visibly *means*, he is disturbed by the violence that echoes back from it. The poet's insistence on the literality of the water, rather than producing a unified picture of reality and putting an end to the haunting double exposures which we have been witnessing, leads to a violent reassertion of that difference as if despite him: a reassertion which takes the form of an allegorical Hope which comes within a hair's breadth of speaking to him with Echo's borrowed voice. Perhaps Orior is not completely gone, after all, and a conjunction between her—the sister-reader—, and Gaieté, the love-figure, is very likely not what the poet hoped for. And so, to nobody's surprise, the refrain is once more called for . . .

In the last stanza, the final turn is given to the construct:

> Passent les jours et passent les semaines
>   Ni temps passé
>   Ni les amours reviennent
> Sous le pont Mirabeau coule la Seine
>
> (The days they pass the weeks they pass
>   Neither times that have passed
>   Nor the loves return
> Under Mirabeau Bridge flows the Seine)

The general assertion of transitoriness seals away "Hope" as well, commits the "loves" to that general flow of time without return, relative to which he has been struggling to construct his permanence.

Time, motion, gender, loss, and identity are all perceptible only in relative terms. The visibility of the "loves" as they float away into the past now sits like a marker on the flow of time and makes its direction definable. It serves as a point of reference that confirms the "masculinity" of the readers' perspective because it is "feminine," that confirms the presence of the poet because it is "past," his mobility because it is imprisoned, his presence because it absents itself, his voice because it is silent, his subjectivity because it is an allegorical "object," and his inobservability because it is visible. Vis à vis that point of reference, then, the poet can complete the circle of his poem and allow for the return of the piece of trivia which triggered the whole process, and which now has been turned into a line from a famous poem, indeed, the first line of a famous poem. The cycle can start over again:

> Sous le pont Mirabeau coule la Seine
>
> (Under Mirabeau Bridge flows the Seine)

The line has been stabilized in an orbit of return. It has been launched as a "classic."

But the next time around, there may be a woman poet among the readers, who turns this relativistic world on its ear and takes the poet as a point of reference. Then it will turn out that his desire for eternal presence has turned him into a thing of the past, relative to which she can go with the flow of time into a still open future.[21] This slight shift of the point of reference, from the poet on the bridge to the loves that go with the flow, results in a relocation of "subjectivity" in the readership rather than the text. That shift places subjecthood (but a better term for this would now be "mobility" *vis à vis* an existing metaphorics) also at the disposal of the woman poet as reader. It has been performed, as I will go on to argue in the remainder of this essay, by the Austrian poet Ingeborg Bachmann.

As we move on into the new space opened by a different, more self-conscious mode of reading, the last words of the poet we hear are, ironically enough, "je demeure."

Ingeborg Bachmann's "Die Brücken" [22]

The structure of "Le Pont Mirabeau" was that of a chain that traversed four layers or stanzas, articulated by the recurring refrain, and ultimately, with the repetition of the first line, looping back to its beginning. That "chain" was designed to contain the movement of time by which layer after layer is added in the cumulative growth of complex interpretive spaces, striving to commit each successive layer to the previous one, and with the time-arresting goal of establishing predictability, stability, and permanence in it. His poem moved from a metaphoric commonplace via a moment of specular identification in the bridge of metaphor, then to allegory and back to an apparent factuality, while defining each of these moves against an undercurrent of exclusion. By contrast, in Bachmann's poem time operates as a continuously expanding frame. No longer a directional flow away from a poet struggling to "remain," time operates as a readerly horizon at which we are situated as we write and read, adding the latest layer, and thus in a position to make a difference. From that position, too, the ultimate futility of the kind of struggle Apollinaire engages in becomes readable.

Die Brücken

Straffer zieht der Wind das Band vor den Brücken.

An den Traversen zerrieb
der Himmel sein dunkelstes Blau.
Hüben und drüben wechseln
im Licht unsre Schatten.

Pont Mirabeau... Waterloobridge...
Wie ertragen's die Namen,
die Namenlosen zu tragen?

Von den Verlornen gerührt,
die der Glaube nicht trug,
erwachen die Trommeln im Fluß.

Einsam sind alle Brücken,
und der Ruhm ist ihnen gefährlich
wie uns, vermeinen wir doch,
die Schritte der Sterne
auf unserer Schulter zu spüren.
Doch übers Gefälle des Vergänglichen
wölbt uns kein Traum.

Besser ist's, im Auftrag der Ufer
zu leben, von einem zum andern,
und tagsüber zu wachen,
daß das Band der Berufene trennt.
Denn er erreicht die Schere der Sonne
im Nebel, und wenn sie ihn blendet,
umfängt ihn der Nebel im Fall.

(The Bridges

Tauter the wind pulls the band before the bridges.

Against the traverses the sky
has ground down its darkest blue.
Over here and over there our shadows
change in the light.

Pont Mirabeau ... Waterloobridge ...
How do the names bear it
to bear the nameless?

Sounded by the lost ones
who were not borne by the faith
the drums in the river awaken.

Solitary are all bridges,
and fame is dangerous for them
as it is for us, for we presume
to sense the strides of the stars

on our shoulder.
But over the slope of transitoriness
we are arched by no dream.

It's better to live in the application
of the riverbanks, from one to the other,
and to guard during the day
that the band is cut by the one called upon.
For he reaches the shears of the sun
in the fog, and when she blinds him
the fog will embrace him in the fall.)[23]

The most immediately apparent change which this different poetic principle effects concerns the way the poem is organized. Four "frames" or phases can be observed in this poem, each occupying more lines, more space than the preceding one:

phase 1:	line 1	(stanza 1)
phase 2:	lines 2-5	(stanza 2)
phase 3:	lines 6-11	(stanzas 3 &4)
phase 4:	lines 12-25	(stanzas 5 &6)

The first line/stanza/phase makes a beginning that differs from Apollinaire's in that it does not place itself within an existing and named historical/geographical space, but rather in a space-time that is as yet completely undetermined except for the (spatio-temporally ambiguous) reference "before the bridges." No gap has opened yet, but *comparison* is where the beginning is made. The poem opens with an adverb in the comparative ("Straffer." i.e., "Tauter"):

Straffer zieht der Wind das Band vor den Brücken.

(Tauter the wind pulls the band before the bridges.)

In the second phase, the number of lines quadruples. In its four lines emerge differences in time ("zerrieb" is in the past tense, "wechseln" is in the present) and space ("Hüben und drüben," i.e., "over here and over there"), light and shadow.

An den Traversen zerrieb
der Himmel sein dunkelstes Blau.
Hüben und drüben wechseln
im Licht unsre Schatten.

(Against the traverses the sky
has ground down its darkest blue.
Over here and over there our shadows
change in the light.)

A traversal ("Traversen") has in the past "ground down" the sky's darkest blue. That mythic superlative ("darkest"), insofar as it belongs to the past, now comes to function as a limit from which the present begins to differ. That difference in temporality in turn opens a spacing into *here and there*, on which we further find superimposed the variable, mobile difference between light and shadow ("wechseln im Licht unsre Schatten," i.e. "our shadows are changing in the light"). This is also the moment when, for the first time in this poem, a subject of some sort appears: a plural subject that is not itself visible. The present moment, in which the subject clearly situates itself, is filled with experimentation about positioning. The subject is multiple and mobile, it experiments with its own position. This moment is the contrastive counterpart to Apollinaire's "bridge of our arms": mobility instead of entrapment, an awareness of and insistence on the difference between present and past, self-reflexive experimentation instead of mystification and oblivion to the possibility of difference.

In the next phase, a difference that is being created springs open: it encompasses two stanzas, a gap has now been solidified and surfaces in the structure of the poem. That gap is presented as one between a bridge (stanza three) and a river (stanza four)—the founding opposition of Apollinaire's poem. And indeed, this phase is the one that contains an explicit allusion to Apollinaire's poem. But that reference is immediately followed by a transition-translation into a different language, and with that translation, the bridge Apollinaire has constructed is immediately washed out again:

Pont Mirabeau ... Waterloobridge ...

> Wie ertragen's die Namen,
> die Namenlosen zu tragen?
>
> Von den Verlornen gerührt,
> die der Glaube nicht trug,
> erwachen die Trommeln im Fluß.
>
> (Pont Mirabeau ... Waterloobridge ...
> How do the names bear it
> to bear the nameless?
>
> Sounded by the lost ones
> who were not borne by the faith
> the drums in the river awaken.)

If the first of these stanzas deconstructs the "bridge," the second one, by contrast, gives voice to the "lost ones" in the river. The stanzas thus respond directly to the opposition that underlies Apollinaire's text—bridges vs. the lost ones—precisely reversing their operation. It is important that the poetic subject of this poem chooses not to settle on either side of that divide. As Bachmann remarks in prose elsewhere: "Dort werden wir unseren Fuß nie hinsetzen, auf diesen Pont Mirabeau niemals ..." ("We will never set our foot there, on this Pont Mirabeau never ...").[24] But neither does she agree to be simply "lost." So what she does instead is cross the divide, traverse the opposition, and undo both the stability of the bridge and the silence of the lost ones.

The deconstruction of Apollinaire's "bridge" is articulated via a laconic juxtaposition of two names—"Pont Mirabeau ... Waterloobridge ..." Two names for bridges on which poets have stood in order to create what they consider "beauty," but their juxtaposition already points out that there is a perspective from which that type of "beauty" spells defeat and dismissal. But more important than what they "say" is the very fact of translation that governs their relation and that proves fatal to the stability of the bridge. For the two names lead us from one context to another, from one language to another. As we read them, we go from French to English. We also go from Paris to London and thus inadvertently cross the Channel. For the first time in this poem, we enter into determinate geographical and historical dimensions—but only to identify such certainty as both a passing moment in a larger scheme, and only to immediately leave them again. For we find no ground to stand on. So what do we do with these names?

We may of course begin to remember. We remember events through the names of bridges which are named after a man and a place: we are reminded of the French Revolution and Napoleon's defeat. We also remember a number of works of art: not just the bridge in Paris, but also the poem by Apollinaire. Not just a bridge in London, but also a number of paintings by John Constable which repeatedly portrays the moment of the "Opening of Waterloo Bridge" in a successive series of paintings, each larger than the preceding one. Or the title of a film ("Waterloo Bridge") made in the 1950s about a woman's suicide, narrated through the memory of her lover as he stands on the bridge. In other words: the names immediately lead us into an infinite regress of "traverses" and translations between places, men, "historic" events, "private" events, countries, languages, bridges, and art forms. They dissimulate their signification by multiplying it, and they establish it by leading us off into an already specific historical discourse swarming with interlocking associations.

But we can also forget for a moment about these memories, this infinite regress into history in which the very multiplicity of its cross-referenced significations cancels them out and turns them into a mere white noise. We can move in a different direction and start listening to the names across language boundaries. If we do, we hear a description of the mode of operation of the "bridge": a traversal, a two-directional exchange between glances from motion at stasis, and vice versa, the gaze of the (deaf) subject from bridge to river, and from river to bridge, and thus of nothing but the mutually stabilizing relationship between two opposed directions of view. We hear a once more laconic description of that functional superposition which we have observed at work in the refrain of "Le Pont Mirabeau": *Mira* is Spanish for "look!" or "lo!" And so, if we listen across languages and forget about memory, we get

Pont - mira (b) - eau ... Water - lo (o) - bridge ...

In English:

Bridge - see - water ... Water - see - bridge ...

But the three dots following each of the names also suggest that there is yet something else, something lost, forgotten, or at the very least unnamed at play here. Something lost, something to be found in another, the next, crossing.

A poetic subject such as Bachmann's requires a poetry that always speaks more than one language, that can listen when other poets and their readers only see, and which can also see when they only listen. Hers must be a different sense of "beauty."

As such a subject discovers that the names do not bear it—and that it cannot bear having to rely on them—it discovers a different sense in the river. What in "Le Pont Mirabeau" appeared as a "wave of glances" ("des éternels regards, l'onde si lasse") appears here as a drumskin awakened by the *lost ones*, who may well have something to do with Apollinaire's "amours" which were going down the drain in such a poetically constructive way.

> Von den Verlornen gerührt,
> die der Glaube nicht trug,
> erwachen die Trommeln im Fluß.

> (Sounded by the lost ones
> who were not borne by the faith
> the drums in the river awaken.)

The stability that was lost when "Pont Mirabeau" turned into "Waterloo Bridge," has reappeared as the surface of the river has solidified into a membrane that can be "sounded." What Bachmann is after is thus also far from being a simple (and necessarily mystified) recuperation of the lost loves, either. Her interest is not in the past but in the future, and her revision of the existing poetic language is fundamental and very ambitious in scope. The challenge for her readers is to learn from her, so that it becomes possible for them to benefit from her pioneering work,

Once our ears have opened up to these drums, we start to remember differently than before. Rather than remembering official history through names, now we remember that there was indeed once again something lost, bracketed in our translation of those names. Lost were two letters, "b" from Mira(b)eau, and "o" from Waterlo(o), two letters which now are heard together to become audible as a delicate bridge across the gap between poem and painting—"b-o," the sound of *beau*—and restore that other sense to the text. Beauty is what arises in the transition, in the crossing, at the moment when the old becomes readable in a new way, in the realization that it is possible to differ.

From the point of view, or rather, from the arc of sound as which the realization arises here, we can now look back and appreciate a kind of beauty which in its tenuousness and unrepresentability is very different from one based on a countercurrent of rejection whose ugliness it has to constantly dissimulate:

> Pont Mira *beau* vs. Water *loo* bridge

At the moment when beauty is no longer founded on an opposition to waste or refuse, but arises out of the illumination and sense of discovery that attends the shedding of old and limiting models and the opening of new possibilities, we enter into a very different regime in aesthetics.

This different regime leads us into the last two stanzas, the last phase in Bachmann's poem. It encompasses once more two stanzas, these yet longer than the preceding ones, and once again opening a difference between them:

> Einsam sind alle Brücken,
> und der Ruhm ist ihnen gefährlich
> wie uns, vermeinen wir doch,
> die Schritte der Sterne
> auf unserer Schulter zu spüren.
> Doch übers Gefälle des Vergänglichen
> wölbt uns kein Traum.
>
> Besser ist's, im Auftrag der Ufer
> zu leben, von einem zum andern,
> und tagsüber zu wachen,
> daß das Band der Berufene trennt.
> Denn er erreicht die Schere der Sonne

im Nebel, und wenn sie ihn blendet,
umfängt ihn der Nebel im Fall.

(Solitary are all bridges,
and fame is dangerous for them
as it is for us, for we presume
to sense the strides of the stars
on our shoulder.
But over the slope of transitoriness
we are arched by no dream.

It's better to live in the application
of the riverbanks, from one to the other,
and to guard during the day
that the band is cut by the one called upon.
For he reaches the shears of the sun
in the fog, and when she blinds him
the fog will embrace him in the fall.)

"Solitary" are the bridges, and fame is dangerous to them, because they rely on the obliviousness of their readers to their most profound principle of operation, and to their limited and limiting nature. The "bridges" need to avoid "fame" in the sense that they cannot announce their procedures, that they rely on readers who unselfconsciously follow their lead. But the first-person plural subject of the first of these two stanzas, the danger that comes with "fame" has different reasons. It is in a strange position, first of all, because, its plurality notwithstanding, it has only one "shoulder"—in the singular. However plural, then, this indexical first person pronoun in which textual and readerly subject can coincide as they did in Apollinaire's "bridge of arms" ("uns," or "us"), and does here consciously offer its support to future readings and readers, also clearly points out that it is incomplete. Someone in the position of Bachmann similarly cannot "say" what she sees, not only because this would call down the wrath of an order that has banked on the obscurity of what she has to say—insofar as that order still has the strength to assert itself. The more profound reason is that the "b-o" she needs to articulate cannot be accommodated by any one language, and that it cannot in principle arch itself over the "gradient of transitoriness." Beauty of this type needs the occurrence of something new and unforeseen, the arrival of a new time, a new language. It needs to be invented in the future, by us as we read. If the first of these two concluding stanzas thus articulates both its support for and its necessary disconnection from us insofar as we position ourselves as consciously revisionary readers, the next stanza concerns the place which writing can still assume in this arrangement.

> Besser ist's, im Auftrag der Ufer
> zu leben, von einem zum andern,
> und tagsüber zu wachen,
> daß das Band der Berufene trennt.
>
> (It's better to live in the application
> of the riverbanks, from one to the other,
> and to guard during the day
> that the band is cut by the one called upon.)

Better is a life in the application of banks, of limits, a life, simultaneously, in the opening of a divide. As we have seen throughout Bachmann's poem, she insistently opens the gap that has been at the heart of this discussion, to make it palpable, but not in order to take sides, but to deconstruct any attempt to do so. She always builds up the river banks on both sides, writing and reading, vision and sound, traversal and separation, conscious of every shadow on the other side that is cast by the light on the one. But this is not a simple disintegration into incoherence, but on the contrary a methodical and extremely precise deconstruction. Writing in her case also, and this is the second way to read this first line, applies a limit or edge ("Ufer") to the old order, from one to the other, from Nietzsche to Celan to Kafka to Apollinaire ... Each of these types of deconstructive readerly texts of hers understands itself as a limit set to the sway of the pernicious poetics she has so thoroughly understood and undone. The one who is "berufen" ("called upon") eventually reaches the "shears of the sun," the moment of crossing and deconstruction. At that moment, illumination arrives, and it arrives once again as a translation:

> Denn er erreicht die Schere der Sonne
> im Nebel, und wenn sie ihn blendet,
> umfängt ihn der Nebel im Fall.
>
> (For he reaches the shears of the sun
> in the fog, and when it/she blinds him
> the fog will embrace him in the fall.)

The one who feels called upon to make that "decision," to divide the band or cut the "ribbon" ("Band" translates as *band* or *ribbon*, and thus can refer either to a "band" of electromagnetic waves, a certain specific frequency, or to the "ribbon" which is cut at the opening of a new bridge—perhaps the "Opening of Waterloo-bridge"?) and open a new bridge for himself, he will find that what he was used to finding reliable is so no longer. He "reaches the shears of the sun," the point where the crossings and traversals do not simply lead to the old "superposition," but rather allow us to "cross" over into a strange new order where the old order of reality and metaphor, of well-directed loss and gain has been reversed. A new order with new kinds of illuminations, where whatever we say will only be half the story, the second one taking place in a language which we cannot yet know, while everything we read seems to speak our language, even though that contradicts every historical or national "reason."

In Apollinaire's poem, the "cutting" of the band was achieved in important ways by the regular recurrence of the "sounding" of the hour, which separated each layer from the next:

> Vienne la nuit *sonne* l'heure
>
> (May night arrive the hour strike/sound)

In Bachmann's poem, the sounding of that hour ("sonne") has been muted by a simple translation, and converted into the sun ("Sonne") of an illumination that occurs always in the transition from one context or language into another. The text we are handed must be transported into a different language—one that in this case happens to be our own.

Bachmann's poem "Die Brücken" consciously positions itself as a deconstructive reading of the type of poetics exemplified by "Le Pont Mirabeau." In her poem, the attempt to "bridge" (possible only on the basis of an enforced separation elsewhere) is replaced by an exploration and opening up of a divide at the heart of her poem, a divide, however, that is always already traversed, as well. Her writing articulates a poetics that differs radically from Apollinaire's. The latter labors to contain that gap through the complex manipulation of divides and crossings, traversals and inversions, and through the recuperative recursivity of the "chain." Bachmann's poem asserts the potential for revision available at every moment as we read and write, adding a layer to the language we have been handed, translating it into something new. Her poem ends on the alternative between two orientations in writing: to offer support to future self-reflexive reading, and to add another layer to the evolving space of writing. In both of these ways, her poem contributes toward a macroscopic demise of the oppressive logic of the "bridges." But, of course, closures of that kind ultimately come about not through a line drawn by anybody in particular, but by a shift in the statistical preponderance from one way of thinking and reading to another, from a poetics of bridging to one of applying "Ufer." Transformations of this type can only occur as the cumulative effect of many particular decisions and readings, rather than one big one. Bachmann's poem clearly understands itself as a contribution toward such a larger change. Her little text is a small but powerful theoretical tool (as her texts tend to be). In studying it in its difference from, in this case, Apollinaire's poem, it can help us achieve a greater readability of the limits of the old, and it can help us discover the possibilities of the new. The use and amplification of the possibilities that open here, in short, is up to us.

NOTES

1. This essay was originally conceived and written in the fall of 1987, but was in some places rewritten to develop aspects that are clearer to me now than they were then. However, I have not changed the overall conception of the essay. The latter has affinities to the way I proceed in my book *The Split Scene of Reading: Nietzsche/Derrida/Kafka/Bachmann* (Atlantic Highlands, New Jersey: Humanities Press, 1998). The latter is also organized around a use of Bachmann's texts in contrastive readings with other texts whose theoretical stance I see her as critiquing.

Due to the extremely close attention that my mode of reading pays to the texts under discussion, I had to supply my own working translations of the texts. Other translations, of course, exist, and I make reference to at least one of them for each of the poems in the footnotes.

2. "Die Brücken," Ingeborg Bachmann, *Werke*, 4 vols., ed. Christine Koschel, Inge von Weidenbaum and Clemens Münster (München: Piper, 1978), 1:50.

3. See for instance Eva Meyer, *Zählen und Erzählen. Für eine Semiotik des Weiblichen* (Wien: Medusa, 1983), 24: "Das heißt, daß die vollständige Beschreibung der Sprache mindestens zwei Kontexte berücksichtigen können muß, ... innerhalb eines erweiterten Systems, das nun *komplex* genannt werden kann, denn 'ein System heißt komplex, wenn zu seiner vollständigen Beschreibung mehr als ein Kontext nötig ist'."

4. For a more developed version of that critique of deconstruction, see my "One Must Go Quickly From One Light Into Another: Between Ingeborg Bachmann and Jacques Derrida." In *Borderwork: Feminist Engagements with Comparative Literature*, ed. Margaret Higonnet (Ithaca: Cornell University Press, 1994), 207-223.

5. Guillaume Apollinaire, *Alcools* (Paris: Gallimard, 1984), 15f.

6. For a published translation see Guillaume Apollinaire, *Alcools*, trans. Anne Hyde Greet (Berkeley: University of California Press, 1965), 15:

Mirabeau Bridge

Past Mirabeau bridge flows the Seine

And our love
Must I remember
Joy followed always after the pain
Let night come sound the hour
Time draws in I remain
Hand in hand let us stay face to face
While past the
Bridge of our embrace
Flows one long look's weary wave
Let night come sound the hour
Time draws in I remain
Love creeps by like the flowing tide
Love slips by
How slow life is and
Expectation how violent
Let night come sound the hour
Time draws in I remain
Days creep by and the weeks creep by
Neither past
Time nor love returns
Past Mirabeau bridge flows the Seine
Let night come sound the hour
Time draws in I remain

    7. Michel Décaudin, *Le Dossier d'"Alcools." Edition annotée des préoriginales avec une introduction et des documents* (Genève: Librairie E. Droz; Paris: Librairie Minard, 1960), 90.
    8. Cf. Décaudin, 212.
    9. *Alcools*, 128.
    10. For a published translation see Apollinaire, trans. Heyde, 189:

> Every morning I pace
> My pit like a bear
> Turn turn again turn
> Sky glitters like a chain
> Every morning I pace
> My pit like a bear

    11. Ibid., 189:

> In the cell next to mine
> A fountain gurgles
> The jailer clinks his keys
> As he comes and goes
> In the cell next to mine
> A fountain gurgles

12. See Julia Kristeva, *Powers of Horror: An Essay on Abjection*, trans. Leon S. Roudiez (New York: Columbia University Press, 1982).

13. See my "Reading in the Twilight: Canonization, Gender, the Limits of Language—and a poem by Ingeborg Bachmann," *New German Critique* 47 (1989, Spring/Summer): 29-52. There, I have elaborated at some length on this intrusive, daemonic HE which is tradition, and pointed out the importance of the motion of "coming and going" for this figure. This motion is also invoked in "A la Santé," III, as "Que le geôlier aille et revienne," which corresponds to Bachmann's line "Er geht, eh es tagt, er kommt eh du rufst, er ist alt," as well as to Rilke's assertion: "Ein für alle Male / ist's Orpheus, wenn es singt. Er kommt und geht," which I have discussed there. The "it," which sings and reminds, which intrudes with the supplementary "Et nos amours," this "it" is a "He" that has the power of a "geôlier" to open one cell and close another. It is NOT anything of the type of a "subject," but it is immensely profitable to those who want to be "subjects" of the specific type that is the object of our inquiry.

14. See Jacques Derrida, "White Mythology: Metaphor in the Text of Philosophy," *Margins of Philosophy*, trans. Alan Bass (Chicago: University of Chicago Press, 1982), 207-71.

15. This argument itself might be read as an echo of the voice of Harold Bloom, or: Bloom's work provides a useful sounding-board for this argument. Bloom would probably attribute the reaction "Faut-il qu'il m'en souvienne" to the (e)motion of "anxiety of influence." That seems adequate insofar as that motion can indeed be read as expressing the irritation of someone who would like to speak in his own "voice," and thus must resent the realization that he does not. At the same time, the addressee of this irritation, even though he is addressed as "il," is not one, but many, a "he" and an "it" at the same time, and the defensive move against

Him is foundational and thus necessary for any poetic voice. Poetry is dependent on the richness of a metaphoric tradition, which grounds it in being pushed aside.

Bloom's concern with the threat to the poet's voice presented by the influential presence of precursors thus has to be supplemented in turn: "Et vos amours . . .?" That is: we must pose the second and at least equally interesting question concerning the function served by the lost "loves" in this scenario as that focus of loss in which all poets can feel united.

The hypothesis (or suspicion) which is put forth here and which differs from Bloom's concerns, then, is not only that the return of the voices of the past is precisely that which *supports* the emergent poet in his effort to dispatch the "loves" that *return with them*. It is also that, vice versa, this return of the "loves," of the—by implication through the "il" of the impersonal tradition—*feminine* component of that hovering wave, were it read differently than it has been, would present a threat not merely to any individual poet's voice, as Bloom's "anxiety of influence" would have it, but to the canon of a male poetic tradition as a whole. To the canon, that is, not in the sense of an ensemble of texts which would need to be rearranged a bit, so as to accommodate a few women writers, but to the canon as the coherent presence of the dead in the living, as a circulating language, as a weapon against "her," as precisely that selectively empowering reservoir of memory which produces HIS "truth," both poetic and "real," and which is held in place through its focus on the continual and continuing loss of "nos amours." For since they—the voices of the tradition and the lost loves— always return *together*, there must be a way to change around the effect from which the poet profits and use the loves to dispatch the tradition to the profit of a reader who is no longer "woman" or his "love," but who is merely and definitely *not he*.

16. —a reading which could also be described as a translation of the name of that river into German, where "seine" is the possessive pronoun "his," as applied to a feminine object. As such, the word "looks" the same as the name of that river, but it doesn't "sound" like it . . .

17. Paul de Man, "Autobiography as De-Facement," *The Rhetoric of Romanticism* (New York: Columbia University Press,

1984), 67-81.

18. Guillaume Apollinaire, *Œvres Poétiques* (Paris: Gallimard, Bibliothèque de la Pléiade, 1956), 1034: "M. Mario Roques a rapproché ce poème d'une chanson de toile du début du XIIIe siècle, *Gaieté et Oriour*, publiée dans la *Chrestomathie du Moyen Age* de Gaston Paris et Ernest Langlois, qu'Apollinaire connaissait certainement: c'est le même dessin rhythmique, la même position des rimes, le même mouvement du refrain." ("M. Mario Roques has connected this poem to a work song from the beginning of the 13th century, *Gaieté and Oriour*, published in the *Chrestomathie du Moyen Age* by Gaston Paris and Ernest Langlois, which Apollinaire definitely knew: it has the same rhythm, the same positioning of the rhymes, the same movement of the refrain.") For pointing me in the direction of that welcome footnote I am indebted to Abby Zanger.

19. Cited from: *Gaston Paris: Chrestomathie du Moyen Age*, 12th revised edition (Paris: Hachette, 1922), 278-280, here: 28. The passage is translated into modern French as follows: "Hélas!" fait Oriour, "à quelle mauvaise heure je suis née! J'ai laissé ma sœur dans le vallon."

20. The mediaeval poem also names the moment in time when this event occurs. Its first line is: Le samedi al soir faut la semaine: (Saturday evening is the end of the week:), which is interesting if we remember the two lines from Apollinaire's first poem from prison:

    Quand donc finira la semaine
    Quand donc finiront les amours
    (Oh when will the week be done
    Oh when will the loves be done)

In the economy of Apollinaire's own recycling of lines, the return of this line occurs in the poem entitled "Marie" in *Alcools* (55f.), with the help of which this reading could explore yet a different dimension. The poem is concerned with the question "Quand donc reviendrez-vous Marie"—*Marie* being both the first name of the woman painter Marie Laurencin who was leaving Apollinaire at the time, and the Old French adjective which characterizes Orior's sadness as she is sent away: "Or s'en va Orior teinte et *marie*" (Oriour s'en va, pâle et triste). The final stanza of the poem reads:

> Je passais au bord de la Seine
> Un livre ancien sous les bras
> Le fleuve est pareil à ma peine
> Il s'écoule et ne tarit pas
> Quand donc finira la semaine
> (I passed the banks of the Seine
> An old book under the arms
> The river resembles my pain
> It flows away and does not dally
> Oh when is the end of the week.)

The threat of the return of Marie/Orior, i.e. of the woman as reader, is countered by the trust in the "river," which will keep taking care that such a thing "flow away" ("s'écoule") and thus assure the continued stability of the "old book" to which he clings, and which he has once more rewritten . . . But we also remember that only one poem ago, what was to be found under those arms was not a book, but precisely that very "river" which "Sous le pont de nos bras passe." And so it does.

21. In other words: the poet has set his hopes on *remembrance*, while the shift of which I am speaking and which I see in Bachmann is made possible not by the remembrance, but by the *repetition* of the past which becomes possible only once it has been broken with . . . (Both terms are used in Kierkegaard's sense.)

22. An earlier and in some respects more detailed reading of this poem can be found in my dissertation "Legenda Feminina: Die verschwindende Poetik der Ingeborg Bachmann" (Ph.D. diss., Cornell University, 1987), 43-54.

23. For a published translation of this poem see Ingeborg Bachmann, "Die Brücken"/"The Bridges," in *Songs in Flight: The Collected Poems of Ingeborg Bachmann*, trans. Peter Filkins (New York: Marsilio, 1994), 48-51:

> *The Bridges*
>
> Wind tightens the ribbon drawn across bridges.
>
> The sky grinds on the crossbeams
> with its darkest blue.
> On this side and that our shadows

pass each other in the light.

Pont Mirabeau... Waterloo Bridge...
How can the names stand
to carry the nameless?

Stirred by the lost
that faith could not carry,
the river's drumbeat awakens.

Lonely are all bridges,
and fame is as dangerous for them
as it is for us, yet we presume
to feel the tread of stars
upon our shoulders.
Still, over the slope of transience
no dream arches us.

It's better to follow the riverbanks,
crossing from one to another,
and all day keep an eye out
for the official to cut the ribbon.
For when he does, he'll seize the sun's scissors
within the fog, and if the sun blinds him,
he'll be swallowed by fog when he falls.

24. Ingeborg Bachmann, *Werke*, 4:240.

4 / To Live with an Instinctive Resistance to Language: Bachmann on Wittgenstein

Barbara Agnese

After her dissertation on the reception of Heidegger's existentialist philosophy (1949-50) and her essays about the Vienna Circle,[1] Ingeborg Bachmann's non-academic and independent encounter with the philosophy of Wittgenstein was a decisive moment in the young author's intellectual formation: Wittgenstein not only offered a compelling solution with respect to the clarity and exactness demanded by the neopositivists, but also provided answers to the existential questions that lay at the heart of Heidegger's reflections in *Being and Time*.

What was most original about Bachmann's interpretation of the *Tractatus Logico-Philosophicus*[2] was not so much her understanding of it, which is in and of itself quite remarkable, but the fact that her reading was guided by the themes found in the *Philosophical Investigations*,[3] a work that had only recently appeared in 1953 as part of Wittgenstein's unpublished works. Ample evidence of her understanding of Wittgenstein's work in its entirety can be found throughout her work, not only in the final section of the radio essay "Sagbares und Unsagbares" ("The Sayable and the Unsayable," 1953), but also in the conclusion of the essay "Ludwig Wittgenstein—Zu einem Kapitel der jüngsten Philosophiegeschichte" ("Ludwig Wittgenstein—On a Recent Chapter in the History of Philosophy"), although in this essay the reference is less obvious. At the end of the radio essay, the significance of Wittgenstein's philosophical position becomes clear: his silence is to be read as a protest against both Heidegger and "the specific anti-rationalism of the times" on the one hand, and against Carnap on the other:

> against the tendency of this era to have faith in science and progress, against the ignorance with respect to "complete reality," an idea which was often put forth by the neopositivistic school which took his [Carnap's] ideas as their basis for

thought and the scientistic thinkers who were closely aligned with them.[4]

Bachmann saw in Wittgenstein an answer to these two opposing views. He overcame the central antagonism inside the philosophical thought of his century through his therapeutic vision of philosophical activity: not "with a feeble prescription for synthesis which was in high demand, but instead with a prescription for healing—as therapist" (Bachmann, 4:127). The philosopher's treatment of a question is like the treatment of an illness (*PI*, §255).[5] Here we find the first incontrovertible proof that Bachmann read Wittgenstein in the way I am proposing: the therapeutic undertaking which first appeared in the *Philosophical Investigations* is projected back onto the *Tractatus*. The radio essay in fact ends with a quote from the *Tractatus*, which Bachmann presents as commentary on the phrase "prescription for healing":

> We feel that even after *all possible* scientific questions be answered, the problems of life have still not been touched at all. Of course there is then no question left, and just this is the answer. (Wittgenstein, *TLP*, 6.52)

We also find a reference in the essay to the famous final statement in the *Tractatus* ("Whereof one cannot speak, thereof one must be silent") which Bachmann interprets in light of the relationship between language and language games, and which without question constitutes one of the cornerstones of the second phase of Wittgenstein's philosophy. What is remarkable here is that the concept of a language game first appears in the *Blue Book*, from which Bachmann had quoted shortly before (Bachmann, 4:22). In the concept of the language game, we find Wittgenstein's answer to the "craving for generality" and the "contemptuous attitude towards the particular case" which found expression in philosophy's use of language.[6]

As I will show in the following discussion, the theoretical basis for Bachmann's reception of Wittgenstein is no longer shaped by the neopositivistic position, nor by the existential questions raised by Heidegger. Rather, we see that her reading of the *Tractatus* is always with an eye to the philosophical views of the later Wittgenstein. Bachmann presents to us a Wittgenstein who is still centrally concerned with the *Tractatus*, but this Wittgenstein is seen through the lens of his two most important works, viewed together as a whole. Based on her reading of the *Philosophical Investigations*, Bachmann was able to recognize certain elements in the *Tractatus* which no one else up to that point had completely grasped and which thus were nowhere to be found among neopositivistic interpretations, and which were also free from any Heidegger-Wittgenstein contamination.

There is no question that we have Bachmann to thank for "discovering" that Wittgenstein was not just a logician, as per the neopositivistic stereotype, but rather a complete philosopher—logician, ethicist, and critic of aesthetics. She is to be credited with this discovery because she provided one of the first interpretations of his work which looked at his philosophy as a whole, made possible in part by her ability to discuss ideas found in both the *Tractatus* and the *Philosophical Investigations*.[7]

We can learn a great deal by analyzing Bachmann's reading of Wittgenstein with the goal of understanding Wittgenstein's philosophical ideas via her interpretation, instead of the other way around, as we often find in scholarship on Bachmann. It is common, for example, for Bachmann scholars to emphasize the so-called "problem of the limit" relative to her skepticism of language; while there is no doubt that this is an important subject, most of the scholarship limits itself only to the *Tractatus*, and sometimes only to a few statements of the *Tractatus*.[8] What I propose to do instead is to broaden the scope of analysis by taking into account the connections between the *Tractatus* and the later, more decisive phase of Wittgenstein's thought. Without such a broadening of scope, it is impossible to understand the transition from Bachmann's dissertation and her essays on the Vienna Circle to her first Wittgenstein essay and finally to the radio essay. Furthermore, this approach allows us to identify the actual influence of Wittgenstein's thought on her literary work much more clearly.[9]

Around the time of her dissertation, Bachmann still maintained a neopositivistic perspective in her reading of the *Tractatus*; by 1953, she has distanced herself from a logical positivistic interpretation and presents instead a comprehensive study of the *Philosophical Investigations* in her radio essay "Sagbares und Unsagbares." In the radio essay, the implicit elements of her earlier understanding are now clearly displayed: philosophical problems as "misfirings of language," Wittgenstein's conception of philosophy, the relationship between hypothesis and verification, the commingling of logical form with ethical form and of ethics with aesthetics, and the analogies between philosophical activity and art.

The continuities and the conceptual affinities which can be established between Bachmann's work and Wittgenstein's thought go far beyond the statements made by the author herself on the subject and any biographical similarities which both sparked and warranted her interest in Wittgenstein.[10] Their shared intellectual position, formal similarities and the continuities which first became evident in Bachmann's original and insightful reading of the *Tractatus* and the *Philosophical Investigations* are of particular interest to this discussion. On the one hand, Bachmann's study of philosophy and her dissertation were strongly influenced by Viktor Kraft and the logical positivism of the Vienna School (hence the "anti-Heidegger" tendency of her dissertation, which was shaped by the criticism of Rudolf Carnap). On the other hand, the most important sections of Wittgenstein's *Tractatus* to which Bachmann refers in both essays point in the opposite direction of such neopositivistic interpretations. Here Bachmann displays a command of the entirety of Wittgenstein's work as shown by her intuitive understanding of his critique of philosophy, especially the much debated and highly controversial relationship between the so-called "positive" and "negative" parts of the *Tractatus*. Even the ideas of the "plunges into silence" and "return from silence" (Bachmann, 4:188), found throughout her first Frankfurt Lecture (1959) and pointing to her own understanding of the role of language, can be regarded as an implicit reference to the famous conclusion of the *Tractatus* as well as to Wittgenstein's own departure and subsequent return to the study of philosophy.

Bachmann chose to analyze modernity's dissolution of the subject via literary signifiers as her point of departure in "Fragen und Scheinfragen" ("Problems and Pseudo-Problems"). This same phenomenon was explored earlier in her radio essay, "Sagbares und Unsagbares," where she offered a logical analysis of linguistic forms that led to an inner dissolution of the relationship between language and the world. Beginning with the work of Bertrand Russell—as emphasized by Bachmann—one had to conclude that not all linguistic expressions functioned uniformly as names and that therefore the apparent logical form of a proposition was not necessarily its actual form. "All philosophy is a 'critique of language' (though not in Mauthner's sense)," writes Wittgenstein. "Russell's achievement was that he had shown that the apparent logical form of a proposition did not have to be its actual form" (*TLP*, 4.0031). In other words, Russell's innovation was to examine the source of metaphysical paradoxes—namely a misunderstanding of the logical structure of propositions—through logical and mathematical analysis. This was the first time that someone had pointed out the necessity of analyzing the formulation of a question in order to arrive at its solution.

It therefore became imperative to examine the sense of propositions and questions rather than to question the truth-value of propositions; in fact, the goal of the logical turn of philosophy was to expose the "hidden nonsense" within language (Bachmann, 4:106-7). Bachmann opens her radio essay, "Sagbares und Unsagbares," with a statement made by Wittgenstein in the *Philosophical Investigations*, situating it within the cultural context of the earliest phase of his thought: "The hidden nonsense—that which is hidden within the language itself—must be thoroughly investigated" (Bachmann, 4:107). "My aim is: to teach you to pass from a piece of disguised nonsense to something that is patent nonsense" (Wittgenstein, *PI*, § 464).

The young interpreter of the philosopher discerned the continuity between the early and the late phases of Wittgenstein's philosophy by underscoring his interest in language and in particular his discovery that philosophical problems lay in language itself, that is to say, within our use of language. This was not self-evident, considering that an understanding of language as both the creation and solution of all philosophical confusion (*PI*, §132) constitutes one of (the later) Wittgenstein's most significant and relevant ideas concerning the purpose of philosophy. From a philosophical perspective, this transition in Wittgenstein's thought which Bachmann pointed out was not at all self-evident. One can find no trace of this idea in the *Tractatus*, where philosophy is viewed as a critique of language and conducted via an analysis of the logical form of propositions. Instead, we find in the *Tractatus* a conceptualization which can be traced to Russell's influence on Wittgenstein, namely a hierarchical distinction between the ideal language of logic and the inexactness of ordinary language.

According to G.E. Moore, Wittgenstein's position with regard to the role of an analysis of language as a philosophical endeavor can be explained as follows:

> But he said, more than once, that he did not discuss these questions because he thought that language was the subject-matter of philosophy. He did not think that it was. He discussed it only because he thought that particular philosophical errors or "troubles in our thought" were due to false analogies suggested by our actual use of expressions; and he emphasized that it was only necessary for him to discuss those points about language which, as he thought, led to these particular errors or "troubles."[11]

In her radio essay, Bachmann takes issue with the neopositivistic standpoint and the idea that the clarity of the logical form of language could effect a change in language itself.[12] Instead, Bachmann was able to identify and elaborate upon the ideas of the *Tractatus* which foreshadowed the philosophical position of the later Wittgenstein, placing greater importance on the completeness of ordinary language and the self-manifestation of its logical form, rather than on a theory of representation and logical atomism (both of which were rejected by the later Wittgenstein). A careful examination of the practical, living aspect of everyday language rather than its apparent clumsiness, was paramount to any relevant discussion about language. Despite its appearances to the contrary, everyday language still offered the possibility of expressing one's inner reality. Wittgenstein formulated it thus:

> When I talk about language (words, sentences, etc.) I must speak the language of every day. Is this language somehow too coarse and material for what we want to say? Then how is another one to be constructed?—And how strange that we should be able to do anything at all with the one we have! (*PI*, § 120)

At this point, Bachmann takes up where Wittgenstein left off. Even though neither propositions of ordinary language, nor mathematical formulas find their basis in the reality which they represent, they still allow us some grasp of that reality.

> In other words, propositions composed of ordinary language as well as mathematical formulas represent reality, even though neither has the slightest bit to do with this reality. Rather, they are only symbols of representation that have nothing in common with what they are representing. The question remains as to how we can operate via such symbols, that is to say, via our language in the broadest sense of the term. (Bachmann, 4:108)

In the *Tractatus*, Wittgenstein provides an answer to the question of how to work with the symbols of language: what the proposition and the state of affairs (*Sachverhalt*) which the proposition represents have in common is their logical form. Bachmann chose to underscore the intransitive nature of language and its ability to create meaning on its own, as Wittgenstein had already written in 1914:[13]

> In the scientific method, for example, scientific propositions are written in such a way as to provide a possible model of the natural world, thereby emphasizing the intransitive nature of the relationship of a statement to that which it represents. We also find the term "model" in the discipline of modern physics, where for example one refers to atomic models in order to make clear that the description of an atom in fact has little to do with an actual atom, since an atom cannot be experienced directly. Rather, according to Wittgenstein, the "model" corresponds only to its own logical form. (Bachmann, 4:109)

Bachmann intuitively understood that the essence of the concept of logical structure in the *Tractatus* was that an "inner relationship" exists between representation on the one hand, and ineffable reality on the other. When Bachmann refers to scientific propositions as models of reality, Wittgenstein's philosophical views of the 1930s immediately come to mind, when he asserted that hypotheses should be viewed as the starting point for the construction of individual and verifiable scientific propositions rather than as scientific propositions (statements of fact) themselves which had simply not yet been proven.[14] Even the concept of logical form, which is the basis of a theory of representation in the *Tractatus*, is in Bachmann's view representative of the inexpressible strength of an inner linguistic gesture. In this case, her intuition proved once again to be on target: the theme of self-manifestation [*sich zeigen*], that is, the inability of logical form to create meaning which can only be achieved contextually in conversation is one which is taken up again in Wittgenstein's later work. Other examples include the concepts of arbitrariness, intransitive grammatical structures in a system of representation whose propositions are not determinable without a grounding in grammar itself, and finally, the idea of the language game and its grounding in actual practice.[15] According to Bachmann, Wittgenstein's later work is largely a continuation and elaboration of the task already set forth in the *Tractatus*: "This clarification of propositions was to be expanded further in the *Philosophical Investigations*. The investigation begins with the statements of everyday language, with an eye toward his one and only philosophical ideal: complete clarity" (Bachmann, 4:123).

Even though her thought was still influenced by a few "conventionalist" viewpoints put forth by Carnap, Bachmann was nevertheless able to draw such conclusions about Wittgenstein's work because she had discovered that he ascribed an important role to both the method and function of philosophical activity. Like the early Wittgenstein, Bachmann considered it essential to distinguish between "actual propositions" and "pseudo-propositions."[16] By drawing this distinction, one could then realize the goal of philosophical endeavor (i.e. complete clarity). Wittgenstein never advocated for a theory to transform or reform language; his philosophical activity "consisted only of method" (Bachmann, 4:122), and by method he did not mean the analytical methods of the traditional rationalist model. What remains then of a philosophy "in which statements that express something" belong to a science of reality and are of an empirical nature? What remains is a method, that is to say, a method of logical analysis, and not philosophical propositions, a theory or a system (Bachmann, 4:112).

A philosophy limited only to method was to achieve independence and leave reality "consciously untouched and indeterminate" so that it could then concern itself with the resolution of arbitrary questions about the essential nature of things, questions which created philosophical confusion. Bachmann describes the condition in which philosophy now found itself after Wittgenstein's newfound perspective as follows:

> There is no longer any attempt to interpret the world; reality is left consciously untouched and "indeterminate," because it does not lie within our power to determine its character. If we can represent things accurately and usefully, then there is no need to raise questions about "essence" or "appearances," neither of which have furthered any progress about representation, but instead have only created obstacles and even led to useless or incorrect results within the empirical sciences. (Bachmann, 4:112-113)

Bachmann also touches on another very important aspect of Wittgenstein's philosophical understanding when she exposes the misleading character of "questions about essence" (*Fragen nach dem Wesen*).[17] In order to create a perspective from which the world can be represented accurately, one must eliminate the source of the philosophical problem; a correct answer within philosophy should cause philosophy itself to fall silent. In Bachmann's terms, this "unphilosophical attitude" results from the conviction that our life's problems would remain untouched even if all possible scientific questions could be answered (Bachmann, 4:113). Even if an effective and accurate representation of reality could be created, one would still not have achieved any philosophically relevant results.

> So what do we have to gain by achieving an accurate and useful representation and image of reality? He gives us the answer on the final page of the *Tractatus*, an answer which allows us insight into the adventure and the challenge which this book takes up: "absolutely nothing." (Bachmann, 4:113)

Bachmann's reading is all the more compelling because she recognized both the sense and the spirit of Wittgenstein's "unphilosophical attitude" toward philosophy. Bachmann understood the real meaning of the answer given in the *Tractatus*: there are no more questions left to ask and, indeed, this is the answer.[18] With regard to his ban on formulating ethical statements (*TLP*, 6.42, 6.421: "It is clear that ethics cannot be expressed"), the "critic" of Bachmann's radio essay sees a dissolution of ethics and the impracticality of propositions about morality. On the contrary, Bachmann understood the positive character of silence in the *Tractatus* and recognized the implicit pathos contained within a negative formulation of ethics.

> It is not the clarifying, negative statements which limit philosophy to a logical analysis of scientific language and which reveal an investigation of reality in the natural sciences, but rather Wittgenstein's "futile" attempts to approach the inexpressible (*TLP*, 6.522) which create a tension in the *Tractatus* and which consume his thoughts—his failure to cast philosophy in a positive light, whereas other neopositivists remain blissfully unaware yet productive—this is worth rethinking again and again. (Bachmann, 4:13)[19]

The parallel structure of logic and morality proved to be the key to Bachmann's understanding of the relationship between the written and unwritten parts of the *Tractatus* ("My work consists of two parts: the one presented here plus all that I have not written," Ludwig Wittgenstein to Ludwig von Ficker, Fall 1919). In her commentary on the transcendental nature of ethics ("Ethics is transcendental," Wittgenstein, *TLP*, 6.421), Bachmann wrote the following in "Sagbares und Unsagbares": "What Wittgenstein meant by this is that the moral structure which does not belong to actual reality is analogous to logical structure" (Bachmann, 4:115). Each provides the necessary counterpart to the other, respectively. The correctness of Bachmann's analysis is confirmed by the following passages found in Wittgenstein's *Notebooks* (first published in 1960):

> The world and life are one. (TLP 5.621)
> Physiological life is of course not "life." And neither is psy-

chological life. Life is the world. Ethics does not treat of the world. Ethics must be a condition of the world, like logic. Ethics and aesthetics are one. (TLP 6.421)[20]

The connection of a proposition to its content parallels the relationship between action and ethical reward. On the one hand, the proposition represents the state of affairs on its own, as it were, while on the other hand, ethical reward and punishment, if they exist at all, can only "be found within the action itself."[21] The implication for logic and ethics comes directly from the concept of the ineffable nature of reality.

> The world is neutral in value and consists of things which are of equal rank. . . . We are left to draw our own conclusions as far as existential questions are concerned. He doesn't mean that there are no values or that ethics is an impossibility . . . he simply means that it is impossible to speak about such things, if one is to be exact about it. . . . The limits of the world occur where language does not suffice and therefore thought also does not suffice (Bachmann, 4:118).

The neutrality of meaning and of value with respect to reality corresponds to the impossibility of attaining with the sayable anything beyond the sayable itself, which limits the unthinkable only to the inner realm and thus hints at the "limits" ["Entgrenzung"]. The drama which plays out in Wittgenstein's thought leads Bachmann to mention Pascal's "mystique of the heart" and the verse from Baudelaire quoted at the conclusion of her dissertation on Heidegger ("Ah, ne jamais sortir des Nombres et des êtres"). "Nombres, êtres, the things which have no consciousness but only exist quantitatively"—these things open the drama of self-manifestation:

> We are thus unable to answer any of the questions which we are used to posing in philosophy. We can only look to ourselves when we are asked about our "reason for being." The "movement" which is behind a philosophy but which cannot help us solve any real problems and which can only offer the bleak, formulaic "eternal" truth of logic—propositions which must be overcome in order to see the world in its true

form—this "movement" is the same one that Baudelaire evokes in his poem *Le Gouffre*. Wittgenstein moves in and with his despair in the same manner as Pascal; he is beset from all sides by that which he cannot name, leading him to a "drame cardinal". "Ah, [ne] jamais sortir des nombres et des êtres!" (4:21)[22]

The controversial conclusion of the *Tractatus* clearly contains the suggestion that "silence on a subject does not simply mean silence" (Bachmann, 4:120). Bachmann takes this interpretation of silence to refer to Wittgenstein's own text, although it could also be applied to his life.[23] We find confirmation of this interpretation in a letter Wittgenstein wrote to Ludwig von Ficker in the fall of 1919, which is often quoted in the scholarship: "My book draws limits to the sphere of the ethical from the inside as it were. . . . In short, I believe that where many others today are just guessing, I have managed in my book to put everything firmly into place by being silent about it."[24] The *polemical* component of Wittgenstein's silence with respect to his contemporaries was also not lost on Bachmann. She recognized that his silence was a reaction not only to irrationalism, but also to scientism and its philosophy. Wittgenstein had described his own attitude toward European civilization in a similar fashion in the early 1930s.[25]

> We can find the reasons for this attitude by examining the historical situation in which Wittgenstein found himself. His silence is almost certainly a protest against a specific anti-rationalism of his time, against the metaphysically contaminated ideas of Western thought . . . . And the silence is also understood to be a protest against the tendency to have faith in science and progress that was prevalent at that time. (Bachmann, 4:126)

It was no coincidence that Bachmann was able to take up the suggestion made by Wittgenstein in his preface to read one text with the other in mind:

> Four years ago I had occasion to reread my first book [the *Tractatus Logico-Philosophicus*] and to explain its ideas to some-

one. It suddenly seemed to me that I should publish those old thoughts and the new ones together: that the latter could be seen in the right light only by contrast with and against the background of my old way of thinking (*Philosophical Investigations*, "Preface," WA 1:232).

The young reader of Wittgenstein highlighted the continuity between the "unphilosophical attitude," which characterized the *Tractatus*, and the "ironic" task of philosophy which was to become the therapy for philosophical problems in the *Philosophical Investigations*.[26] Philosophical problems are seen as diseases that have their roots in language, resulting from a "misfiring" of language:

> herewith we have discovered Wittgenstein's purpose, the same one that comes to light in the *Tractatus*: to show that problems of philosophy are problems of language, in other words that "misfirings" of language create philosophical problems. (Bachmann, 4:123)

In this sense, the philosophical activity and the description of our use of language are one and the same for Wittgenstein. The "conceptual" investigations of philosophy, which are carried out on a much broader basis in the *Philosophical Investigations*, take leave of abstraction in order to provide concrete images (*Bilder*). The later phase of Wittgenstein's philosophy consists of a series of thought-experiments, representing a new conception of language which has been characterized as a multiplicity of language games (*PI*, §§ 10, 23-24).

> It is Wittgenstein's conviction that we must bring peace to philosophy so that it will no longer be "whipped" by questions which themselves cast doubt on philosophy itself, and he believes that we can silence these problems, if our language can function in a decent and sensible way, which is to say when our language lives and breathes in usage [*PI* 432: "Every sign by itself seems dead. What gives it life? In use it is alive. Is life breathed into it there? Or is the use its life?"] Only where language, which itself is a form of life, is taken out of context and is left to idle [*PI*, 132: "The confusions

which occupy us arise when language is like an engine idling, not when it is doing work."]—and this occurs when ... philosophy is applied to language in the conventional way—when this happens, problems arise. These problems should not be solved but instead should be eliminated.

These investigations revolve around the *Tractatus* but at the same time expound upon it in all directions through more detailed investigations. They take leave of abstraction and provide concrete images. Language is now no longer called a system of signs—which of course it remains—but instead, in its multiplicity, is compared to an old city." (Bachmann, 4:124)

By comparing language to a city, the heterogeneity of language games and the relative perfection of language is emphasized. Bachmann provides a more detailed explanation of this allegorical image as follows:

If one were to compare language to a city, then there is the old city center, and newer sections of the city are added to it, and at the outskirts there are gas stations and arterial roads, and perhaps the edges of the city are ugly when compared to the city center, but all of it still belongs together, and this is what makes up a modern city.[27]

The question that Wittgenstein raises in this passage is not about the search for the essence of language; rather, the question is concerned with the perfection and completeness of language.[28] The problem of the limit has by no means been solved but has been emblematically relativized in an anthropological sense. Bachmann connects the commingling of language with a form of life in the *Philosophical Investigations*, to the themes of self-manifestation and idea of the *inexpressible* which themselves are commingled with the limits of the world in the *Tractatus*.[29] In a statement typical of her theoretical writings, we find that Bachmann has already condensed her entire argument in a surprisingly enlightening comment at the conclusion of her 1953 essay, "Ludwig Wittgenstein—zu einem Kapitel der jüngsten Philosophiegeschichte:"

But doesn't Wittgenstein inform us that the moral form, which just like the logical form cannot be represented, makes itself manifest and is reality? "Whereof one cannot speak, thereof one must be silent," he states in conclusion and refers precisely to this reality that we find ourselves unable and even prohibited from creating an image of. Or does he conclude instead, that we have mis-played our language game, because it does not contain any word(s) upon which we can really depend? (4:22-23)

Philosophical errors lead us to become victims of a *mystification of our language*—what matters is not so much the language itself as *our reaction to language*. We can only achieve an overview of language, albeit limited to specific instances, by doing away with broad, conclusive explanations. *Therapy* is called for in order to clarify the grammar of a language segment: "he does not of course offer a feeble prescription for synthesis which was in high demand, but instead a prescription for healing—as therapist" (Bachmann, 4:127).

Upon closer examination, we see that this is not a demand to lower one's expectations of philosophy but instead an attempt to liberate thought from the *sublimation* of ordinary forms of language. If we read Bachmann's essays on Wittgenstein from this perspective, it is not difficult to recognize three essential elements within them:
- first of all, we find a clear reference to a description of language as language game and thus the attempt to provide an explanation for the final statement of the *Tractatus* based on later developments in Wittgenstein's thought;
- secondly, there is considerable overlap between Wittgenstein's conception of philosophical activity and Bachmann's own conception of the linguistic work of art (*sprachliches Kunstwerk*) which she illustrates in her "Frankfurt Lectures";
- thirdly, we are given a preview of Bachmann's own future development: if one seeks the redemptive phrase in language, then one is condemned again and again to mis-play language, to lose the "language game." Language will avenge itself for this unjustifiable demand upon it; herein lies the seed of the idea of language as "punishment," an idea which will be developed later in her literary work.[30]

"Kein Sterbenswort, / ihr Worte" ("Do not breathe a single word / you words")—Bachmann composed this line at the end of one of her last poems ("Ihr Worte," 1:163). "Silence," the motif that recurs throughout Bachmann's poetic works, represents the necessary departure from the usual misuse of language in order to find one's own way in language. Bachmann's "suspicion" (4:190) with regard to language and the unavoidable "conflict with language" (4:191) play a central role in her lecture "Fragen und Scheinfragen," where she characterizes the human condition of the poet/writer in a linguistic *and* existential sense. Again, Bachmann's approach seems to be closer to Wittgenstein than to Heidegger. Indeed, it is not far removed from the following note found in Wittgenstein's unpublished works:

> People are deeply embedded in philosophical, that is to say, grammatical confusion. In order to liberate them, one needs to tear them away from the unbelievable multiplicity of connections in which they are trapped. One must so to speak rearrange their entire language. Yet this language developed in this way because people had an inclination—and still do—to think *like this*. This is why the process of tearing away occurs only to those who live with an instinctive rebellion against language. It does not happen to those who according to their entire instinct live in *the* herd which has taken this language to be its *actual* form of expression.[31]

Nevertheless, this shows Bachmann's lucid understanding of Wittgenstein and also suggests the existence of an affinity of attitude which goes beyond theory and permeates her literary work and aesthetic achievements in an original way. A similar attitude was shared by several idiosyncratic intellectuals who lived during the cultural age of Viennese modernity and emphasized the central role of the connection of language and morality.[32] One particularly significant aphorism collected in Hofmannsthal's *Buch der Freunde* (*The Book of Friends*) seems to epitomize this special kind of affinity: "Wahre Sprachliebe ist nicht möglich ohne Sprachverleugnung" ("A real love of language is not possible without a repudiation of language"). In other words, the poet and the philosopher experience the two sides of a *single* tragedy—they share a common "drame cardinal" because, in as far as they possess an extreme sensitivity to the use of words, they both perceive and live silence as an instinctive act of rebellion against language.

[Translated from the German by Linda Hsu]

NOTES

1. The radio essay, "Der Wiener Kreis—Logischer Positivismus—Philosophie als Wissenschaft" (1952/53; unpublished), was broadcast on April 14, 1953 by Hessischer Rundfunk. There is also another unpublished essay entitled "Philosophie der Gegenwart" (1948). Cf. Sara Lennox, "Bachmann and Wittgenstein," *Modern Austrian Literature* 18, no. 3-4 (1985): 243-44.

2. Ludwig Wittgenstein, *Tractatus Logico-Philosophicus*, German text with an English translation *en regard* by C.K. Ogden, introd. Bertrand Russell. First edition: 1922 (London: Routledge, 1996). Hereafter cited as *TLP*, followed by the paragraph-number.

3. Ludwig Wittgenstein, *Philosophical Investigations* (Oxford: Blackwell, 1988). Hereafter cited as *PI*.

4. Ingeborg Bachmann, *Werke*. 4 vols., ed. Christine Koschel, Inge von Weidenbaum and Clemens Münster (München: Piper, 1978), 4:126. Hereafter cited by volume- and page-number.

5. On the topic of philosophy as therapy see also *PI*, § 109, 111, 119, 133.

6. Cf. Ludwig Wittgenstein, *The Blue and Brown Books* (Oxford: Blackwell, 1989), 16-19) (*Das Blaue Buch*, in *Werkausgabe*, 8 vols. [Frankfurt am Main: Suhrkamp, 1989]. Here: vol. 5, p. 36-39. Hereafter cited as *WA*); cf. *PI*, § 65-66.

7. The fact that Bachmann's reading is based on the connections between the *Tractatus* and *Philosophical Investigations* and not on a blend of Heidegger/Wittgenstein proves that the Wittgenstein essays (composed 1952-1953) belong to the phase in which she was already emancipated from academic-scientific philosophy. (Cf. Ingeborg Bachmann, *Wir müssen wahre Sätze finden. Gespräche und Interviews*, ed. Christine Koschel and Inge von Weidenbaum [München: Piper, 1983], 135, where Bachmann explained her discovery of Wittgenstein as follows: "There was no professor, no one suggested him to me, rather I looked around myself and found this book . . .").

8. On the subject of the "problem of the limit" cf. Peter Kampits, "Ingeborg Bachmann oder Das Ringen um die Grenzen der Sprache," *Ludwig Wittgenstein. Wege und Umwege zu seinem Denken* (Graz: Styria, 1985), 189-93. There is now a relatively large body of literature on the subject of the relationship between literature and

philosophy in Bachmann, which focuses specifically on the influence of Heidegger and Wittenstein on her work. For a recent presentation of the main issues in the scholarship, see Monika Albrecht and Dirk Göttsche, ed., *Bachmann Handbuch: Leben, Werk, Wirkung* (Stuttgart: Metzler, 2002).

9. For a detailed account of this influence, see Barbara Agnese, *Der Engel der Literatur: Zum philosophischen Vermächtnis Ingeborg Bachmanns* (Wien: Passagen, 1996), chapter 2 and passim. On this subject see also the interesting remarks by Majorie Perloff, *Wittgenstein's Ladder. Poetic Language and the Strangeness of the Ordinary* (Chicago: University of Chicago Press, 1996), 148-52.

10. Bachmann often discussed the significance of her "intellectual encounter" with Wittgenstein, cf. *Wir müssen wahre Sätze finden*, 12, 58, 83, 136.

11. G. E. Moore, "Wittgenstein's Lectures in 1930-1933," *Philosophical Papers* (London: Allen and Unwin, 1959), 257 (see also 323-324). Cf. also *PI*, § 111.

12. In Bachmann's radio essay, "Der Wiener Kreis: Logischer Positivismus—Philosophie als Wissenschaft" (1952/53), we find an introduction to a position which offers a reading of Wittgenstein that distances itself from logical positivism, although it does not yet stand in open opposition to it: "Where is a good place to start? Perhaps with Ludwig Wittgenstein, who has yet to be discovered, one of the greatest and at the same time one of the most unknown philosophers of our era. On the final pages of his *Tractatus Logico-Philosophicus* we find statements that could bring about the turn, the end of positivism, without having to relinquish its insights." Quoted in Lennox, "Bachmann and Wittgenstein," 244-245.

13. Cf. Bachmann, 4:109 and Wittgenstein, *Notebooks 1914-1916* (Oxford: Blackwell, 1961), p. 26e ("Tagebücher 1914-1916" [5.11.1914], *WA*, 1:115): "In this way the proposition represents the situation—as it were off its own bat."

14. See "Ludwig Wittgenstein und der Wiener Kreis," *WA*, 3:158-159.

15. On this point, see Wittgenstein, "Philosophische Bemerkungen," *WA* 2, § 225-230; "Philosophische Grammatik," *WA* 4, § 56, p. 97; *PI*, § 1-25.

16. The title used for her first Frankfurt Lecture was "Fragen und Scheinfragen" ("Problems and Pseudo-problems"), which calls to mind the philosophical terminology of the Vienna Circle.

17. See Wittgenstein, *The Blue and Brown Books*, 26, 169 (*WA*, 5:50, 261). For a detailed commentary on Wittgenstein's text and philosophical issues, see G. P. Baker and P.M.S. Hacker, *An Analytical Commentary on Wittgenstein's Philosophical Investigations*, vol. I-II (Oxford: Blackwell, 1980).

18. Cf. Wittgenstein, *TLP*, 6.52. Bachmann quotes this statement twice in the radio essay; see "Sagbares und Unsagbares," 4:119, 127.

19. See also Bachmann, 4:116: "In what context are we to place the other components of Wittgenstein's thought, his futile efforts centered on the inexpressible, the 'unsayable'?"

20. Wittgenstein, *Notebooks 1914-1916*, 77e ("Tagebücher," *WA*, 1:172).

21. See Wittgenstein, *Notebooks*, 26e ("Tagebücher," *WA*, 1:115); *TLP*, 6.422, 6.421.

22. See Bachmann, *Die kritische Aufnahme der Existenzialphilosophie Martin Heideggers* (München: Piper, 1985), 130-131; "Sagbares und Unsagbares," *Werke*, 4:117, 120. Bachmann's reference to Pascal's "mystique of the heart," on the insignificance of the human value of conceptual argumentation which is not guided by any moral necessity, corresponds to several comments by Wittgenstein which Bachmann could not have known. For instance, in a 1946 note, Wittgenstein makes a similar remark: "An observation in a poem is overstated if the intellectual points are nakedly exposed, not clothed from the heart." See Wittgenstein, "Vermischte Bemerkungen," *WA*, 8:527 (quoted in *Culture and Value*, ed. Georg H. von Wright and Heikki Nyman, trans. P. Winch [Oxford: Blackwell, 1984], 54e). We should add that whenever Wittgenstein quotes Pascal in his notes, he views him as a mathematician who admires the beauty of a theorem in *number theory*. We can almost find validation of Bachmann's intuitive sense of Wittgenstein's mystical connection with „nombres et êtres" in a note (1942) from the "Vermischte Bemerkungen," *WA*, 8:508: "The mathematician (Pascal) who admires the beauty of a theorem in numbers theory; . . . One might

say: what wonderful laws the Creator built into numbers!" (quoted in *Culture and Value*, 41e). See also *WA*, 8:562 (*Culture and Value*, 79e). Many Wittgenstein critics have underscored the relationship of Wittgenstein to Pascal; see Georg H. von Wright, *Wittgenstein* (Oxford: Blackwell, 1982); Kurt Wuchterl and Adolf Hübner, *Ludwig Wittgenstein in Selbstzeugnissen und Bilddokumenten* (Reinbek bei Hamburg: Rowohlt, 1979), 15-16.

23. See Bachmann, 4:120: "This interpretation of Wittgenstein's concept of silence goes beyond that which he himself articulated; but we believe that we are allowed to draw such conclusions in order to make the *TLP* understandable, and also because Wittgenstein's life gives us a point of reference for all that he believed could be silently performed."

24. Wittgenstein to Ludwig von Ficker, Oct.-Nov. 1919, *Briefe* (Frankfurt am Main: Suhrkamp, 1980), 96-97. See also Brian McGuinness, *Wittgenstein: A Life* (London: Duckworth, 1988), 288.

25. See "Ludwig Wittgenstein und der Wiener Kreis," *WA*, 3:68-69; Wittgenstein, "Vermischte Bemerkungen," *WA*, 8:458-59 ("Zu einem Vorwort"); *Philosophical Remarks*, "Preface" (Oxford: Blackwell, 1975)/"Philosophische Bemerkungen" ("Vorwort"), *WA*, 2: "This book is written for such men as are in sympathy with its spirit. This spirit is different from the one which informs the vast stream of European and American civilization in which all of us stand. That spirit expresses itself in an onwards movement, in building ever larger and more complicated structures; the other in striving after clarity and perspicuity in no matter what structure. The first tries to grasp the world by way of its periphery—in its variety; the second at its center—in its essence. And so the first adds one construction to another, moving on and up, as it were, from one stage to the next, while the other remains where it is and what it tries to grasp is always the same." On this point, see also Lennox, "Bachmann and Wittgenstein," 254.

26. Original documents lend credibility to this philosophical analysis; the relevant sections (*PI*, § 81-133) which take stock of a logical understanding of the *TLP* and above all point to Wittgenstein's new philosophical views are marked by Bachmann in the copy of the *PI* found in her private library.

27. *Gespräche und Interviews*, 16. See also ibid., 17: "Language itself, I believe, is as it were a city, and new phrases grow externally onto it, and the old poems are created from the old 'word materials' and the new poems from old and new, I would say. Some also only from new (material)." Mauthner's analogy (cf. *Sprache und Leben* [Salzburg: Residenz, 1986], 76), as elucidated by M. Swiderska (*Die Vereinbarkeit des Unvereinbaren* [Tübingen: Niemeyer, 1989], 31), has a negative connotation in contrast to Wittgenstein's and Bachmann's analogy, which has a positive connotation. We have thus further confirmation that Wittgenstein's critique of language is almost never "in Mauthner's sense."

28. See Wittgenstein, *PI* § 18: ". . . ask yourself whether our language is complete;—whether it was so before the symbolism of chemistry and the notation of the infinitesimal calculus were incorporated in it; for these are, so to speak, suburbs of our language. (And how many houses or streets does it take before a row begins to be a town?) Our language can be seen as an ancient city: a maze of little streets and squares, of old and new houses, and of houses with additions from various periods; and thus surrounded by a multitude of new boroughs with straight regular streets and uniform houses."

29. See *TLP*, 6.522: "There is indeed the inexpressible. This *shows* itself; it is the mystical."

30. See Bachmann, "Rede zur Verleihung des Anton-Wildgans-Preises," 4:295, 297; and *Malina*, 3:97). For an extensive analysis of this motif and of the relationship between Bachmann and Heidegger, see Agnese, *Der Engel der Literatur*, chapters III and VIII.

31. Wittgenstein, TS 213, quoted in: "'Philosophie'—from the so-called Big Typescript," ed. Heikki Nyman, *Revue internationale de philosophie*, no. 169 (1989): 194. Cf. *The Big Typescript: TS 213* (Oxford: Blackwell, 2003; in print).

32. On Bachmann's relationship to Viennese modernity, see Agnese, *Der Engel der Literatur*, especially chapter IX.

5 / Ingeborg Bachmann's "Eyes to Wonder": Towards a Structural Interpretation

Robert Pichl

Since the 1980s, a new trend of interpretation has been noticeable in Bachmann scholarship that has largely ignored the epistemological value of systematic structural analysis. As such, this trend is part of a current fundamental skepticism of structural analysis as the historically established method of the so-called "work-immanent interpretation" with its aim of demonstrating inner structural harmony as an expression of the timeless aesthetic values inherent in the textual body.[1] Today this kind of interpretation—if it is pursued solely for its own sake—is considered as obsolete as the positivistic collecting of data and facts or the humanistic categorization of literary texts based on the intended "intuition of essence" common in the first part of the 20th century.[2]

The following essay has a twofold purpose: on the one hand, it attempts to show paradigmatically the epistemological value of a structural analysis through a reading of Ingeborg Bachmann's narrative "Ihr glücklichen Augen" ("Eyes to Wonder") (without suggesting this to be a "model interpretation"). On the other hand, this method of interpretation will document the structural complexity of Bachmann's text, which makes a multi-perspectival interpretation necessary. Underlying such an interpretation is a concept of the literary text as a complex entity with potentially multiple poetic functions and with its own historicity. As such, the text can play with elements from different non-literary discourses and arrange them aesthetically, without, however, completely becoming accessible to interpretation. The interpretation of such a text must then necessarily be provided from a holistic perspective. What is at stake here is the uncovering of several thematic aspects whose various functions of expression and poetic effect are mediated by structural elements or structural constellations (such as striking motifs, individual or stereotypical style of speech, or a multi-layered narration).

These thematic aspects in their complexity are already evident even in a first detailed reading of the text, and they are even deepened, or, rather, broadened, and modified in a second reading.[3] On the one hand, these readings are to be understood as individual points of discourse and can be further explored with the proper and adequate methodical questions. On the other hand, their common anchoring within the textual structure also causes a mutual relativity of thematic references through flashbacks upon the narrative method that are recognized as multi-dimensional. Therefore, the detailed thematic aspects can be integrated in the reading process in the deepened connective meaning of a differentiated discourse.[4]

The conventional poetic analysis of the story "Eyes to Wonder," according to its "structural forms" [Bauformen], provides at first the layout of an interplay between two levels of plot. First, there is an apparently stereotypical foreground plot, often used in a clichéd manner within trivial literature: a woman of good character is left by her lover for another woman, who is presented as an evil competitor.[5] This foreground plot is set in opposition to and into play with the psychological reactions of the three protagonists (Miranda, Josef, Anastasia), which offer different narrative perspectives. Yet the narrative course of events appears to be incomplete and not proceeding toward any logical conclusion. What is missing is the catchy moral to the story, a manifestation of an image of the world and of mankind offering sociologically or even ideologically critical perspectives. Instead, the narrative contents itself somewhat with mere allusions, then capriciously turns to symbolism and poses questions concerning the logical connections of events, resulting in a climactic, though ambiguous and open ending. In this way, a plausible relation between the loose structure of events and its idealistic background remains in suspense even in the end.[6]

The characters themselves, in particular the protagonist Miranda, are characterized with great psychological skill in their individuality, for example, such as Miranda's habit—already developed and explained in a rough draft [text level I]—of conversing in disjointed sentences: "Miranda always speaks in quarter sentences, as she considers them long enough . . . ."[7] At the same time, the very same characters receive through their "speaking" names a touch towards a typifying general approach, e.g. Miranda, Latin: the admirable; Anastasia, Greek: the resurrecting; Josef, the bearer of a protective role associated with his Biblical namesake. The semantic aura thus spun around the characters is, however, at times in contrast to their behavior in the story which appears partly trivial, partly as psychosomatic failure.[8]

Dimensions of space and time are realized in loosely connected narrative episodes presenting sequences of snapshots. In this way, topographic details of the city of Vienna become increasingly the focus: for example, the great concert hall of the *Musikverein* as a place of Miranda's transgressive self-realization in her enjoyment of beauty, or the top-class restaurants "Roman Emperor" and "Eden Bar" as an adequate ambiance and meeting place of the so-called "high society."[9] This topography also includes Miranda's apartment in the "Blutgasse," a street that supposedly was named after a massacre of the members of the Templars in 1312, which allows enigmatic associations of violence and death.[10] The same is true for glasses, as a central requisite that increasingly takes on symbolic meaning and suggests manifold connotations within the context of the foregrounded plot. With the arbitrary use of the glasses, Miranda succeeds in manipulating the perceptions of her environment according to the corresponding degree of her willingness for apperception. Without her glasses, she confuses actual places and people (as is the case with the "Leopoldsberg," which is located on this side of the Danube with the "Bisamberg"[11] on the other side of the Danube, or Herr Kopetzky with Herr Langbein). However, precisely in this way, she may see only whatever she wants to, and how she wants to see it. Thus, her subjective understanding of identity is illustrated by her perception of the external world.

The narrative and the dialogues of the characters are, for the most part, presented in a pleasant conversational tone.[12] As a result, in decisive moments, essential and less pleasant points remain undiscussed between Miranda and Josef, such as the problems of their relationship. When Miranda draws the attention of her newspaper-reading friend to a striking change in the behavior of Stasi—"Stasi has calmed down a lot, she never used to be so nice, I think she's in love, at least something must be doing her good . . ." (Bachmann, *TPL*, 78)—Josef is "distracted, as though he doesn't know who she's talking about," and then assumes that the reason must be, among others, that Stasi, who had been worn down by her divorce procedures, would now be granted custody of her child after all:

> That is the first Miranda has heard of this, and she hears it from Josef. She wants to call Stasi right away and rejoice, but then suddenly feels cold; she checks to see if the window is open, but it's shut. Josef looks back down at his newspaper, Miranda at the roof across the street. (*TPL*, 78)

While essential things remain undiscussed, seemingly unimportant or unclear details sometimes appear emphasized in an unmotivated manner, for example, the advertising slogan "Never lose sight of the best things in life" of the optical company in the opening part of the narrative (*TPL*, 80), or Miranda's spontaneous, yet contextually unclear remark about Anastasia: "She's just more beautiful than I am" (*TPL*, 85).

From the perspective of conventional structural principles, the narrative fails to be organized around any central stance and does not follow the principle of hypotactic unity. Instead, we find a textual conglomerate that is loosely spun around the foregrounded plot and, with its numerous allusions, obscurities and symbolic turns partly asks for supplementation or completion. Accordingly, several discourses can be recognized, while their thematic coherence can at best be reconstructed by the reader in individual association and without certainty for a general liability.

An interpretation of this textual structure could consequently take place from several different extreme positions, according to the aforementioned trends of more recent Bachmann research. On the one hand, one could selectively observe the foregrounded plot as the only structural element that is more or less logically reconstructable. This would lead to the interpretation of a not particularly original love story that, with its remaining structural elements, expresses the pleasant local color of Vienna and a picture of its society that is faintly reminiscent of Schnitzler. In this way, the narrative would at least be granted some "higher level" entertainment value. This reading is precisely the essence of a negative review of the "Simultan-cycle" by Marcel Reich-Ranicki; in addition, the 1992 film adaptation was also undertaken from this point of view.[13]

On the other hand, given some knowledge about the problematic perspectives of Ingeborg Bachmann's late prose, one could also choose as a starting point for an interpretation the well-known topic of the destruction of feminine concepts of identity in the masculine-organized present-day society. The narrative, indeed, deals with the subject, but the latter is only alluded to from different perspectives, and nowhere is this topic shaped into a uniform model with statements regarding solution or dissolution. As a result, many parts of the text must appear superfluous if one takes this issue as the starting point of an interpretation. Also, a reading of the story "with Wittgenstein against Heidegger or from Derrida's perspective," will find, undoubtedly, evidence for corresponding philosophemes, partly immediate, partly per analogies. But again, this kind of reading will not be able to present a unified perspective. None of these methods will disclose the poetic text in its multifaceted unity, which in my opinion is the precondition for understanding its historical relevance.

An integrative perspective of interpretation, based on the textual concept defined at the beginning, is to be constructed from the central motif of vision.[14] Miranda's bad, Anastasia's decent, Josef's normal vision, the loss, the forgetting and the breaking of the glasses, the torturing contact lenses, the hurting eyes, the substitution of vision with other sensory perceptions, the looking at Josef, the ignoring of Josef, the looking away, the seeing of what others do not see and at last the overlooking of a glass door of a coffee house at the beginning and the end of the narrative as well as the advertisement slogan "Never lose sight of the best things in life" as a leitmotif of the eyeglass company: in semantic variation, metaphorical deepening and manifold connotations, the meaning of seeing penetrates all structural levels of the story. It weaves together individual and disparate narrative episodes; due to different valuations of seeing by individual characters, it attributes values to their characteristics; at last, it serves Miranda as a means to establish her subjective concept of identity in opposition to her external world. Thus, it also motivates her illogical pre-decision that—according to the inner logic of the narrative—affects the as yet hidden crisis of her relationship:

> Because she knows that her glasses didn't fall into the sink by accident—she will have to lose Josef and would rather lose

him voluntarily—she sets herself in motion. She takes the first steps toward an end she will one day discover, blinded by fear. She mustn't allow Josef and Anastasia to guess that she is letting them drift toward each other, Stasi in particular, and thus she must invent a story for all of them which is more bearable and better than the real one: .... (Bachmann, *TPL*, 87)

From the integrative perspective, focused on the motif of vision, the functionality of the remaining ambiguities, obscurities and symbols that appear structurally striking becomes obvious: they are elements of a creative principle of "allusion" which organizes a loosely linked, multilayered text,[15] a concept partly based on Ingeborg Bachmann's reception of Wittgenstein's philosophy. The earliest documentation of this reception may be the "summary" in her dissertation (1949): existential questions of man cannot be made understandable through rational explanations with abstract concepts, but only through art, that is, in the image. (Bachmann refers to the following images as examples: Goya's painting "Kronos Devours His Children" and Baudelaire's sonnet "Le gouffre").[16]

It is not Bachmann's point to show Miranda's destiny in a uniform model of life, with clearly identified factors of cause and effect, or to summarize the idealistic background of the narrative in a concise moral of the story. In the latter case the reader could be mislead into an affirmative reception, and would hardly be provoked to draw further conclusions. The "alluding" narrative functions as a formal reflection of a painful certainty which develops from Miranda's subconscious on the basis of irrational and yet compelling circumstantial evidence that her subjective concept of identity cannot be maintained in opposition to the reality of life. It is precisely through this indirect, alluding presentation of this process of realization, that the reader is able to carry it out individually and in an operative way.

In addition, the narrative causes the reader to further follow through on thematic aspects that are partly associated with them; thus, for instance, the question arises about the role of the subconscious in human behavior, when Miranda suddenly knows that she is going to lose Josef without having any particular reason for this insight at that time. Also, there is the question, identified already as the feminist perspective, of how to put feminine concepts of identity

"Eyes to Wonder" 121

into practice in a male-dominated present-day society. Or the question about the valuation of Miranda's concept of identity under the aspect of social responsibility that would at least put her suggestive assessment as an exploited victim into perspective. Or, with regard to the generally typical approach to the "speaking" names of characters, the question of whether the obvious, feministic perspective could not be extended to a more general agenda concerning modern man's existential loss of experience with its corresponding social or ideological consequences.[17] Thus the discourse, building upon the so-called incomplete narrative method, produces further detailed discursive points of origin that can be pursued with specific, methodic procedures, which, however, always remain tied to "Miranda's case" as both the starting point and exemplary case. A differentiated methodological analysis of thematic details therefore cannot be carried out in the form of an eclectic combination of several procedures, but rather as a dialogue of questions that contributes to multidimensional results. A far broader and more evident perspective is to be gained if we, in contrast to more recent trends in criticism, approach the text with a range of coherent topics developed on the basis of its structure, which will also illuminate the text's historical significance.

Finally, two particularly striking structural elements shall be pointed out that will support the previously presented analysis by highlighting the narrative's intertextual aspect. I am referring to the title of the narrative and its dedication to Georg Groddeck. The story's title refers very clearly to Lynceus' Song from the Watch-Tower in Goethe's "Faust Part Two" (V. 11288 and following verses):

Zum Sehen geboren	For sight I was born
Zum Schauen bestellt	For viewing was set;
Dem Turm geschworen	To watchtower sworn,
Gefällt mir die Welt.	I love the world yet.
Ich blick in die Ferne	I gaze out afar,
Ich seh in der Näh,	I see what is near,
Den Mond und die Sterne,	The moon and the star,
Den Wald und das Reh.	The forest and deer.
So seh ich in allen	Thus splendor of ages

Die ewige Zier	On all sides I view;
Und wie mir's gefallen	As I found them all good,
Gefall ich auch mir.	So I find myself too.
Ihr glücklichen Augen	You eyes to wonder,
Was je ihr gesehen.	For all you have seen,
Es sei wie es wolle,	Whatever it was
Es war doch so schön!	It still was so fine![18]

According to Albrecht Schöne's *Faust*-commentary in the edition of Goethe's collected works published by *Deutscher Klassiker Verlag*, Goethe differentiates very often in his use of language between the non-reflective sensual perception of seeing and seeing as intuition grasping the essence of things.[19] The intertextual perspective reveals a reflective constellation: Miranda is placed in opposition to the watchman Lynceus whom we recognize from the referential indication of the quote and who is also equipped with a "speaking" name—that is "lynx-eyed." Lynceus enjoys the world from the highest point of the tower where he lets his eyes wander across the land and absorbs it in this way. Miranda retreats with her manipulated bad eyesight into the protective "tower" of her subjectivity, which is established in opposition to the objective course of history. To allude to Ingeborg Bachmann's famous quote from her "Kriegsblindenrede" ("Speech to the War Blind"), Miranda does not succeed in the unfolding of possibilities by and through a counter-play between conscious seeing and unconscious perceiving due to destiny; there is no re-negotiation of identity leading her from a position against the very reality of life toward a position within the reality of life, for example by fighting for her endangered love, regardless of its uncertain success. She avoids the existential confrontation and looks for a way, in reverse response to the course of history, to remodel it subjectively: against her most inner desire, she paradoxically drives Josef into Anastasia's arms. Thus, in the end, Lynceus' "eyes to wonder" become for her a symbol of destructive irony that exposes her identity as a grand delusion. This irony culminates in the pointed final sentence that is repeatedly used as a leitmotif and suggests to "Never lose sight of the good things in life," at the moment when the glass door of the coffeehouse hits her face. Confronted with this incident, the reader is stimulated both to think about what "the good" would actually be for Miranda and to continue further reaching reflection about the relativity of all good. In her substantial analysis of the *Simultan* cycle, Ingeborg Dusar points out that the psychosomatic Georg Groddeck also established a parallel between his theory of the double character of visual work and the opposition of seeing and perceiving in Lynceus' tower song.[20] Significantly, the narrative "Eyes to Wonder" is also dedicated to his memory. This second intertextual aspect suggests the cross-link to Groddeck's most famous work, the *Book of the It (Das Buch vom Es)*[21] with which Ingeborg Bachmann occupies herself as well in greater detail in a draft for an essay about Groddeck.

> This "It," the unknown, something only, therefore, . . . full of secrets, because life is it, because nature is it, for Groddeck would reject any other secret . . . the "It" for him is a helping word, it is nothing in itself, but is there to point out, there is something there and it is stronger, much stronger than the I, as the I is not even able by will to interfere in our breathing system, our digestive system, in our circulation, the I is a mask, the court manner, with [which] each of us walks around, and we are ruled by the "It," the "It" does it, and it talks in symbols through illness. [Again a dangerous word. Not for Groddeck. The symbol and the thing are one].[22]

One can easily establish the analogy to Miranda's presumptuous autonomy on the basis of which she wants to domesticate the incommensurable course of history (especially in terms of destiny) according to her own, in a double sense, limited point of view that condemns her to failure. Considering this aspect, the narrative becomes a parable that does not dogmatically impose any formulated world- or human view, but rather invites, in an allusive manner, to participate in the experience and exploration of an existential and problematic horizon that is highly diversified in perspectives and intertextual connections.

[Translated by Nicole Franke]

NOTES

1. Cf. Jost Hermand, *Synthetisches Interpretieren. Zur Methodik der Literaturwissenschaft* (München: Nymphenburger Verlagshandlung, 1968), 143ff.
2. Ibid., 41ff.
3. Cf. Umberto Eco, *Das offene Kunstwerk*, trans. Günter Memmert (Frankfurt am Main: Suhrkamp, 1977), 81.
4. Ibid.
5. Cf. Marcel Reich-Ranicki's rhetorical question: "Should these stories . . . indeed be nothing more than reading material for those ladies who skim through magazines at the hairdresser or in the waiting room of their dentist? That means consciously and cynically aimed at trivial literature?" (Marcel Reich-Ranicki, "Ingeborg Bachmann—Die Dichterin wechselt das Repertoire," in Reich-Ranicki, *Entgegnung. Zur deutschen Literatur der siebziger Jahre* [München: dtv2, 1985], 173f).
6. Cf. Robert Pichl, "Ingeborg Bachmanns 'Offene Kunstwerke.' Überlegungen zu ihrer poetischen Verfahrensweise," *Kritische Wege der Landnahme. Ingeborg Bachmann im Blickfeld der neunziger Jahre*, ed. Robert Pichl and Alexander Stillmark, Londoner Symposium 1993 (Wien: Hora, 1994), 97f.
7. Ingeborg Bachmann, *Todesarten-Projekt. Kritische Ausgabe*, 4 vols. in 5 vols., ed. Monika Albrecht and Dirk Göttsche (München: Piper, 1995), 4:209.
8. Cf. Robert Pichl, "Rhetorisches bei Ingeborg Bachmann. Zu den 'redenden Namen' im *Simultan*-Zyklus," *Akten des VI. Internationalen Germanisten-Kongresses Basel 1980*, Part 2, ed. Heinz Rupp und Hans-Gert Roloff (Bern: P. Lang 1980), 298-303.
9. Ingeborg Dusar's interpretation of these localities in the sense of Biblical associations, seems to be not convincing here (the established connection between the "Roman emperor" and King Herod the Great is also factually incorrect). Cf. Ingeborg Dusar, *Choreographien der Differenz. Ingeborg Bachmanns Prosaband "Simultan"* (Köln: Böhlau, 1994), 59, footnote 65.
10. Cf. Felix Czeike, *Das große Groner Wien Lexikon* (Wien: F. Molden, 1974), 406.

11. Ingeborg Bachmann, "Eyes to Wonder," *Three Paths to the Lake*, trans. Mary Fran Gilbert (New York: Holmes & Meier, 1989), 81, 83. Hereafter cited as *TPL*.

12. Cf. Marcel Reich-Ranicki (quoted in endnote 6).

13. The television production "freely adapted from Ingeborg Bachmann's narrative of the same name" was produced in a co-production of ORF and ZDF in 1992. (Screenplay: Christian Jordan; Direction: Margareta Heinrich; Characters/Actors: Miranda: Cornelia Köndgen; Josef: Peter Sattmann; Stasi: Andrea Eckert). It may be considered proof for the lacking resonance to this adaptation that this film was not rebroadcast despite the well-known inclination of the ORF to repeat its productions many times.

14. Cf. Pichl, "Ingeborg Bachmanns 'Offene Kunstwerke'," 104. For other discursive relations, cf. Ingeborg Dusar, *Choreographien der Differenz*, especially 92ff.

15. Cf. Eco, *Das offene Kunstwerk*, 37.

16. Ingeborg Bachmann, *Die kritische Aufnahme der Existentialphilosophie Martin Heideggers (Dissertation Vienna 1949). Based on a comparison of the text with the literary estate*. Edited by Robert Pichl. With an afterword by Friedrich Wallner (München: Piper, 1985), 127-131.

17. Cf. Tanja Schmidt, "Beraubung des Eigenen. Zur Darstellung geschichtlicher Erfahrung im Erzählzyklus 'Simultan' von Ingeborg Bachmann," *Kein objektives Urteil—nur ein lebendiges. Texte zum Werk von Ingeborg Bachmann*, ed. Christine Koschel and Inge von Weidenbaum: (München: Piper, 1989), 479-502.

18. Johann Wolfgang Goethe, *Faust: Part One and Two*, trans. Charles E. Passage (New York: The Bobbs-Merrill Company, 1965), 383-384, translation modified (Passage's translation of "Ihr glücklichen Augen" as "You fortunate eyes" was changed to "You eyes to wonder"). "Faust," *Sämtliche Werke*, vol. 7.1, ed. Albrecht Schöne (Frankfurt am Main: Deutscher Klassiker Verlag, 1994), 436.

19. Albrecht Schöne, commentary to "Faust," *Sämtliche Werke*, by Johann Wolfgang von Goethe, vol 7.2, 728f.

20. Dusar, *Choreographien der Differenz*, 89.

21. Georg Groddeck, *Das Buch vom Es. Psychoanalytische Briefe an eine Freundin. Eingeleitet von Laurence Durrell* (Wiesbaden: Limes, 1961). A copy of this edition is included in Ingeborg Bachmann's private library.

22. Ingeborg Bachmann, *Werke*, 4 vols., ed. Christine Koschel, Inge von Weidenbaum and Clemens Münster (München: Piper, 1978), 346-53. Here: 351f.

6 / "A man, a woman . . .":
Narrative Perspective and Gender Discourse in Ingeborg Bachmann's *Malina*

Monika Albrecht

In the late fall of 1971, Suhrkamp Publishing House once more organized a tour across the Federal Republic for its successful author, the focus of which were readings from the novel *Malina*, published in March of the same year. The interviews given on the occasion of this second reading tour[1] show a distinctly disillusioned Ingeborg Bachmann[2] who answers questions such as: "Is *Malina* an autobiographical novel?" by now as categorically as: "I would not say so, no"[3] and explains the "confusing variety of reality levels and references" in her novel only by saying that "it . . . cannot be presented in any other way."[4] Her initial willingness to comment on the composition of the novel had obviously yielded to an attitude of refusal at this point. From today's point of view, the lack of comprehension on the part of then contemporary commentators is rather understandable, as Bachmann's detailed attempts to explain her novel in her interviews, right after its publication, were often just as hermetical and in need of interpretation as *Malina* itself. Critical approaches to her first and only novel *Malina* have therefore oscillated between interpretations of the complex texture of the novel, on the one hand, and of the author's own explanations on the other. This is particularly true for the question of narrative perspective, a question to which Bachmann pointedly responded in an interview in late fall 1971 by saying that "one [cannot] want the perspective, one has it."[5] Even in an earlier interview, she had already described the perspective as necessary and noted that she could "only narrate from a male point of view" (*GuI*, 99).

Since the beginning of a more intense critical discussion of Bachmann's work in the 1980's, the narrative perspective of *Malina* has become the focus of interest. The basis for the controversial problematic of narrative perspective is located in the novel itself, in the "imaginary autobiography" of an author (*GuI*, 73) who reflects under gender-specific portents, the conditions and possibilities of her writing; the text is written in the first person, and this first person seems to be female; there is, however, also a male *"Doppelgänger"* (*GuI*, 71, and passim). Until now, the question of narrative perspective has usually been approached from two different points of view. On the one hand, the author's gender alone has been taken as a sure indicator for the novel's female perspective, for example, in arguments that suggest that Bachmann tries "decidedly... to side with women while describing a female world view."[6] However, it seems appropriate[7] to question the validity of arguments that use the author's gender for an analysis of narrative perspective, especially in the case of *Malina*, at the center of which is the constellation of a male-female *Doppelgänger*. On the other hand, critics have—particularly through an engagement with poststructuralism[8]—sought for starting points for an *"écriture féminine,"*[9] and, in this sense, for a "new language" in Bachmann's novel.

Based on the assumption of the "impossible location of a female subject in the dialectic of enlightenment," what is at stake in a general sense is the "paradox of a female author's position"[10] and therefore the question of whether and how Bachmann has found a solution for this dilemma. The spectrum of positions ranges from the thesis that Bachmann did not even have the intention "to realize a redemption of a superceded female experience on the level of language and discourse,"[11] to its opposite, namely the attempt to read in the "affective... emotional and expressive movements" of the self "the other language of the feminine," which withdraws "from the prisons... of male genres."[12] What frequently determines the interpretation of Bachmann's novel, even when it is not assumed that it represents a "model of feminine writing,"[13] is the claim or even the wish that such a mode of narration could lead out of dualistic thinking and thus "out of gender discourse."[14] This view is affirmed in Bachmann research, where textual evidence is presented that indicates that the novel has been written "from the perspective of a female I" who occupies the position of the Other of reason."[15] The novel could then, so to speak, be read as a "representation of the dialectic of enlightenment from a feminine perspective,"[16] an interpretation that might be suggested in the preface of the novel:

Then it seems to me that his [Malina's] calm comes from my ego being too familiar, too unimportant for him, as if he had rejected me as waste, a superfluous something-made-human, as if I were merely the dispensable product of his rib, but at the same time an unavoidable dark tale accompanying and hoping to supplement his own bright story, a tale which he, however, detaches and delimits.[17]

Bachmann, however, named the novel after Malina, after the male double of the female "I," and made him the "protagonist." Moreover, in an interview with Toni Kienlechner, she claimed that the perspective of the female "I" was anything but the dominating one. The frequently quoted statement that she had "always looked for this protagonist" and at the same time knew that "it will be male," does not refer to Malina's future role as narrator of the *Todesarten* novel-cycle. Bachmann had been asked how she came across the idea of the *Doppelgänger*-constellation; she subsequently outlined her search for the figure of Malina and afterwards discussed its role in the novel:

For me this is one of the oldest, although almost buried, memories; that I always knew I had to write this book—already very early while still writing poetry. That I continuously looked for the protagonist. That I knew: it will be male. That I can only narrate from a male position. But I often wondered: why so? I did not understand, not even in my narratives, why I had to use the male "I" so often. It was for me now like the discovery of my own person, not to deny this female "I" and yet to put emphasis on the male "I." (*GuI*, 99f.)

Applied to the collection of short stories, *The Thirtieth Year*, the fundamental statement that she could only narrate from a male position would suggest that all narratives of this collection are presented from a male perspective, even those two in which female figures are at the center.

I would like to defer the problem of narrative perspective in *Malina* at present and instead pursue the search for the adequate narrative position, of which Bachmann has spoken in this and other interviews. Considering that she, in retrospect, professed not to have known why she earlier "had to use the male 'I' so often," and claimed to have only understood why while working on *Malina*, it is probably accurate to assume that the very gesture of self-stylization that was characteristic for the interviews after the publication of *Malina* is here highlighted as well.[18] Because, essentially, Bachmann had answered the question why she could "only narrate from a male position" in "A Step Towards Gomorrha" at the latest, even if it was not before the auto-reflexive novel *Malina* that Bachmann combined the problematics of identity and narration under gender-specific portents.[19] She obviously had been already aware of the fact that her narrative perspective was determined by the male-dominated order, which is the reason that she later persistently called it a male position. On the level of "plot," in "A Step Towards Gomorrha," the protagonist Charlotte is pushed into the masculine role by the homosexual Mara. The "process"[20] described in this narrative circles, however, around the question of why the search of the female protagonist for an independent identity has to fail in Bachmann's view, and, in this respect, foreshadows the "intellectual process" (*GuI*, 88) which *Malina* represents. In western society of the twentieth century, faced with the choice between the "standardization[s] of polar complementarity and the *equality* of men and women," Charlotte has "submitted," corresponding to her status as an intellectual, "to the offers of equality," that is, to "act and think, as it corresponds to a patriarchal logic, and to misunderstand it as human logic."[21] The narrative takes its departure from this basic situation. It is not the encounter with Mara as such that leads Charlotte to assume the "male" position; it is rather the constellation of the figures Charlotte/Mara that reveals the situation of the intellectual woman in modern western society, who has internalized the pattern of thought dominant in the latter. Charlotte believes that she lives in an "order that is not hers,"[22] but in the end understands how much she has been mistaken.

The protagonist's search for identity is presented as a nocturnal process of realization at the beginning of which—marking also the beginning of the narrative—Mara is introduced as Charlotte's figure of projection[23] and as her—at least up to that point—unnoticed female alter ego: "just for once the world was in red. The girl's eyes opened up, two moist, dark, drunken objects that met the woman's eyes."[24] Seduced by the Undine-like creature Mara to "thoughts of fiasco,"[25] Charlotte fantasizes about withdrawing from the male-dominated order. However, the way this female alter ego is put into concrete terms provides for a counter-movement that exposes Charlotte's adherence to precisely this pattern of thought. For in the projection "Mara," Charlotte reproduces the ruling gender dichotomy in which male and female are associated with the counter-pairs reason/feeling, active/passive, spirit/nature, strong/weak etc.[26] In this way, Charlotte, from her "male" perspective, assigns her female alter ego everything that is traditionally considered feminine. Moreover, she adopts the hierarchy of values that is tied to the social stereotypes of male/female; here we can see a starting point for an answer to the question as to why, according to Bachmann, her search for identity has to fail.

In this context, I would like to quote Max Frisch, not because of his role in Bachmann's life but because he articulated, with unusual clarity, the stereotypical view of the other side and in such a way that it also describes the position of Charlotte. In a section "about women" in his novel *Gantenbein*, Frisch writes:

> What one despises in women: their passivity, the coquetry they still keep up where quite other things are at stake, the permanence of their woman-man position, all other interests reveal themselves as pretext or camouflage or interlude, their insatiable need for love . . . their ability to keep silent, they wish and are able to remain a mystery to themselves,...their awful ability to be consoled at any moment . . . the ease with which they are offended, their need for protection and security and with it the wraithlike inconstancy on their part, in a word: their magic . . .[27]

In the narrative "A Step Towards Gomorrha," Mara is described from the same perspective. Charlotte's projection-figure, the character onto which she transfers the very aspects of her personality that she perceives as feminine, is the product of a structure of consciousness that is marked by the dominant hierarchy of values. Thus it happens that the "woman with the name Mara, whom she detects inside of herself,"[28] turns into a being "full of ignorance"[29] who is "so much smaller, more fragile, more insignificant" than men,[30] not to be taken seriously with her "useless little words"[31] and despicable with her subservient tactics and her "stupid chatter."[32] However, Charlotte reproduces only one side of this perspective in the figure of Mara; the traditional ambivalence of exclusion and desire, represented in Max Frisch's work as the simultaneity of contempt and fascination, is in Charlotte's case reduced to mere contempt and leads to the projection of a subordinated alter-ego figure with connotations of inferiority. This projection, however, makes it all the clearer to what extent her perspective is marked by her identification with the male dominated order, and thus highlights what was not least important for Bachmann in the narrative, namely, to show the forms of opposition that a woman encounters in her search for her own identity; more precisely, not so much the external forms of opposition in patriarchal society, which the female protagonist (with an ease unusual for the 1950s) almost casually dismantles during her nocturnal process of realization, but rather the internal ones. For Charlotte, the integration into the social order means that she, like any other human being, has internalized the ways and manners in which this order structures the world and subjects individual areas to its values. Grounding her identity in these patterns of thought also means, however, devaluing herself to the degree to which the internalized criteria define those areas as detestable. Characteristically, Charlotte speaks of the fact that she would be *"at home . . . in herself"* if she "loved Mara," if she could see her alter ego in a different light and that then "everything would change."[33] According to Bachmann, this possibility seems, however, imaginable at best, but is doomed to fail in reality. In the third chapter of the novel *Malina*, when the title character and the "I" look at *"this* I" together from the outside, the "I" still objects: "But I'm just now beginning to love it" (*Malina*, 208); yet, this claim, made almost at the end of the novel, also remains a vague starting point. Charlotte resists being gauged "by an alien measure,"[34] and yet, in her confrontation with her alter ego, she herself reproduces this alleged "alien measure." The process of realization presented in this narrative last but not least consists of the disclosure of women's participation in the existing order, in particular of the "devaluation of woman . . . by woman herself."[35]

In this context, one should be reminded of the interview quoted at the beginning in which Bachmann talked about her success in "not *denying* this female I" in *Malina* (*GuI*, 99ff.; emphasis added). Regardless of whether the word was chosen unconsciously or if it was meant to be self-ironic, "denying" means not to confess to something, not to stand up for something, and even when one speaks of not-denying, the choice of words testifies to a basic recognition of dominant norms and its hierarchy of values. For Bachmann, then, there seems to be no way out of the dichotomous patterns of thought, despite her realization and aesthetic representation of the problematic.

A telling example is "Undine Goes," the final story in the volume *The Thirtieth Year*, where she clearly expresses her dualistic understanding. Undine, as a literary figure, is a male fantasy about the female *par excellence* and as such also part of the collective stockpile of images;[36] precisely because Bachmann's Undine simulates a "representation of the site of the Other,"[37] her speech, at the same time, preserves the separation of the world into a male and a female realm. In her monologue, Undine reinforces the traditional dichotomous understanding,[38] for example, by claiming for herself "water and veils and whatever cannot be fully determined."[39] However, in doing so, she commits herself to the very "undecidability," that is, precisely to that which had been assigned to her from a male perspective in fairy tales and their literary adaptations, particularly in the Romantic Movement.[40] Correspondingly, in a draft for the third chapter of *Malina*, Bachmann writes: "I am the flow and Malina is the substance,"[41] and even in the printed version, she still speaks of the "stability of [Malina's] existence and the instability of my own" (*Malina*, 8). At the end of "A Step Towards Gomorrha," the structures of consciousness of modern man and therefore the patterns of thought of today's society are traced back to ancient mythical images that are "timeless" and, as Bachmann says in her *Frankfurt Lectures*, "cannot be undone."[42] Just as Horkheimer and Adorno equate the beginning of enlightenment with that of world history,[43] Bachmann seems to locate the origins of today's gender problematic in prehistoric times when myth developed. It seems, therefore, doubtful that Bachmann, as it has been claimed, does bring up for discussion the "incompatibility of the male and female principle . . . as an 'eternal' conflict that equally concerns man and woman."[44] After all, in *Malina* she even goes one step further; in the last dialogue with Malina, just before the disappearance of the

"I" in the wall, it is noted, in reference to Malina and the "I": "Something must have gone astray with the primates and later with the hominoids. A man, a woman . . . strange words, a strange mania!" (*Malina*, 220).

It seems therefore appropriate to exercise caution when, as a result of the discovery of a dimension in Bachmann's work that offers a critical perspective on culture, it is assumed that Bachmann had been searching for a narrative mode suitable to lead us out of the dualistic thinking of gender hierarchy. The previously discussed connections between the collection of short stories, *The Thirtieth Year*, and the novel *Malina* suggest rather that Bachmann's position did not essentially change in the ten years in between. In "A Step Towards Gomorrha," she vividly shows how the projection of a female alter ego falls into the trap of interiorized patterns of thought and hierarchies of values, with the result that the projected figure becomes a faithful image of precisely the same dominant pattern of thought. If one follows the trace suggested by the narrative, a hint can be found at the end of *Malina* that the figurative constellation "Charlotte/Mara" can principally be transferred to the "Malina/I" constellation. In the second to last dialogue with Malina, the "I" says that it has "become a caricature," which remarkably is immediately followed by the introduction of a "we" position that combines Malina and the "I": "Are we satisfied now?" (*Malina*, 220). If one follows this trace further, what needs to be examined above all is the question whether it is indeed the case—as it is generally assumed[45]—that Malina's view increases in dimension only in the third chapter. In other words, the question is essentially from which overall perspective the narrative is told when the female voice seems to speak. When, for example, early in the novel, the "I" emphasizes the difference between herself and Malina and says that Malina had, in contrast to the female "I," never "wasted his time on trivialities" (*Malina*, 8), then useful and banal actions are thereby already assigned to the male and female realm respectively. The novel type-casts the female "I" to a large extent as that which is generally considered feminine and, therefore, establishes the polarity male/female in the first place; above all, the novel judges the actions of the female "I" from the perspective of reason, as was already the case with the figure of Charlotte, and determines them as "banalities," or a waste of time.

It is precisely this kind of value judgment, namely the recognition of Malina's superiority and the devaluation of the female "I,"[46] that permeates the entire novel; from the allusion to the book of "Genesis"[47] at the beginning of the novel—symptomatically, the "I" there calls itself "waste" and a "superfluous something-madehuman," an image that does not appear in the book of Genesis—to the declaration in the third chapter that "I am the first perfect extravagance, ecstatic and incapable of putting the world to any reasonable use" (*Malina*, 165).[48] Sigrid Weigel described it as the basic problem "for the self-understanding of woman" that "she looks at herself by seeing *that* and *how* she is looked at, meaning that her eyes see through the glasses of man."[49] In light of the narrative perspective in *Malina*, this statement might need to be modified to the extent that the male "I," the Malina-I, is part of the *Doppelgänger*-figure and therefore anything but a pair of glasses that could be taken off.

Extensive studies have been dedicated to the thesis that Bachmann's narrative style can lead out of the dualistic thinking of gender hierarchy,[50] that is to say, that the author developed a specific feminine narrative perspective. Challenging this view in detail would, however, exceed the scope of my essay. Therefore, I have to confine myself to the refutation of one of the examples commonly used to argue for the emergence of a female voice in Bachmann's novel.

The grotesque answers of the "I" in the Mühlbauer-interview have been included among those parts of the novel in which the voice of the female "I," in distinction from Malina's rationality, is supposed to clearly express itself.[51] Taking into account a parallel scene[52] that existed just before the printing of the novel, could have prevented the erroneous assumption that Bachmann wanted to express a female narrative perspective in and through the answers of the "I" in the Mühlbauer-interview. Methodologically speaking, it only seems as if I am walking on uncertain ground because what I intend to do with my comparison can, if not quite as clearly, in general also be shown in the final version of the text.[53] The scene, erased shortly before the completion of the novel, was supposed to show the same ironical and grotesque gesture of presentation that completely contradicts usual performances, but this time as a gesture of the other "I," the Malina-I. The "I" is visited by two Englishmen and an Irishman who would like to "receive information about Vienna" and want to know above all "how much flower power we have and where to find our flower children." Malina joins them and answers the guests instead of the female "I" in words that could well be stated literally in the Mühlbauer interview; he says "flowers we would have, children and youngsters of course as well"; however, "especially in our areas you can hardly expect the power of flowers" (*KA*, 3.2, 712). While the Mühlbauer-interview can be found in the first chapter, the just-quoted "flower power" scene was supposed to be included in the beginning of the third chapter. The mirror-function of this second scene would have been even more pronounced insofar as the "I" immediately afterwards opens up a newspaper and checks whether the interview with Mr. Mühlbauer has already been published; thus, originally, a clear reference from Malina's "flower power"-answer back to the first chapter and the corresponding answers of the "I" was intended.[54] Even in the finished text, the Malina-I occasionally expresses itself in this grotesque-ironic way that caricatures usual performances, for example when saying that "All these people renting opinions, and at such high rates, [will] wind up paying dearly" (*Malina*, 82). Incidentally, the published version of the novel includes the statement that "it's *someone else* inside me, . . . someone who never allowed answers to be forced out of *him* to questions which had been forced upon *him*" (*Malina*, 89; emphasis added). With the Mühlbauer interview, Bachmann did not intend, then, as it has been claimed, to create "a new way of writing from the point of the absent-minded and the buried-alive I-narrator;"[55] rather, what is at stake in these interview-answers[56] is to present the *continuous presence* of the Malina-perspective *as such* even at points where Malina is not even present at the level of plot.

The most recent response to the question concerning the idea behind the male/female *Doppelgänger* constellation was the suggestion that *Malina* shows "the impossibilities to think of femininity as a positive, determinable category"[57]—an answer which comes very close to my argumentation so far; however, I would like to differentiate still further. In Bachmann's interviews for *Malina*, a general categorization of the figures into emotionality on the one hand and intellect on the other, served as the starting point for the definition of the perspective of the female "I" and that of Malina. In the meantime, this categorization has been considerably differentiated in Bachmann research. Malina is still considered the representative of the principle of rationality, as the stand-in for "reason and self-preservation."[58] In addition, however, the figure of Malina can be read as presenting various, partly contradictory allusions to philosophical and literary positions of European modernism[59] in which the principle of rationality is already rendered problematic. Also, Malina is someone—and this descent to the banality of everyday life follows a purpose—who feeds the cats when the "I" forgets all about it (*Malina*, 75) and makes suggestive remarks about former lovers of the "I" (*Malina*, 175). These are behavioral patterns which probably do not follow philosophical or literary positions, but also do not necessarily fit into patterns of thought of gender difference. The contradictions inherent in the Malina-figure can most likely only be resolved through a very simple model: one could view the male figure Malina, the Malina-I, as a representation of all that has been accumulated under the portent "male" in the course of the narrator's life. The "I" herself suggests this interpretation in a dream, when she lies down among the books scattered on the floor and says, "Good night, *gentlemen*" (*Malina*, 120; emphasis added). On the other hand, the female "I," whose common features are generally identified as "emotionalism and affectivity,"[60] would be a representation of all that, in the course of life, has been accumulated under the category of the "feminine." An "I" that defines itself as "male" and one that defines itself as "female" distinguish themselves from each other and—above all—mutually evaluate each other. Indeed, there are only a few aspects which are equally ascribed to both versions of the "I," for example the need for discretion (*Malina*, 177), which is therefore to Bachmann obviously neither a male nor a female characteristic but rather a human one; and here lies for me the problematic of the male/female *Doppelgänger*-constellation.

One cannot deny the logical consistency of a depiction of the dichotomous relations between the sexes and the corresponding hierarchy of values as an inner state of the narrator;[61] however, the socially-established ideas of what generally is to be labeled as "male" and "female" is once more reinforced—corresponding to social stereotypes, reason and self-preservation continue to have a male connotation, emotion and affect a female one, with the result that the hierarchy of values remains intact.[62]

In "A Step Towards Gomorrha," Bachmann had shown how the protagonist becomes a slave to the very patterns of thought from which she tries to escape. In *Malina* this problematic is radicalized insofar as the gender dichotomy is shifted to the interior setting of the "theater of my thoughts" (*Malina*, 188). The novel thus highlights the effects of hierarchic gender relations in modern Western society, but it does not question the dualism itself and thus merely reproduces what it renders problematic. Even if Bachmann occasionally introduces playful elements, for example, when the ascriptions "male and female, reason and feeling" are put into the mouth of an astrologer (*Malina*, 163), irony does not lead beyond that to which it is applied.

The question therefore arises as to why Bachmann persistently characterizes features and forms of actions as "male" and "female." The novel does not offer any answer to this question; the split of the narrator is presented as given and insurmountable.[63] In this context, however, it seems important not to forget when the novel *Malina* was written and to which generation the author belonged, for even if the problematic described in her novel has not lost its relevance, it nevertheless is marked clearly by historical specificity. Bachmann was ahead of her time insofar as she described in her novel women's participation in the patriarchal order and in their own degradation,[64] decades before the rise of the complicity-debate.[65] This might explain also why she emphasized in interviews that she does not "believe in the whole idea of emancipation" (*GuI*, 109), for she obviously recognized that the mechanisms underlying the problematic of gender go a lot deeper than public debates at the beginning of the 70s revealed it to be. Bachmann's rejection of the emerging emancipation movement, however, can not solely be explained with her greater vision, nor with the fact that she generally tended to resist repeating "phrases" of her time.[66] Bachmann's defensive attitude also reveals something about the blind spot in her analysis of gender conflicts, especially when the latter is articulated as a polemic against the currents of time, as for example in her poetological sketches for the volume *Simultan*.

Bachmann's characterization of Viennese women and earlier generations of women in Austria in these texts is at first sight quite irritating. She claims, for example, in regard to her "great-aunts and grandmothers" and leaving their imprisonment in rigid role expectations completely aside, that they "would have laughed a good deal about the problems that young girls create for themselves today. They were so entirely free, ...they [were] not sexually educated but knew already everything" (*KA*, 4:13). And what appears to be said about Viennese women in all seriousness is that "liberation" is for them "no category, as they have been free for a long time." Viennese women are, for Bachmann, "women . . . who . . . sometimes even know how to think yet do not show it;" furthermore, one learns that women in Vienna do "not" owe their freedom to "a particular fighting spirit," as they would be ashamed to have one," but to their men. The quotations speak for themselves.[67] At the latest, when Bachmann juxtaposes the "[loud] emancipation" of Italian women, "which drives every sensitive human being crazy," (*KA*, 4:14) and the "magic" and the "charm of Viennese women" (*KA*, 4:16), it becomes clear what it was that she saw threatened by the abandonment of traditional roles. Here, a conflict completely different from the one in *Malina* is expressed, a seemingly banal one, which, however, seems to be also somewhat responsible for Bachmann's clinging to the traditional dualism of "male" and "female" in her novel. This conflict is, by the way, the one which Zelda Fitzgerald described very precisely forty years earlier in her novel *Save Me the Waltz* (1932): "it's very difficult ... to be two simple people at once, one who wants to have a law to itself and the other who wants to keep all the nice things and be beloved and safe and protected."[68]

[Translated by Nicole Franke]

NOTES

1. The interviews Bachmann gave during the second reading tour have not been included in the collection of interviews, *Wir müssen wahre Sätze finden: Gespräche und Interviews,* ed. Christine Koschel and Inge von Weidenbaum [München: Piper 1983] [Hereafter cited as *GuI*]). In addition, the collection of interviews lists the date of the first interview about *Malina* as 23 March 1971, after the radio interview of March 22. This former date is, however, the publication date of the interview in the *Kölner Stadtanzeiger* (cf. *GuI*, 152); the interview was first printed in the "Abendzeitung" (München) of March 16, 1971; Cf. Otto Bareiss and Frauke Ohloff, *Ingeborg Bachmann—Eine Bibliographie* (München, Zürich: Piper, 1978), 62.

2. For example, cf.: "Some critics have pointed out the esoteric character of the novel: the book reflects private details, the political and social reality would only appear as a caricatured, dull and puzzling background phenomenon. She sighs, thinks for a long time and holds her hands in front of her eyes: 'usually something like this is written by German critics who like to call something esoteric. . . .'" *Kölner Stadtanzeiger,* 26 November 1971.—The irritation caused by the complexity of the text, directed critics' attention to more familiar spheres at first. Even though Hans Mayer had warned in his review in the Zürich newspaper *Die Weltwoche* ("Malina oder Der große Gott von Wien," 30 April 1971) that one should not be deceived by autographical details, hardly anyone could resist the temptation of reading the novel *Malina* as an autobiography. An evaluation of the interviews about the novel *Malina* in chronological order shows Ingeborg Bachmann's increasing indignation, concerning a reading that was more interested in her person than in her work, in the successive withdrawal of alleged concessions. In her first interview in March 1971, she "explicitly" called the novel "an autobiography" even if not in a "traditional sense" (*GuI*, 73). A few days later, she already used a more careful formulation: "If one could call this an autobiography at all, then it is for sure not one in the traditional sense" (*GuI,* 71). And in May, asked once more, if one could see "in the first person narrator . . . the author herself" (*GuI,* 107), she already objected more clearly: "Please forgive me when I openly admit that I always end up in a dead-end street with

these kinds of questions. The book was not supposed to be and can probably not be understood as an autobiography. There is a double, no curriculum vitae, no story" (*GuI*, 108). Finally, in the late fall, she did not address this question, as quoted above, any longer.

3. *Frankfurter Neue Presse*, 1 December 1971. In this context, Bachmann referred her interview-partner to the discussion of the novel by Hans Mayer: "At this point, I must mention a critic whose review I liked very much ... He said more or less: 'If somebody lays out his cards so openly on the table, he most likely will not play with them.'"

4. *Kölner Stadtanzeiger*, 26 November 1971.

5. *Kölner Stadtanzeiger*, 26 November 1971. In this context, however, narrative perspective in a general sense was discussed. The complete statement reads as follows: "I would imagine the book of an American to be different—or of a German author. I am from Austria, a country which resigned from history. The perspective is inevitably a different one. One cannot want it; one has it."

6. Christa Gürtler, "*Der Fall Franza*: Eine Reise durch eine Krankheit und ein Buch über ein Verbrechen." In *Der dunkle Schatten, dem ich schon seit Anfang folge. Ingeborg Bachmann—Vorschläge zu einer neuen Lektüre des Werks*, ed. Hans Höller (Wien: Löcker 1982), 82. Hans Höller (*Ingeborg Bachmann—Das Werk* [Frankfurt am Main: Athenäum, 1987]) starts from the point that Bachmann has given the female self "a voice," that she brought it literally to life (236). Susanne Baackmann (*Erklär mir die Liebe. Weibliche Schreibweisen von Liebe in der Gegenwartsliteratur* (Hamburg: Argument [AS 237], 1995) talks in her interpretation also about the "female perspective" of the author Ingeborg Bachmann (15, and passim) and interprets Malina at the same time as a representative of "female participation in a male order of thought and significance" (83).

7. Also several male interpreters seem to have no difficulty with this kind of partiality and the emphatic rendering of Bachmann's "female world view"; cf. e.g. Hans Höller, *Ingeborg Bachmann—Das Werk*.

8. See Barbara Becker-Cantarino's "Feministische Germanistik in Deutschland: Rückblick und sechs Thesen," in which she retrospectively determines that "(quite different) positions of

French poststructuralism . . . were selectively applied" in the feminist studies of German language and literature (223); this also applies to Bachmann research. In *Women in German Yearbook 8* (1992), 219-33 Cf. Sara Lennox' outline in the same yearbook ("The Feminist Reception of Ingeborg Bachmann," 73-111).

9. The title of a study by Hélène Cixous (Berlin: Merve, 1980).

10. Sigrid Weigel, "Zur Polyphonie des Anderen. Traumatisierung und Begehren in Bachmanns imaginärer Autobiographie," *Ingeborg Bachmann—Die Schwarzkunst der Worte*, ed. John Pattillo-Hess and Wilhelm Oetrasch (Wien: Wiener Urania Schriftenreihe 3, 1993), 9.

11. Sigrid Schmid-Bortenschlager, "Spiegelszenen bei Bachmann: Ansätze einer psychoanalytischen Interpretation" *Modern Austrian Literature* 18, no. 3/4 (1985): 45.

12. Hans Höller (*Ingeborg Bachmann—Das Werk*, 251) following Hélène Cixous. Höller, however, concedes an equally important meaning to Malina's position (ibid.).

13. Gudrun Kohn-Waechter, *Das Verschwinden in der Wand. Destruktive Moderne und Widerspruch eines weiblichen Ich in Ingeborg Bachmanns "Malina"* (Stuttgart: Metzler, 1992), 12. In regard to the work *Simultan*, Ingeborg Dusar also starts from the fact that "Bachmann's stylistic experiments ... lead to another choreography of difference, which exceed the old binary categories, among them first of all the opposition male/female" (*Choreographien der Differenz. Ingeborg Bachmanns Prosaband Simultan* [Köln: Böhlau, 1994], 12).

14. Sigrid Weigel, "Zur Polyphonie des Anderen," 11.

15. Gudrun Kohn-Waechter, *Das Verschwinden in der Wand*, 12.

16. Sigrid Weigel, *Topographien der Geschlechter. Kulturgeschichtliche Studien zur Literatur* (Reinbek bei Hamburg: Rowohlt, 1990), 19. Cf. also the differentiation of her earlier interpretation in the essay published in 1993, "Zur Polyphonie des Anderen," 12.

17. Ingeborg Bachmann, *Malina. A Novel*, trans. Philip Boehm (New York: Holmes & Meier, 1990), 8/9. Hereafter cited as *Malina*.

18. One of the most important things at that time was to present the ten-year silence of the legendary author to the public as

a period of productive work on the novel cycle; cf. also Bachmann's repeated asseveration that she had "written almost 1000 pages before this book" and that "these 400 pages from the very recent years... would have only been the beginning (*GuI*, 96).

19. Cf. on the other hand Sigrid Weigel: "In Bachmann's work as a whole... this story is the site of departure toward a new female narrative perspective." ("'Ein Ende mit der Schrift. Ein anderer Anfang.' Zur Entwicklung von Ingeborg Bachmanns Schreibweise." *Text und Kritik-Sonderband Ingeborg Bachmann* [München: edition text und kritik, 1984], 74).

20. In an interview on the occasion of the volume *The Thirtieth Year*, Bachmann said that the "plot" in these narratives... plays an insignificant or infinitesimal role" and that "there [were] processes that take the place of the storyline" (*GuI*, 27).

21. Christina Thürmer-Rohr, "Aus der Täuschung in die Ent-Täuschung. Zur Mittäterschaft von Frauen" in Thürmer-Rohr, *Vagabundinnen. Feministische Essays* (Berlin: Orlanda 1992 [1987]), 41f.

22. Bachmann, Ingeborg. "A Step Towards Gomorrah," *The Thirtieth Year*, trans. Michael Bullock (New York: Holmes & Meier, 1987).

23. Cf. among others Ritta Jo Horsley, "Ingeborg Bachmann's "Ein Schritt nach Gomorrha": A Feminist Appreciation and Critique," *Amsterdamer Beiträge zur Neueren Germanistik 10 (1980)*, 280ff.; Kurt Bartsch, *Ingeborg Bachmann*, Sammlung Metzler, Realien zur Literatur Bd. 242 (Stuttgart: Metzler, 1988), 122; Karen Achberger, *Understanding Ingeborg Bachmann* (Columbia: University of South Carolina Press, 1995), 84.

24. *The Thirtieth Year*, 106. Translation modified. As later in *Malina*, the metaphors of looking up and down refer generally here to the wish to perceive and yet not to perceive the other (Bachmann, *The Thirtieth Year*): "With her head bent... to the table.... When she looked up again, Mara had stood up" (109ff.). "She turned away... Charlotte... finally compelled to give her gaze an unmistakable direction, followed her every movement" (110). "Charlotte closed her eyes... She... kept her eyes fixed unwaveringly on the table top in front of her (110/111).... so that she didn't have to look up and see Mara" (116). "She looked at Mara

and smiled" (119). Mara opened her eyes" (126). "Mara ... stared at her impudently" (128). In *Malina*, the same metaphors are used when Malina confronts his female alter ego in prominent parts of the novel. At the first close encounter "by the Stadtpark" it is said the self "wanting to force [Malina] to look up": . . . already at the streetcar stop . . . by the Stadtpark when something could have happened, and almost did. There he stood holding a newspaper; I...kept staring over my paper in his direction, without fliniching" (*Malina* 5). At the end of the novel, just before the vanishing of the self in the wall, the narrator says: "I stare at Malina resolutely, but he doesn't look up" (*Malina* 223).

25. Bachmann, *The Thirtieth Year*, 175.

26. Mara is assigned to the field of feeling/passivity/weakness etc.; however, there is also an obvious relation to the natural being Undine, when, while dancing, she moves "her body through space as though through water" (Bachmann, *The Thirtieth Year*, 110) or when she claims that Charlotte had called her—like the man named Hans called Undine (ibid,. 114; cf. the narrative "Undine Goes," ibid., 175).

27. Max Frisch, *Gantenbein. A Novel*, trans. Michael Bullock (New York: Methuen & Co., 1965), 198.

28. Karen Achberger, "Bachmann und die Bibel. Ein Schritt nach Gomorrha als weibliche Schöpfungsgeschichte." In Höller, *Der dunkle Schatten*, 97.

29. Bachmann, *The Thirtieth Year*, 117.

30. Ibid., 114.

31. Ibid., 117.

32. Ibid., 128.

33. Ibid., 123/124.

34. Ibid., 126.

35. Christina Thürmer-Rohr, "Frauen in Gewaltverhältnissen. Zur Generalisierung des Opferbegriffs," *Mittäterschaft und Entdeckungslust*, Studienschwerpunkt "Frauenforschung" am Institut für Sozialpädagogik der TU Berlin (ed.) (Berlin: Orlanda 1989), 31.

36. Cf. Susanne Baackmann's interpretation of the "Undine" narrative as a crossing of the literary topoi that underlie love relationships (*Erklär mir die Liebe*, 15-43, here 15). In her interpretation (following New Historicism), Baackmann assumes that "the

limitation of the position of this I [Udine], to be the 'other' in opposition to the 'one',... provides the figure with an extended perspective" (16); this reading, however, in my opinion, is supported only by one reference to the narrative with the (indeed enigmatic) sentence: "The wet frontier between me and me" (Bachmann, *The Thirtieth Year*, 172). On the other hand, she concedes: "Does Undine indeed formulate her own desire . . . or is her covetous 'calling' simply a female voice created by male desire . . . ? As Undine's speech crosses first of all the established discourse to which she owes her existence, a distinct fixation of these two poles is difficult and tentative inasmuch as Undine attempts to speak in her own voice" (Baackmann, 38).

37. Sigrid Weigel, "Zur Polyphonie des Anderen," 12.

38. Cf. also Ritta Jo Horsley, "Re-reading 'Undine geht': Bachmann und Feminist Theory," *Modern Austrian Literature* 18, no. 3/4 (1985), 234: "Perhaps because the pattern of polarity is so deeply set, 'Undine geht,' despite its multiple deconstructions of the traditional material, never explicitly challenges the dualism that pervades it."

39. Bachmann, *The Thirtieth Year*, 178. Translation modified.

40. Cf. Anna Maria Stuby, "Vom Kommen und Gehen Undines. Ein feministischer Blick auf die Rezeptionsgeschichte des Wasserfrauenmythos," *Feministische Studien*, Heft 1 (1992), 12ff.

41. Ingeborg Bachmann, *Todesarten-Projekt. Kritische Ausgabe*, 4 vols. in 5 vols., ed. Monika Albrecht and Dirk Göttsche, (München: Piper, 1995), 3.1:209. Hereafter cited as *KA*.

42. Ingeborg Bachmann, *Werke*. 4 vols., ed. Christine Koschel, Inge von Weidenbaum and Clemens Münster (München: Piper, 1978), 4:195.

43. Theodor W. Adorno and Max Horkheimer, *Dialectic of Enlightenment*, trans. Edmund Jephcott (Stanford: University Press, 2002), 36ff.

44. Sigrid Weigel, "Der schielende Blick. Thesen zur Geschichte weiblicher Schreibpraxis," *Die verborgene Frau. Sechs Beiträge zu einer feministischen Literaturwissenschaft*, ed. Inge Stephan und Sigrid Weigel (Berlin: Argument (AS 96), 1983), 123.

45. Cf. more recent works, for example Sigrid Weigel, "Zur Polyphonie des Anderen," 11, Ingeborg Dusar, *Choreographien der Differenz*, 57f. and Susanne Baackmann, *Erklär mir Liebe*, 57f. and 64.

46. Cf. also Sigrun D. Leonhard, "Doppelte Spaltung: Zur Problematik des Ich in Ingeborg Bachmanns *Malina*," *Ingeborg Bachmann. Neue Richtungen in der Forschung? Beiträge zur Robert-Musil-Forschung und zur neueren österreichischen Literatur*, Bd. 8, ed. Gudrun Brokoph-Mauch and Annette Daigger, 156f.

47. Cf.: "as if I were merely the dispensable product of his rib" (*Malina* 8). Bachmann hints here also at the famous opening scene in Marcel Proust's *Remembrance of Things Past*, vol. I: *Swann's Way*, trans. C. K. Scott Moncrieff and Terence Kilmartin (New York: Vintage Books, 1981), 4: "Sometimes, too, as Eve was created from a rib of Adam, a woman would be born during my sleep from some strain in the position of my thighs."

48. Here also exists a cross connection to the figure of Undine, which also defines itself as "undetermined for any use" (Bachmann, *Werke*, 2:258).

49. Sigrid Weigel, "Der schielende Blick," 85. This "metaphor of the glasses implicates" for Sigrid Weigel "the utopia of a set-free, glass-free view" (ibid.).

50. For example Inge Röhnelt, *Hysterie und Mimesis in 'Malina'* (Frankfurt am Main: Peter Lang, 1989); Gudrun Kohn-Waechter, *Das Verschwinden in der Wand*; Ingeborg Dusar, *Choreographien der Differenz*; Susanne Baackmann, *Erklär mir Liebe*.

51. Cf. for example Gudrun Kohn-Waechter (*Das Verschwinden in der Wand*, 187, annotation 23).

52. Bachmann had crossed out this scene during the final revision together with four other usually short passages from the novel (Ingeborg Bachmann, *KA*, 3.2:697-716). This included, among others, also the passage "Besichtigung einer alten Stadt," published in the magazine *TEXT + KRITIK* in 1971. Cf. the critical commentary *KA*, 3.2:872 and 892, as well as Dirk Göttsche, "Die Strukturgenese des *Malina*-Romans—Zur Entstehungsgeschichte von Ingeborg Bachmanns *Todesarten-'Ouvertüre'*," *Ingeborg Bachmann—Neue Beiträge zu ihrem Werk. Internationales Symposium Münster

1991, ed. Dirk Göttsche and Hubert Ohl (Würzburg: Königshausen & Neumann, 1993), 163f.

53. The cut passages were, with one exception, of a humorous kind, which suggests that the reason for the deletions is probably to be looked for in the tightening of the novel to the central motif of the *Todesarten*. On the other hand, it can hardly be assumed that Bachmann took out the parallel scene to the Mühlbauer-interview from the novel in order to fundamentally revalue the constellation of figures shortly before its completion. Therefore, in this case, it seems justifiable to bring the two passages into opposition because of heuristic intention.

54. One can agree on the one hand with Dirk Göttsche's final commentary in his essay "Die Strukturgenese des *Malina*-Romans" ("Although one may regret the deletions of humorous and satiric passages in light of the prevailing image of Bachmann, they nevertheless doubtlessly contribute to the condensation of the 'composition' and, therefore, are congruent with the change in the conception of the *Todesarten*" [165]). On the other hand, knowing what the previous version looked like, one should wonder whether Bachmann, with the cuts (obviously encouraged by the publisher and Martin Walser) immediately before the printing of the novel (*KA*, 3.2:872) did not tear one or several holes into the dense texture of the text; Bachmann might not have been aware of this, as the text was not edited again after the deletions. Besides the abovementioned example, one might think of the connection between the deleted episode about neo-fascist activities of Austrian youngsters (*KA*, 3.2:713-716) and the dream chapter. Karen Achberger (*Understanding Ingeborg Bachmann*, 100) has indicated, that—if Bachmann had not deleted "Murder or Suicide" (*KA*, 3.1:141; 142)—then the first and last word of the novel would have been "murder." Bachmann herself expressed a feeling of unease in view of the printed text, after the publication of the volume *The Thirtieth Year* in 1961: "contrary to poetry, one has the feeling with prose . . . even when seen in print, that it could be changed once more, be rewritten" (*GuI*, 29).

55. Gudrun Kohn-Waechter, *Das Verschwinden in der Wand*, 123.

56. Ingeborg Dusar, *Choreographien der Differenz*, 168.

57. Cf. e.g. Sigrun D. Leonhard's interpretation of the Mühlbauer interview as "a critique of the stereotypical way of thinking offered by Mr. Mühlbauer "("Doppelte Spaltung," 148).
58. Sigrid Weigel, "Zur Polyphonie des Anderen," 10.
59. Cf. Hans Höller, *Ingeborg Bachmann—Das Werk*, 258; Gudrun Kohn-Waechter, *Das Verschwinden in der Wand*, 19f.
60. Hans Höller, *Ingeborg Bachmann—Das Werk*, 256.
61. Kurt Bartsch (*Ingeborg Bachmann*, 144) considers Malina to be "a critical controlling authority, as an *auctor* . . . in possession of *auctoritas*." And this authority must consequently be male in a society in which men have the "*auctoritas*."
62. Furthermore, the almost entirely positive connotation of the male "I," the Malina-I, in the novel itself but also in interviews, may signal the fact that the feminine is reduced "to a simple complementary function." (Cf. Sigrid Schmid-Bortenschlager, "Spiegelszenen bei Bachmann: Ansätze einer psychoanalytischen Interpretation," *Modern Austrian Literature* 18, no. 3/4 [1985], 45). An early draft of the "Malina" novel from the summer of 1966 describes this function still quite openly, when it is said that "a shadow falls over [Malina's] shoulder," which has "this Martin Ranner," the literary figure, with whom he is occupied in the draft, "jump out of his head" and let him "walk up and down in front of his desk" (*KA*, 3.1:9).
63. Cf. also Sigrun D. Leonhard, "Doppelte Spaltung," 156f.
64. Cf. also Kathleen L. Komar: "'Es war Mord.' The Murder of Ingeborg Bachmann at the Hands of an Alter Ego," *Modern Austrian Literature* 27, no. 2 (1994), 100: "Bachmann presents an even more challenging depiction than the straightforward suppression of the female by patriarchal culture."
65. Cf. *Mittäterschaft und Entdeckungslust*, Studienschwerpunkt "Frauenforschung" am Institut für Sozialpädagogik der TU Berlin (ed.) (Berlin: Orlanda, 1989); Christina Thürmer-Rohr, *Vagabundinnen. Feministische Essays* (Berlin: Orlanda, 1992 [1987]).
66. Cf., for example, the speech on the occasion of the awarding of the Anton-Wildgans Prize (Bachmann, *Werke* 4:294-7, in particular 297) and *GuI*, 72, 91.

67. Cf. Leo A. Lensing: "Joseph Roth and the Voices of Bachmann's Trottas: Topography, Autobiography, and Literary History in 'Drei Wege zum See'," *Modern Austrian Literature* 18, no. 3/4 (1985), 56: "However tempting it may be to explain or dismiss this statement as a gesture of provocative irony, it clearly expresses Bachmann's reserve toward the militant women's movements forming in the early 1970s."

68. Zelda Fitzgerald, "Save Me the Waltz," *The Collected Writings of Zelda Fitzgerald* (Tuscaloosa: University of Alabama Press, 1997), 56.

7 / *Senza pedale:*
Metaphors of Female Silence in *Malina*

Karen R. Achberger

Ingeborg Bachmann's novel *Malina*[1] is a collage of texts on the theme of female absence. It traces the journey of a female protagonist to her painful realization that she does not exist as a woman in contemporary society, a fact announced unambiguously by her male *Doppelgänger* at the novel's close: "There is no woman here."[2] In this acoustically focused novel, where sounds and especially music ring throughout all three chapters, the narrator's absence is not so much a visible as it is an audible one. She is above all silent, speechless. When at the novel's close she slips into a crack in the wall, the penultimate sentence interprets for us the meaning of this event, not as a disappearance from view, but as a silencing, a permanent and long-standing inability to make herself heard: "It is a very old, a very strong wall, from which no one can fall, which no one can break open, from which nothing can ever be *heard* again (my italics, *Malina*, 225).[3] It is the wall of silence and speechlessness that surrounds her as she struggles in vain to be heard within the structures of patriarchal discourse. Furthermore, this silencing of her as a woman is the "murder" referred to in the novel's next (and final) sentence. The wall is the last of the novel's many metaphors for female alienation and absence in contemporary patriarchal society, a truth that continually seeps through the cracks of the narrative in such things as dreams and parapraxes, and most decisively in the novel's subtextual musical allusions.

Using music to show female silence is the audial counterpart to the visual absence that Bachmann had shown in earlier texts. In *Das Buch Franza (The Book of Franza)*, for instance, she was able to let female absence become visually decipherable by invoking the Egyptian wall drawings of Queen Hatschepsut, in which the latter exists today only as the lack of an image in all those places where her brother attempted to eradicate every trace of her: "that in the place where he obliterated her, she is still left standing. She can be seen because there is nothing in the place where she is supposed to be."[4] In *Malina* Bachmann found the audial analogy to this visual absence by denying her narrator a name and a voice adequate to express herself.

That final act of slipping into the wall is not the sudden silencing of the novel's protagonist and narrator, but rather the ultimate manifestation of a condition she has been confined to all along, her dead silence sounding repeatedly as the novel's main theme. Bachmann may be pointing to this lack of a linear progression into the wall when she begins her novel with two paragraphs on the time being "today," to which she also draws attention in an interview: "The entire book is today, in each moment present time, now. It has a unity of time and place—I don't know if there has ever been that in a book."[5] The narrator's inability to be heard is not a new development. The wall is a "very old" one, we are explicitly told. The fact that language makes no provision for her is a "very old" phenomenon, just as the "very old" Egyptian wall drawings document a condition existing for thousands of years. Through music, Bachmann is able to give a gender-specific slant to the painful awareness of linguistic shortcomings that Hugo von Hofmannsthal lets Lord Chandos describe in "A Letter" ("Ein Brief," 1902). Music serves Bachmann as the central metaphor to underscore the shortcomings of patriarchal language for women.

The central importance of music for the novel and for Bachmann's writing in general has been well documented.[6] A close examination of the novel's many musical intertexts shows some of the ways Bachmann has underscored the novel's main theme of female silence and absence through musical allusions, particularly in the final dialogue with her male *Doppelgänger* Malina, a section of the novel that Bachmann called attention to in her interviews at the time of its first appearance (cf. *GuI*, 75). It is music, paradoxically, that allows Bachmann to show female silence and speechlessness.[7]

One of the most striking metaphors for the narrator's speechlessness comes in the final dialogue, one in which "Malina gains the upper hand, tries to make it clear to the female I that she cannot go on" (*GuI*, 75). It is here, in the novel's final turning point, that the narrator realizes that she does not exist in this world as a woman and, unable to narrate as a woman, turns over the role of narrator to Malina: "Go ahead and take over all the stories which make up history. Take them all away from me" (*Malina*, 221). Bachmann has composed the dialogue, as she emphasized in her interviews, "like a musical score" ("wie eine Partitur") for "two voices in harmony or in opposition . . . governed by marks as in music: sotto voce, con sentimento, etc."[8]

Actually, it is only the *female's* lines that are governed by Italian tempo and expression marks. Why then would Bachmann show the narrator struggling to express herself using Italian marks that one would expect to find in a musical work, while no such marks govern Malina's speech? What role does she want music to play here in this lopsided "score"? Scholars have generally interpreted these marks as an expansion of the narrator's spoken text in order to show the entire spectrum of excitement in her delivery through the addition of a rhythmic and gestic dimension. Her expressiveness, which here embraces the gestic-physical, rhythmic and sonorous, is viewed as being thus contrapuntally juxtaposed to the linear, rational voice of Malina. The final dialogue has been interpreted as one last recapitulation of the earlier, more heterogeneous, androgynous, simultaneous way of narrating, which must now make way for the new narrative position of Malina.[9]

The Italian marks serve as more than a mere enhancement of the narrator's expression, however. In fact, their function is precisely the opposite: far from affording her *more* expressive possibilities than her male counterpart, they are a haunting reminder that she has at her disposal far fewer. In fact, it is these marks that are, if not directly killing her, then at least making her non-existence discernible. A closer examination of these marks reveals that many of them, like *senza pedale,* refer to the use of pedals in a work for the piano. The mark *una corda* (literally, "one string"), for instance, calls for the muting of the piano by depressing the soft pedal, which shifts the hammer so that it hits only one of the three strings available for each key on the piano. *Tutte le corde* (literally, "all the strings") calls for the release of the soft pedal, which then allows the hammer to hit all three strings. Similarly, *senza pedale* ("without pedal") instructs the pianist to play without the use of the damper pedal (the right-hand, or loud pedal).

Beyond signaling the use of pedals, some of the marks serve to quote unmistakably the late piano sonatas of Ludwig van Beethoven. The last two marks, *con sordino* (literally, "with mute") and *tutto il clavicembalo* ("all the harpsichord / keyboard") are relatively rare and are associated specifically with Beethoven, who used the term *con sordini,* for instance, in his final piano sonatas (Opus 109-111), instead of the customary circular, asterisk-like symbol, to call for the release of the damper pedal, and who wrote *tutto il cembalo* in his Opus 101 piano sonata to call for a fuller sound, presumably without the use of the soft pedal.

What then does it mean that the female narrator's speech is shaped by Italian marks governing the depression and release of piano pedals, while that of her male counterpart Malina is directed by no such marks? And what is the reference to Beethoven's late piano sonatas supposed to signify? Beyond the standard interpretation that these marks serve to contrast the narrator with Malina—to portray her way of being and speaking as somehow more musical, more lyrical,[10] suspended in another realm as it were, while Malina remains firmly rooted in prosaic discourse—, beyond this more positive sign of her otherness, suggesting that not words but music is her medium, and beyond the concomitant theses of contrapuntal interaction and recapitulation of narrative simultaneity, how are we to explain the pedal marks, and the reference to Beethoven's Opus 111?

What Bachmann seems to be suggesting here through the use of these Italian marks is not an utopian glimpse of another realm of being, but a blatant incongruence: a human voice is being directed by marks intended for another instrument, an instrument with pedals. One could conclude that a woman's potential for self-expression within the confines of patriarchal language is about as great as that of a human voice responding to pedal marks. Thus, by showing a woman's speech governed by marks intended for the piano, Bachmann is offering a striking metaphor for female alienation in patriarchal language structures. A female voice, lacking pedals, struggles in vain to express herself using marks designated for an instrument with pedals, and the incongruence is apparent whenever she tries to speak. She has no recourse but to avail herself of the "pedalocentric" tradition. As her own words suggest, she would have to be "somebody else," ("eine Andere"), to "become someone completely different" ("noch eine ganz Andere," *Werke*, 3:311 and *KA*, 3.1:662)—e.g., an instrument with pedals—in order to fit the tradition in which she finds herself. Actually, we should say: the tradition in which she does *not* find herself, since she is absent, speechless and nameless in this tradition, a condition that she finally comes to realize, when the novel ends and she disappears into the ever-widening crack in the wall. That she is left to deliver her lines *senza pedale* and *una corda* shows her position—or rather her *lack* of a position—in a musical language system that makes no provision for her own (pedalless) voice.

If Bachmann, as it seems, has used multiple references to piano pedals in order to subvert the symbolic order of musical language and allow female silence to become discernible, what then could be the significance of quoting Beethoven for the novel? Invoking Beethoven's piano sonatas in particular adds an additional layer of resonance to the text: these late sonatas seem directed toward a break with traditional tonality and as such would appear to offer glimpses of a new mode of musical expression, a new musical language, just as the quotes in musical notation from Arnold

Schönberg's Opus 21 *Pierrot lunaire* motif that frames the novel ("O ancient scent from far-off days." *Malina*, 4 and 212) offers a faint atonal whiff of another time and another musical language.[11]

Bachmann offers this new order glimpsed in Beethoven's Opus 111 and Schönberg's Opus 21 as a counterpoint to the novel's main theme of female silence, which in the final sentence is unequivocally labeled a murder: "It was murder" (*Malina*, 225). The reader, so accustomed to the subtle resounding of the murder theme throughout the novel, is taken aback by this blatant proclamation. The destruction has been so gradual as to be nearly imperceptible in a narrative where on the surface almost nothing appears to be happening as the narrator moves among the three men who, it now appears, have "murdered" her: her Hungarian lover (Chapter 1: "Happy with Ivan" ["Glücklich mit Ivan"]), her abusive father and the patriarchal society he represents (Chapter 2: "The Third Man" ["Der dritte Mann"]), and, most pernicious of all, her other self, Malina, whose name appears on her mailbox (Chapter 3: "Last Things" ["Von letzten Dingen"]).

While the murder at the narrative's surface remains subtle and metaphoric, the novel's subtext is saturated with references to the most brutal murders ever imagined or recorded in history or literature. Thus, the brutality of a setting like the large dining hall of Vienna's Sacher Hotel, for instance—a setting which, filled with the city's high society, epitomizes for Bachmann that "greatest of all murder scenes" ("größte(r) aller Mordschauplätze")—is signaled through an allusion to the beheading of John the Baptist, as recreated in Richard Strauss' opera *Salome*. After breathlessly refusing to be seated at a small corner table where a piece of wall juts out—a foreshadowing of her ultimate disappearance into a crack in the wall of her apartment—, the narrator, still not knowing what it was that she glimpsed, reenters the restaurant for her execution:

> This is the table where it happens and where it will happen, and this is the way it is before they strike off your head. Beforehand you're permitted one last supper. My head rolls onto the plate in the restaurant of the Sacher Hotel, spraying the lily-white damask tablecloth with blood, my head has fallen and is exhibited to the guests. (*Malina*, 200)

After mention of dancing with an explicitly destructive purpose ("I went dancing, that I wanted to destroy something," *Malina*, 209), Herodias' words at the end of the opera, "Kill this woman!" ("Man töte dieses Weib!") also resonate in the novel: "Malina whispers inside me: Kill them, kill them!" (*Malina*, 209). The murder theme is sounded repeatedly in the titles of works that surround her, titles that Bachmann has frequently emphasized through capitalization, for example, the French film "L'ASCENSEUR A L'ECHAFAUD" ("Elevator to the Gallows," *Malina*, 185), the book that she comes across at Altenwyl's and is already familiar with, "MURDER IS NO ART," *Malina*, 105), the piano score for "Death and the Maiden," (*Malina*, 105), the book Ivan objects to, "NOTES FROM A MORGUE" (*Malina*, 30), the book she had begun to write, "DEATH STYLES" (*Malina*, 30) and the one she had wanted to write about three men she knew personally, "Three Murderers" (*Malina*, 186). The murder theme is sounded in the dream of her father's performance at the cemetery of the murdered daughters, "WHEN WE DEAD SHALL ARISE" (*Malina*, 144), once again when she suddenly finds herself standing on the street corner in a "puddle of blood " (*Malina*, 200), and in her recollection of what she hears and reads about the world around her, news that also serves to foreshadow her own end:

> The news is often filled with such ghastly reports. In Plötzleinsdorf, at the Prater, in the Vienna Woods, on every periphery a woman is murdered, strangled—it almost happened to me, too, but not on the periphery—strangled by some brutal individual, and then I always think to myself: that could be you, that will be you. Strangers murdered by strangers. (*Malina*, 183)

Her thoughts revolve around the precariousness of her existence in her relationships with men: "I don't know how long Ivan has been shortening my life. . . . Because someone has killed me, because someone has wanted to kill me constantly" (*Malina*, 184).

The title of the novel's central chapter, "The Third Man" ("Der dritte Mann"), also sounds the murder theme. In quoting here the title of the classic 1949 film thriller set in Vienna,[12] Bachmann is connecting the dark Vienna of the novel with that dangerous city of the early postwar years, a connection she also made explicit in her interviews: "For me it would be more important to show how the actual black market developed from the black market of the postwar years—which at the time wasn't all that black as the one today" (*GuI*, 99). By invoking the film, she is also underscoring the novel's mystery character, originally introduced in the jacket text that she intended as the novel's introduction: "Murder or suicide?" When this introduction is included, the novel has the same structure as the film, each beginning with an unsolved murder, which then becomes the focus of the entire work. Other striking parallels between film and novel serve to reinforce the criminal brutality sounded repeatedly in the novel's subtext. Set against the seedy background of shattered postwar Vienna, the film follows the suspenseful uncovering of a murder after the mysterious hit-and-run death of racketeer Harry Lime. The writer narrating the story, Holly Martins, comes to realize that his old friend was in fact the "third man" at the scene of the accident, that he is still alive and is in fact a villainous murderer, not only of the medical orderly who worked for him and was buried in his stead, but also of the many sick children dying in Vienna's hospitals after receiving the penicillin he had diluted for sale on the black market. With Holly's assistance, Harry is chased and shot to death in the dark sewers of the moral wasteland that is postwar Vienna.

In addition to the common tone, setting, and thematic focus, the film, like the novel, suggests a kind of doubling or splitting of the protagonist into two halves: in the film, the good Holly and evil Harry; in the novel, the emotional female narrator and rational male title figure. This *Doppelgänger*-effect is underscored by the similarity of the protagonists' names (Harry-Holly) and backgrounds (old American friends), their complementary placement in the frame (Holly on the left of the screen, Harry on the right, in accordance with the double letter in their names), as well as several verbal slips[13] where the truth is accidentally expressed: Harry's girlfriend Anna absentmindedly calls Holly by Harry's name on more than one occasion, and Holly once says "I" in reference to Harry, then corrects himself quickly by saying "he." Anna comments at one point that Harry used to come to visit her at the same time of day as Holly did, and that Harry used to say the same thing that Holly just said. Holly decides after Harry's death not to return to the U.S., but to continue living in Vienna, as if he were somehow a replacement or continuation of Harry.

An additional parallel between the novel and the film lies in the fact that both have as their central constellation a love triangle between two men and a woman: Malina-Ivan-Ich in the novel; and Holly-Harry-Anna in the film. In each case, one of the male names has a sexually ambiguous ring. "Holly" is an unusual name for a man, although it is a common woman's name, just as the feminine sounding ending of the name "Malina" has similarly androgynous overtones. In both works, the male protagonist bears a feminine sounding name. Furthermore, both the film and the dream chapter of the novel have as their central outcome the realization that someone who had been close and trusted was, in fact, a murderer. Beyond the allusiveness of the chapter title, the dreams themselves depict the narrator's unending destruction at the hands of the prototypical "murderer we all have" (*GuI*, 89). After discovering the "cemetery of the murdered daughters" surrounding a lake where hearty men's glee clubs had once sung on the ice, the narrator is subjected to a series of violent acts by her father, perpetrator of her "death styles." Like the "Company President" ("Generaldirektor") in Bachmann's first radio play, "A Deal in Dreams" ("Ein Geschäft mit Träumen," 1952) and "the Good God" in her last, "The Good God of Manhattan" ("Der gute Gott von Manhattan," 1958), the father here represents the patriarchal principle that destroys women. Subsequent nightmares depict "every imaginable kind of torture, of ruin, of assault" (*GuI*, 97). The narrator is annihilated in a gas chamber, blinded as her father drives his short, hard fingers into her eyes, disemboweled, frozen in ice, plunged into fire, subjected to electric shock therapy, deported, abducted, imprisoned, poisoned, starved to emaciation, bombarded with flowerpots, buried under an avalanche, electrocuted on a high-voltage barbed wire fence, and eaten by a crocodile.

The destruction of the female narrator is repeatedly shown to be a silencing, her absence an acoustical one. Again and again, she is described by metaphors of speechlessness: she has no name; she dreams of losing her voice, of her father tearing out her tongue, taking away her paper and pencil, and giving her no words to sing in his opera. At the same time that she is silent, the novel resonates with the sounds of the metropolis around her, swamping her in a flood of music and voices. More than a visual, it is an acoustical novel. Bachmann has taken care to weave into the narrative an acoustical backdrop and surface noise, which form a rich tapestry of sounds ("Klangteppich"[14]), from the songs on the car radio to the noises of daily life: "One hears strains of Mahler, voices behind a curtain discussing Freud and Wittgenstein, a soprano suddenly interrupted by an advertising jingle, weather and the news, and finally the sound of marching boots and savage war cries."[15] Against this resounding backdrop, the narrator remains silent, a nonparticipant in the sounds of her world.

A narrator without a voice, a silent writer. Putting aside the novel's gender specificity for a moment, this calls to mind Bachmann's compatriot, Hugo von Hofmannsthal, a writer with whom Bachmann shared a great deal.[16] The novel *Malina*, like all of Bachmann's work, is informed by a careful reading of Hofmannsthal and his relationship to language.[17] Like Hofmannsthal, Bachmann unexpectedly stopped writing poetry early in her career and articulated in essays, lectures and interviews the need for a new language, without which she saw no hope for renewal. In her first *Frankfurt Lecture*, she quotes for two pages (!) from the "Letter" of Lord Chandos, which she connects to Hofmannthal's "unexpected aversion to the pure, magical poems of his early years—an aversion to aestheticism" (*Werke*, 4:188). The despair of Chandos is echoed in one of Bachmann's final poems, "No Delicacies" ("Keine Delikatessen"), in which she, too, refuses to go on creating those magical, delectable "first-class word tidbits." As if to reiterate the finality of her decision, the poem begins—as does what is thought to be her final poem, "Enigma"—with the words "Nothing more" ("Nichts mehr"):

> No Delicacies
> Nothing pleases me anymore.
>
> Should I
> dress a metaphor
> with an almond blossom?
> crucify syntax
> on a trick of light?
> Who will beat his brains
> over such superfluities—
> ...
>
> Should I
> take a thought captive,
> lead it into an illuminated sentence cell?
> Feed eye and ear
> with first-class word tidbits?
> Investigate the libido of a vowel,
> ascertain the lover's value of our consonants?[18]

What follows after the refusal to write poetry? For both writers, it was music. For Hofmannsthal, it was a turn to drama, to *Everyman (Jedermann), The Difficult Man (Der Schwierige), The Salzburg Great Theatre of the World (Das Salzburger große Welttheater)*, and to the period of collaboration with Strauss on the operas *Elektra, The Knight of the Rose (Der Rosenkavalier), Ariadne on Naxos (Ariadne auf Naxos),The Woman without a Shadow (Die Frau ohne Schatten), Helen in Egypt (Die ägyptische Helena)*, and *Arabella*. For Bachmann, it was a turn to prose and to a way of writing that is so firmly grounded in music that she consistently referred to it as "composition." She repeatedly referred to *Malina* as an "overture," spoke of her "special relationship to music,"[19] and also used music as a recurrent metaphor for her work as a writer. "I do not write program music" ("Ich schreibe keine Programmmusik"), she once responded to an interviewer's question on the social relevance of the novel. Similarly, the work that Ivan wants the novel's narrator to write is explicitly an "Exsultate jubilate," a title that calls to mind Mozart's motet.

In the absence of a new, adequate language, Bachmann "composed" literary texts with strong musical underpinnings. By "musicalizing" her texts, she was able to expand the limits of what she termed "the faulty language" ("die schlechte Sprache," *Werke*, 4:268) in keeping with Ludwig Wittgenstein's words, which she never tired of quoting: "The limits of my language are the limits of my world." ("Die Grenzen meiner Sprache sind die Grenzen meiner Welt.") We can read the novel *Malina* then as Bachmann's attempt to work with "the faulty language"—since this is all we have, as she goes on to say[20]—and expand its limits through the infusion of music. Musical structures, allusions, even notation serve throughout the novel to help us sense what words cannot adequately convey. Her novel is a multi-layered pastiche of dialogues, interviews, letters, fairy tales, and quotations from literary and musical works,[21] all woven into the narrator's thoughts, memories, and nightmares on her path to the wall. Only music, for her the superior art form, was capable of expression where words fail, as she seems to be suggesting in what is probably her final poem, "Enigma," dedicated to the composer Hans Werner Henze.

> "Enigma"
> For Hans Werner Henze from the time of the Ariosi
>
> Nothing more will come.
>
> Spring will never be again.
> Millennial calendars predict it to everyone.
>
> But summer too, and more, everything with good names
> like "summery" —
> nothing more will come.
>
> You shouldn't cry
> the music says.

> Otherwise
> no one
> says
> anything.²²

The quest for a new language, the contrapuntal and polyphonic "composition" of *Malina* failed to find resonance in critics almost without exception²³ at the time of its appearance in the early 1970s. Its fragmented, Joycean texture, combined with the typically Bachmannesque absence of plot, was lost on its critics, who were receptive to neither its rich allusiveness and intertextuality nor its timeliness and radical depiction of the destruction of female subjectivity.

Rather, they were quick to criticize what they perceived as the novel's sentimentality and lack of social relevance while making superficial connections to persons, settings, and events in Bachmann's personal life.²⁴ The posthumously published collection of conversations and interviews documents the clarity with which Bachmann untiringly explained her conception and way of writing following *Malina's* appearance in 1971 to interviewers oblivious to the novel's philosophical and psychoanalytic underpinnings.²⁵ It was only through the lens of feminist, psychoanalytical and/or poststructuralist theories of the 1980s that readers seemed able to follow the clues that Bachmann had given those interviewers about *Malina*.²⁶

Malina's initial misreception may have been due to the inadvertent obfuscation of the guidance that Bachmann had originally intended to give her readers for understanding the novel's deeper significance. Originally, the work seems to have come wrapped in its own interpretation. The opening lines of the novel's prologue served to focus attention unambiguously on the crime at its center and to prepare the reader for the novel's explicit pronouncement: "It was murder." This final sentence, however, in the absence of the opening text, which was first moved to the novel's back cover and then eliminated entirely, appears almost gratuitous:

> Murder or suicide?
> There are no witnesses.
> A woman between two men.
> Her last great passion.
> The wall in the room,
> with an unnoticeable crack.

A corpse that is not found.
The will vanished.
A pair of glasses shattered,
a coffee cup missing.
The waste paper basket, examined by no one.
Covered tracks. Footsteps.
Someone therefore still walking back and forth,
in this apartment — for hours:
MALINA[27]

When included, this opening text thus makes the first and last word of the novel "murder," thereby interpreting for us unambiguously the criminal nature of the action taking place between these two words. In this context, the final sentence (It was murder.), as if in answer to the question posed at the onset (Murder or suicide?), identifies the crime implicitly as *not* a suicide. This is clearly not a novel about woman's self-destruction. This interpretation stands in sharp contrast not only to Christa Wolf's reading of the novel in her final Frankfurt Lecture,[28] but also to the interpretation offered in Werner Schroeter's film "Malina,"[29] which depicts a woman ready to self-destruct as it aestheticizes human suffering in a series of horrifying images of fire and burning.[30]

Although Bachmann's novel is frequently thought to have been ahead of its time when taken in the context of either contemporary Austrian literature or German women's writing, its development appears as a more gradual progression when viewed in the context of Bachmann's other poetic works. Both formally and thematically, *Malina* was the next step for her in a series of literary experiments. The split character or, as Bachmann preferred to term it, *Doppelfigur*,[31] Malina-Ich, evolved from the earlier sketches of Leda Steiner/Eugen Tobai—in "In Ledas Kreis" (In Leda's Circle)—and the brother-sister pair Franziska/Martin Ranner—in the posthumously published *Franza* fragments, which Bachmann stopped working on during the mid-1960s, as the *"Todesarten"- Projekt* has clearly documented,[32] in order to focus on writing *Malina*. Likewise, the novel's creation of separate layers of text through the use of italics has its precursor in the poem "Reklame" (1956). Similarly, the theme of the impossibility of love surviving in contemporary society, indeed, its systematic destruction by a society that finds it too potentially life-threatening, can be traced back to the radio play, "The Good God of Manhattan" ("Der gute Gott von Manhattan," 1958),[33] just as the silencing of the female, its absence in patriarchal discourse was prefigured in the narrative, "Undine geht" (1961). At the same time that the novel represents a radical break with convention at the time of its appearance, it shows an unmistakable continuity within the larger body of Bachmann's oeuvre.

NOTES

1. Ingeborg Bachmann, *Malina. Roman* originally was published by Suhrkamp in 1971. Besides translations into at least thirteen languages, including English, the novel also appeared posthumously in volume 3 of Ingeborg Bachmann, *Werke*, 4 vols., ed. Christine Koschel, Inge von Weidenbaum, and Clemens Münster, (München: Piper, 1978), hereafter cited as *Werke*, and in volume 3 (3.1 and 3.2) of Ingeborg Bachmann, *"Todesarten"—Projekt. Kritische Ausgabe*, 4 volumes in 5 volumes, ed. Monika Albrecht and Dirk Göttsche (München: Piper, 1995), hereafter cited as *KA*.

2. Ingeborg Bachmann, *Malina*, trans. Philip Boehm (New York: Holmes & Meier, 1990), 224. Hereafter cited as *Malina*.

3. "Es ist eine sehr alte, eine sehr starke Wand, aus der niemand fallen kann, die niemand aufbrechen kann, aus der nie mehr etwas *laut* werden kann." My italics. Bachmann, *Werke*, 3:337 and *KA*, 3.2:694-5. All translations from German texts are my own.

4. My translation. I have not used the published English translation here since Peter Filkin's rendering of this central passage in Bachmann's work eradicates the female gender in two instances of the pronoun "sie" by rendering it with the object pronouns "it," and "something": ". . . that though he had eradicated her, she was still there. *It* can still be read, because nothing is there where in fact *something* should be." Ingeborg Bachmann "The Book of Franza," *The Book of Franza* and *Requiem for Fanny Goldmann*, trans. Peter Filkins (Evanston: Northwestern University Press, 1999), 109, my italics. The original German reads: ". . . dass an der Stelle, wo er sie getilgt hat, doch sie stehen geblieben ist. *Sie* ist abzulesen, weil da nichts ist, wo *sie* sein soll" (Bachmann, *KA*, 2: 274, my italics). The gender-neutralizing translation obliterates the central image that Bachmann is invoking here through the wall metaphor: the Egyptian queen, not as "something," but as a prototypical WOMAN, exists only as absence. Bachmann's text is not about the absence of "something," but about female absence in patriarchy.

5. Ingeborg Bachmann, *Wir müssen wahre Sätze finden. Gespräche und Interviews*, ed. Christine Koschel and Inge von Weidenbaum (München: Piper, 1983), 75. Hereafter cited as *GuI*.

6. See especially Dirk Göttsche, "Musikalische Poetik in *Malina* und anderer Erzählprosa," *Bachmann-Handbuch. Leben—Werk—Wirkung*, ed. Monika Albrecht and Dirk Göttsche (Stuttgart: Metzler, 2002), 303-307. See also Suzanne Greuner, *Schmerzton. Musik in der Schreibweise von Ingeborg Bachmann und Anne Duden*,

Literatur im historischen Prozeß, N.F. 24, Argument-Sonderband AS 179 (Hamburg: Argument, 1990), 73-103 on *Malina*; Hartmut Spiesecke, *Ein Wohlklang schmilzt das Eis*. *Ingeborg Bachmanns musikalische Poetik* (Berlin: Norman Klaunig, 1993), 190-221 on *Malina*; Corina Caduff, "Musik als Erinnerungsfigur bei Ingeborg Bachmann," *Ingeborg Bachmann. text+kritik 6* (Nov. issue, 1995): 99-110, and *"dadim dadam"—Figuren der Musik in der Literatur Ingeborg Bachmanns* (Köln: Böhlau, 1998); Jost Schneider, *Die Kompositionsmethode Ingeborg Bachmanns. Erzählstil und Engagement in "Das dreißigste Jahr," "Malina" und "Simultan"* (Bielefeld: Aisthesis, 1999), 265-293 on *Malina*; Eva U. Lindemann, "'Die Gangart des Geistes.' Musikalische Strukturen in der späten Prosa Ingeborg Bachmanns," *Ingeborg Bachmanns 'Malina,'* ed. Andrea Stoll (Frankfurt: Suhrkamp, 1992), 301-320; Karen R. Achberger, "Der Fall Schönberg. Musik und Mythos in 'Malina'," *Ingeborg Bachmann. text+kritik Sonderband* (München: edition text+kritik, 1984), 120-131, and, "Musik und Komposition in Ingeborg Bachmanns *Zikaden* und *Malina*," *German Quarterly* 61, no. 2 (Spring 1988): 193-212, as well as her, "*Malina* and the 'Death Styles' Cycle," *Understanding Ingeborg Bachmann* (Columbia: University of South Carolina Press, 1995), 96-142.

7. See Elizabeth Boa, "Women Writing about Women Writing and Ingeborg Bachmann's *Malina,"* *New Ways in Germanistik,* Richard Sheppard, ed. (New York: Berg, 1990), 128-144. Boa reads the novel in light of psychoanalytic theory, especially that of Julia Kristeva, and so connects Bachmann's intertextuality and musicalization of writing to a linguistic subversion of the symbolic order.

8. "Es gibt nur noch zwei Stimmen, die mit- oder gegeneinander geführt werden und wie in der Musik Anweisungen bekommen, wie *sotto voce, con sentimento,* etc" (*GuI*, 75). Pages 68-115 contain eight interviews on *Malina* from 1971, six of which are reprinted in *Ingeborg Bachmanns 'Malina.'* suhrkamp taschenbuch materialien 2115, ed. Andrea Stoll (Frankfurt: Suhrkamp, 1992), 70-102.

9. Corina Caduff, "Musik als Erinnerungsfigur," 107-8.

10. Suzanne Greuner refers to a "musicalization of language" ("Musikalisierung der Sprache") in *Malina* (*Schmerzton*, 88), while Dirk Göttsche suggests the term "lyricization" ("Lyrisierung"), and points to its closeness to the *Sprechgesang* of Schönberg's *Pierrot lunaire* ("Musikalische Poetik," 407).

11. Göttsche interprets the use of Italian marks in the final dialog as a reminder of a lost and yet irreplaceable utopia along the lines of the poem "Enigma" ("Musikalische Poetik," 307).

12. The British film by Carol Reed was based on the script by Graham Green and features Orson Welles as Harry Lime, Joseph Cotton as Holly Martins, and Trevor Howard as the British police inspector. To augment Green's script, Welles is said to have written the text for his famous "cuckoo clocks" speech himself, contrasting Italy's great cultural achievements in times of turmoil and political corruption with Switzerland's production of "cuckoo clocks" after "500 years of democracy." The film is one of the novel's many intertexts, from Wagner's opera "Tristan und Isolde" and Offenbach's "Tales of Hoffmann" to Thomas Mann's *Doktor Faustus* and Schönberg's "Moses und Aron," which constitute a fine mesh of interwoven references. See also Monika Albrecht, *"Die andere Seite." Untersuchungen zur Bedeutung von Werk und Person Max Frischs in Ingeborg Bachmanns "Todesarten"* (Würzburg: Königshausen & Neumann, 1989) and Gerhard R. Probst, "Mein Name sei Malina—Nachdenken über Ingeborg Bachmann." *Modern Austrian Literature* 11, no. 1 (1978): 103-119, one of the earliest studies of *Malina's* intertextual relationship with Max Frisch's novel, *Mein Name sei Gantenbein* and Christa Wolf's novel *Nachdenken über Christa T.*

13. That these "Freudian" slips occur in the city of Sigmund Freud's psychoanalytical work is probably not a coincidence and may have been intended, together with the extensive images of men moving through damp, narrow, underground passages, as an "hommage" of sorts to Freud.

14. This is the term that the Austrian composer Otto Brusatti used in describing the novel in a 1986 interview with me in Vienna. The novel's acoustical richness was so obvious to him in reading it for the first time that he composed a "Sprechkammeroper" (spoken chamber opera) for radio, *Malina-Suite,* which was first broadcast by ORF (Austrian Radio) in May 1985.

15. Mark Anderson, "Death Arias in Vienna," afterword to *Malina,* by Ingeborg Bachmann, trans. Philip Boehm, 227.

16. Beyond the language crisis, Hofmannsthal is also one of the first names that come to mind when we think of German writers whose work relates closely to music. A writer who was sensitized to the interrelationship of music and literature in the opera libretto above all through his collaboration with the composer Richard Strauss, his development is not without parallels some half

century later in the work and life of Ingeborg Bachmann. Like her compatriot, Bachmann, too, was a librettist. She worked closely with the composer Hans Werner Henze for whom she wrote two opera libretti and a ballet scenario.

17. See Dirk Göttsche, "Sprachskepsis und Identitätsproblematik," *Die Produktivität der Sprachkrise in der modernen Prosa* (Frankfurt am Main: Athenäum, 1987), 155-222. In the sixth of eight chapters dealing with the twentieth-century "language crisis," Göttsche examines Bachmann's early and late prose, including *Malina*, in light of her critical statements on language.

18. Ingeborg Bachmann, *In the Storm of Roses. Selected Poems by Ingeborg Bachmann*, trans. and ed. Mark Anderson (Princeton: Princeton University Press, 1986), 187 and 189. For a different translation, see also Ingeborg Bachmann, *Songs in Flight. The Collected Poems of Ingeborg Bachmann*, trans. Peter Filkins (New York.: Marsilio, 1994), 321 and 323.

19. Bachmann stressed this in her interviews: ". . . (it) is . . . above all music to which I probably have an even more intensive relationship than to literature" (". . . (es) ist . . . vor allem die Musik, zu der ich eine vielleicht noch intensivere Beziehung als zur Literatur habe"), *GuI*, 107.

20. See Bachmann, *Werke*, 4: 268: "since life has only a faulty language" ("denn das Leben hat nur eine schlechte Sprache," my translation).

21. See Annette Klaubert, *Symbolische Strukturen bei Ingeborg Bachmann. Malina im Kontext der Kurzgeschichten*, Europäische Hochschulschriften 1:662 (Bern: Peter Lang, 1983). In attempting to develop a "key" to the "symbolic structures" in *Malina*, Klaubert examines four characteristic stories from the 1961 collection in search of key words, metaphors, and symbols, and thereby identifies many of Bachmann's concealed allusions to literary, musical, cinematic, and critical works. See also Barbara Kunze, "Ein Geheimnis der Prinzessin von Kagran: Die ungewöhnliche Quelle zu der 'Legende' in Ingeborg Bachmann's *Malina*," *Modern Austrian Literature* 18, no. 3/4 (1985): 105-119. Kunze uncovers Algernon Blackwood's story, "The Willows" ("Die Weiden") as a source for the novel's italicized fantasy, "The Mysteries of the Princess of Kagran."

22. Bachmann, *In the Storm of Roses*, 185. See also Bachmann, *Songs in Flight*, 319. Beyond the role of music as the sole source of consolation in the desolate world depicted here, the specific reference to Gustav Mahler, whose children's chorus from the

Third Symphony is quoted here ("Du sollst ja nicht weinen"—"You should not cry") points to the importance of Mahler for the work of both Bachmann and Henze.

23. One exception is the perceptive review by Hans Mayer, who, with characteristic acuity, recognized at once the novel's strict composition and rich fabric of quotations. See Hans Mayer, "Malina oder Der große Gott von Wien," *Die Weltwoche* 39.17, Zürich: 30 April 1971, page 35. See also Hilde Spiel, "Ingeborg Bachmann: Malina." *Literatur und Kritik* (July/August, 1972): 437-38. Reprinted in *Ingeborg Bachmanns 'Malina,'* 134-135. While Spiel also recognized the work's complexity, she criticized it for its subjectivity.

24. For a well written and carefully researched study of the (mis)reception of Bachmann's novel by German-language critics, see Elke Atzler, "Ingeborg Bachmanns Roman *Malina* im Spiegel der literarischen Kritik," *Jahrbuch der Grillparzer Gesellschaft* 3, no. 15 (1983): 155-171. See also Constanze Hotz, "Erster Roman der Bachmann. 'Malina' in der journalistischen Kritik," *Die Bachmann. Das Image der Dichterin: Ingeborg Bachmann im journalistischen Diskurs* (Konstanz: Ekkehard Fraude Verlag, 1990), 175-204, and Andrea Stoll, "Kontroverse und Polarisierung: Die *Malina*-Rezeption als Schlüssel der Bachmann-Forschung," *Ingeborg Bachmanns 'Malina,'* 149-167.

25. See Bachmann, *GuI*, especially 68-115.

26. Sigrid Weigel was one of the first scholars to examine Bachmann's uniquely "female way of writing" ("weibliche Schreibweise"). She and several of her (mostly female) students in Hamburg and Zürich made substantial contributions to scholarship on *Malina* and the "Todesarten" fragments. See Sigrid Weigel, "'Ein Ende mit der Schrift. Ein anderer Anfang.' Zur Entwicklung von Ingeborg Bachmanns Schreibweise," *Ingeborg Bachmann. text+kritik Sonderband* (München: edition text+kritik, 1984), 58-92, and "Zur Polyphonie des Anderen," *Ingeborg Bachmann. Die Schwarzkunst der Worte*, ed. John Pattillo-Hess and Wilhelm Petrasch, (Vienna: Wiener Urania, 1994), 9-24. See also Caduff, "Musik als Erinnerungsfigur," Greuner, *Schmerzton*, and Lindemann, "Musikalische Strukturen." See also Susanne Baackmann, "Der Diskurs der Liebe. Zu Ingeborg Bachmanns *Malina*," *Erklär mir Liebe. Weibliche Schreibweisen von Liebe in der deutschsprachigen Gegenwartsliteratur*, Argument-Sonderband N.F. 237 (Hamburg: Argument, 1995).

27. Bachmann, *KA*, 3.2:742. This text, which Bachmann originally intended to open the novel, was printed on the back

jacket of the novel's first edition in 1971 and has not been published with the novel since that time. Neither the four-volume edition of Bachmann's works (*Werke*, 1978) nor the published English translation includes this fourteen-line text, which first resurfaced in Hans Höller, "Der Todesarten-Zyklus," *Ingeborg Bachmann. Das Werk. Von den frühesten Gedichten bis zum "Todesarten"-Zyklus* (Frankfurt am Main: Athenäum, 1987), 228-29. Albrecht and Göttsche include it in three slightly different versions, the first written already at the end of her second (of eight) text stages (*KA*, 3.1:141), the second belonging to the corrected manuscript copy of the third stage (3.1: 143) and the final one published on the back cover of the novel's first edition (*KA*, 3.2:742). That Bachmann apparently intended this text to constitute the opening words of the novel, would seem to underscore the significance of its criminal focus for an interpretation of the work, as does the reference to Bertolt Brecht's poem "Verwisch die Spuren" ("Cover the traces"). For a discussion of Bachmann's intertextual relationship with Brecht, see Achberger, "'Kunst als Veränderndes': Bachmann und Brecht," *Monatshefte* 83, no. 1 (Spring 1991): 7-16 as well as "Bachmann, Brecht und die Musik," *Ingeborg Bachmann—Neue Beiträge zu ihrem Werk. Internationales Symposion Münster 1991* (Würzburg: Königshausen & Neumann, 1993), 265-79.

    28. See Christa Wolf, *Voraussetzungen einer Erzählung: Kassandra* (Darmstadt: Luchterhand, 1983) as well as her *Cassandra. A Novel and Four Essays*, trans. Jan van Heurck (New York: Farrar, Strauss, Giroux, 1984). In her fourth *Frankfurt Lecture*, which also includes a rather extensive discussion of Bachmann's *Franza* fragment, Wolf states: "The last sentence reads: 'It was murder.' It was also suicide" (299) ("Es war Mord, heißt der letzte Satz. Es war auch Selbstmord" [149]).

    29. Schroeter's film, starring French actress Isabelle Huppert, was based on the script by Elfriede Jelinek. See Elfriede Jelinek, *Malina. Ein Filmbuch* (Frankfurt am Main: Suhrkamp, 1991). The film's overdeveloped fire imagery apparently is meant to suggest a connection to Bachmann's own death after accidentally setting fire to herself in her Rome apartment, thus reviving once again the posture exemplified in the heading of the German tabloid *Bild* when it brought the news of Bachmann's death on 17 October 1973: "Sie starb, als wär's von ihr erdacht" ("She died as if she had imagined it").

30. See Kurt Bartsch, "'Mord' oder Selbstvernichtung?" *Die Schwarzkunst der Worte*, 85-95. Bartsch dismisses Schroeter's filmic interpretation of the novel as an anachronistic return to the gross misjudgment of the early years before 1978.

31. An additional doubling in the novel, besides the male-female, is that of the narrator-narrated. See Andrea Treude, "'Sich verschreiben—das ist ein schönes Wort,'" *Die Schwarzkunst der Worte*, 76-84. Treude uses the quote from one of Bachmann's interviews as a starting point for a discussion of the double role of first-person narrator and narrated figure in the novel. See also Sabine Grimkowski, *Das zerstörte Ich. Erzählstruktur und Identität in Ingeborg Bachmanns "Der Fall Franza" und "Malina,"* (Würzburg: Königshausen & Neumann, 1992). Grimkowski shows how the split subject (Malina-I) in *Malina* enabled Bachmann to demonstrate the disintegration of the first-person narrator that she had attempted unsuccessfully in *Franza*. See also Gudrun Kohn-Waechter, *Das Verschwinden in der Wand. Destruktive Moderne und Widerspruch eines weiblichen Ich in Ingeborg Bachmanns "Malina,"* Ergebnisse der Frauenforschung 28 (Stuttgart: Metzler, 1992), an examination of Bachmann's novel as the destruction of a dialogic way of writing in favor of a single, superior, objective, male narrative voice.

32. See also Monika Albrecht, "Die Suche nach Malina." *Die Schwarzkunst der Worte*, 46-56. Albrecht traces the development of the Malina figure in Bachmann's drafts going back to the 1950s and early 1960s in his various incarnations (Eugen Franz Josef Tobai, Martin Ranner, Klaus Jonas) and shows connections of the Ich/Malina constellation to earlier sketches of Leda Steiner/Eugen Tobai ("In Ledas Kreis") and Franziska/Martin Ranner (in the "Franza" fragments).

33. It is also no coincidence that in both the radio play and the novel, it is the female who is destroyed while the male survives.

8 / "It was Murder": Who framed *Malina*?[1]

Ingeborg Majer O'Sickey

Preliminary Remarks

One of the pressing questions film theorists have grappled with for the past three decades is deceptively simple: what can the spectator learn about the ways cinematic syntax produces gendered characters?

Perhaps no other film adaptation challenges us to address this question more urgently than the Werner Schroeter/Elfriede Jelinek film adaptation of Ingeborg Bachmann's novel, *Malina*. Although the 1991 film won the German Film Prize, its reception was mostly negative.[2] While many reviewers and critics acknowledge the film's visual and auditory brilliance, most blasted the film's portrayal of the female protagonist played by Isabelle Huppert. Many of their frustrations with the representation of the woman echoes my own. The film transforms the novel's political space into a cinematic *Psychogramm*[3] of Bachmann herself. The result is devastating. The film ultimately fuses the female protagonist with the legend surrounding Bachmann's *Todesart* (way of dying);[4] the depiction of the woman's struggle to write herself into being and her ultimate death are depoliticized and reconfigured as an etiology of "female malady" *tout court*. As a consequence, the film version erases the novel's radical political potential.

How could this happen? After all, Elfriede Jelinek, the well-known feminist *enfant terrible* of Austrian literature, wrote the screenplay.[5] From her *oeuvre* we know that she champions the socially transformative potential of Bachmann's thematization of the violence experienced by *Malina*'s split female protagonist.[6] Not surprisingly, Jelinek called the film adaptation a "disaster." It seems that somewhere along the way—from the pages of the screenplay to the final cut of the film—Jelinek lost control of Bachmann's *Ich-Figur*.[7] To Brenda Bethman she explained that she was frustrated by the reviewers' denigration of her own work. Critics, she noted, were clearly unaware that Schroeter had made significant alterations to her original script and that he did not follow her interpretation of Bachmann's novel.[8] While it is not my goal to trace the differences among Bachmann's novel, Jelinek's screenplay and Schroeter's final cut of the film, I would like to offer an example that may stand as paradigmatic for Jelinek's claim that Schroeter did not understand her interpretation of Bachmann's *Ich-Figur*. The change from Jelinek's screenplay to the final cut results in a dramatic shift in meaning. In Jelinek's screenplay (sequence 53), the woman relates a pivotal moment in her childhood to her alter ego, Malina. The woman explains that a boy had beckoned her under the pretext of wishing to show her something; when she approached, he slapped her hard. The woman tells Malina: "It was my first experience with pain and with the pleasure of another to inflict it."[9] In the film, Isabelle Huppert in her role as the female protagonist, restates the reminiscence as follows: "It was my first experience with pain and with the pleasure in it."

Transformed by Schroeter, the female protagonist emerges as a woman who enjoys being abused. This altered version leads to an impression of the film as an etiology of "female malady." While Jelinek's screenplay presents the masochistic tendencies of the novel's female protagonist in differentiated ways that can, more often than not, be read as critiques of ideology, in Schroeter's final cut, masochism is configured as *"female* masochism." This impression is not simply gained from the sequence above. Its meaning emerges, as I hope to show later on, in the film-in-process.

At first glance, the Schroeter-Jelinek alliance seems ideal for the film adaptation of Bachmann's complex novel. Both artists are very much aware that gendered subjectivity goes beyond the simple understanding of female subjectivity as difference. To Jelinek's interpretation of Bachmann's character and political agenda, Schroeter brings his fascination with opera and opera divas[10] as well as a portfolio of films that deconstruct masculinity and femininity. Indeed, although not as widely known as Jelinek, he had, by the time he undertook *Malina*, developed a cult following with his highly emotive, performance-driven films that draw on a number of genres (among these, opera, popular music, stage melodrama, cabaret and contemporary dance-theatre).[11]

In many ways, Isabelle Huppert's portrayal of the female character in *Malina* recalls Schroeter's portraits of opera divas. Huppert represents femininity with such excess that the character's struggle to signify is palpable. For Jelinek and Schroeter, the woman's alter ego Malina is an internalization of social contexts (codes in the symbolic) and a psychical projection of the body based on the body's social meaning. Both artists' previous representations of femininity as constructed, independent of biology, would seem to augur well for a differentiated portrayal of Bachmann's complex female protagonist.

So what went wrong? How did the film turn into a "disaster," to use Jelinek's description? The answer lies not simply in the complicated production of the film, but rather in the significant differences between the two artists' *goals* in questioning the construction of gender. For Jelinek the depiction of gendered subjectivity more often than not becomes a vehicle to reveal the cultural pressure women experience in the process of signifying.[12] As we see from her explanation to Anke Roeder (1996), Jelinek understands women's speech as an act that takes courage: "As Bachmann shows in paradigmatic ways, the woman must, if she is to speak, create a masculine 'I'. Woman's speech is, to say it with psychoanalysis, an appropriation of the phallus, a transgression, that is, after all, not within her rights."[13]

Schroeter, on the other hand, evidently judges Bachmann's character as rather timid and passive. In an interview with the German television network, ZDF, he opined: "It would be awful if it were filmed as it is written. One bridge is Jelinek, the other is me. One must cross both if one is to come up with a new question. Otherwise, no one is interested in all that whining (Gejammer)."[14] Schroeter's judgment that feminist protest is simply "whining," and the implication that a new age of post-feminism had arrived, not only express his misunderstanding of feminist projects that critique patriarchal culture, but also show how he misjudges late 20th century reality for women writers, as is strikingly evident in his film *Der Tod der Maria Malibran (The Death of Maria Malibran)*, in which Magdalena Montezuma and Candy Darling's portrayal of the diva Malibran is designed to mark gender as a continuum.[15] The result is that while Jelinek, in her screenplay, offers a critique of masculinist notions of female suffering and yearning, Schroeter is rather more interested in having the viewer note the physical experience of the female protagonist's suffering and yearning.

The Speaking Subject in Process/on Trial

Before I return to my opening question—what can the spectator learn about ways cinematic syntax produces gendered characters?—it is important to revisit Bachmann's novel. "Writing comes out of terror," Philippe Sollers says in a terse statement[16] that can be seen as a reformulation of Emile Benveniste's dictum that "it is in and through language that man constitutes himself as a subject."[17] Both statements speak to the violence inherent in symbolic law, a law that sentences the speaking subject to death in the very attempt to signify. *Malina* is part of a trilogy Bachmann called *Todesarten*,[18] which means "ways of dying." *Todesarten* signals her protagonists' struggles with the patriarchal system. Bachmann's transposition of one letter produces "Todes*r*aten,"[19] marking her protagonists' deaths as lingering (*Raten* means "installments").

It is the sheer terror of being silenced that animates the female half of the *Doppelfigur* in *Malina*. *Ich* is terrorized by the notion of performing the act of speaking/writing. Her attempt to create herself as a speaking subject on the battlefield of discourse forces her into dangerous territory. To claim her *Ich* (signified) means that she must enter the fray for a commonly shared signifier (*Ich*). To wrest it from the piles of *Ich*s for her "own" is, perforce, an act of violence. But it is also an act that requires creativity and a (naive?) belief that she can arrest the floating signifier into a unified, static whole. *Ich*'s tragedy is that she rejects the idealist's philosophical belief in the transcendental ego; she understands that to speak is always to simultaneously accept both, a socially given subjectivity and a radical alienation from her "self," which is unknowable to her. *Ich* perishes in the very act of writing herself into and out of a society Bachmann has called the "allergrößte Mordschauplatz" ("the biggest murder scene of all").[20]

The very idea of such a "scene," designed for staging (spectacle) as well as viewing (spectator) murder, must make us pause. It is a concept that invites us to think about cinematic representation. *Ich*'s struggles in terms of performance involve a mise-en-scène, spectators, narrative, a director. The concept also invites a historical and a psycholinguistic reading. The novel's last words, "Es war

Mord"—"It was murder"—refer to *Ich* as a historical subject. Expressing the historical as located in *Ich* is a process that begins in earnest in chapter two, "The Third Man." Here, Bachmann's protagonist names her murderer, who appears to her in dreams: "Es ist nicht mein Vater. Es ist mein Mörder" ("It's not my father. It's my murderer").[21] He is more than her murderer, of course. He represents the principle of violence in patriarchal society. Long before she dies, visions of her father have him appear in judge's robes, in charge of gas chambers, in an SS uniform, in the guise of an opera director, as a book burner, and as a butcher, wearing a bloody apron.[22]

As a psycholinguistic concept, the "allergrößte Mordschauplatz" calls to mind the domain of the symbolic, the place where the prelinguistic self enters a traffic circle/circuit of exchange. Since one's place in this traffic circle/circuit—that includes the Oedipal triangle—depends upon positionality and judgment, mirroring and misrecognition, self-estrangement and identification, it is easy to see why the nomination *Ich* does not save us. Is it any wonder that we long so much to return to a time before the mirror stage?[23] Here, *méconnaissance* firmly places us in our ideal self and we experience, in Lacan's word, "jubilation."[24] The fall into language, then, is a fall squarely into the very middle of the *Mordschauplatz*.

As we have seen, Jelinek refers to Bachmann's narrating *Ich* as necessarily split. In the interview with Roeder (cited above), Jelinek invokes Lacanian psychoanalysis, as variously reworked by French feminists like Cixous, Irigaray, and Kristeva. Her reference seems particularly apt here. Bachmann's work often anticipated or appeared roughly contemporaneously with many of the exciting theories by French feminist theorists and writers. Bachmann, like Julia Kristeva, understands the speaking subject as divided between unconscious (physiological processes) and conscious motivations and responses (characterized by social constraints). Kristeva's explanations of the processes involved in engendering the speaking subject are most helpful in understanding Bachmann's split character.

What follows is a necessarily brief outline of the processes Kristeva describes. Developing Benveniste's insight that "it is literally true that the basis of subjectivity is in the exercise of language" and that "it is in and through language that man constitutes himself as a subject,"[25] Julia Kristeva has pointed out that "the *subject of enunciation* introduces, through categorical intuition, both *semantic fields* and *logical*—but also *intersubjective—relations*, which prove to be both intra- and translinguistic."[26] Kristeva explains intra- and translinguistic relations by positing two modalities that are involved in the production of language: the symbolic and the semiotic. She ascribes the symbolic to the masculinist, and the semiotic to the feminine function. Both types of signifying processes are necessary in the production of language and, hence, in the engendering of the speaking subject. Kristeva relates the symbolic process to the creation of law, social constraints, and thus to the creation of sign and syntax. In contrast, Kristeva locates the semiotic process in the prelinguistic realm. Somewhat idiosyncratically, Kristeva names this site *chora*, a term she borrows from Plato's *Timaeus*. As she explains, "Plato emphasizes 'the receptacle ... which is also called space ... it is unstable, uncertain, ever changing and becoming; it is even unnamable, improbable, bastard.'"[27] Language then, theorized by Kristeva, is the beating out of rhythms involving the two modalities, the symbolic and the semiotic. What is important here is that Kristeva locates revolutionary potential in art at precisely that moment when the semiotic (genotext) disrupts the symbolic (phenotext).[28] Art, she says, is the only means by which the symbolic order can be cracked open, and it can do this by incursions of the semiotic into the symbolic. These incursions can be achieved by nonsensical (agrammatical) elements, such as may be found in certain stream-of-consciousness narratives and nonlinear texts, by insertion of camp, artifice and excess, in other words, by way of any textual operation that destabilizes the unified transcendental speaking subject.[29]

In this conception of the signifying process, *Ich's* masculine alter ego (Malina) has the function of communicating to her the laws and values of patriarchal society. Malina's voice in the novel represents the critical, controlling voice internalized by the female protagonist. Bachmann's novel performs semiotic incursions in a variety of ways. These include disruptions of genre expectations (is *Ich* telling us a murder mystery? A love story? An *Entwicklungsroman*?) that are further complicated by the inclusion of textual fragments (fairy tales, letters, libretti, and segments of dreams). In addition, disruptions of the symbolic on the level of syntax are frequent (*Ich* speaks elliptically and often fragmentarily). And, finally, perhaps the most important mechanism of disruption is that Bachmann split her protagonist into two, a female half (*Ich*) and a male half (Malina).

Semiotic Incursions

In his film adaptation, *Malina*, Schroeter also puts a number of different genres into play; especially brilliant are the sections of the film where the protagonist's volatile interior life (especially, her dreams) is exteriorized, with images of fire and opera performances as its objective correlative. And yet, as intensely as these semiotic elements disrupt the symbolic in the texture of the film, the protagonist is ultimately refused a Bachmannian/Kristevian "revolution." This refusal has, I believe, to do with Schroeter's choice of making visible the female protagonist's internalization of the symbolic modality. Schroeter gives the symbolic a physical body, with Mathieu Carrière in the role of Malina. By making the woman's male alter ego Malina part of the mise-en-scène, that is to say, by moving him from the woman's interior space to the camera, Malina is no longer an index of the woman's analytical abilities.

The woman's narration is perforce taken over by the basic rule of cinematic syntax, where image "A" becomes meaningful by way of image "B" and inversely. As a result of this syntax, the woman is represented as a body that is marked physically by pathological disturbances. In contrast to her male counterpart, whose calm and contained body language represents psychosomatic control and rationality, the woman is literally falling apart. Images that serve as indexes of her psychological disturbance, such as her peripatetic running around the apartment, her incessant and obsessive smoking, her seeming inability to finish sentences, her fascination with fire, her frantic writing and obsessive telephoning, are repeated to such a degree that they mark her as a person whose interior loss of control is shown by her physical disintegration.

It is important to keep in mind that in the novel, *Ich* manifests herself as a critique of ratio in both verbal and non-verbal ways. Her semiotic incursions into the symbolic make her rebellion an integral part of her perceptual world. All the while, *Ich* understands that the symbolic will be the instrument of her death. "I was *subordinate* to him from the beginning, and I must have known early on that he [Malina] was destined to be my doom."[30] But, it would be a grave mistake to assume that Bachmann has created *Ich* as a victim, who indulges in "Gejammer," to use Schroeter's word. Yes, *Ich* dreams that her father has burned her books, has torn out her tongue, and has taken away her words. And, yes, she blames Malina and her lover Ivan for prescribing to her what kind of story she should tell. However, *Ich,* as a split speaking subject, uses a preponderance of genotext to signify her reaction to the symbolic. She stages her alter ego in part *as* protest; she acquiesces to and rebels against it/him.

In the end, *Ich* emerges as a character who problematizes the terms of her situation as a writer. She performs voices and thus oscillates between empowerment and disempowerment. She names the causes of her illness at once as she physically manifests that which makes her ill. More than this: after her disappearance into a crack in the wall, it is left unclear who speaks the last sentences that declare that *Ich* was murdered. *Ich*'s death could therefore be seen as a displacement of the semiotic by the symbolic in the novel.[31] She has removed herself from her alter ego's masculinist rationality. The crack in the wall could also be read, as Jane Marcus does, as a metaphor for *Ich*'s genitalia. *Ich*'s disappearance into her physical body may, in this reading, signify her unwillingness to continue to collaborate with the Law of the Father and express her understanding that *jouissance* is an impossibility for her in the symbolic.[32]

Engendering the Woman on Screen

We can now sharpen the question I posed at the beginning and ask about cinematic syntax as it produces gendered characters by refracting the question through historical and psycholinguistic categories. I believe that Bachmann designates the space, where the gendered subject is produced, as the *"allergrößte Mordschauplatz"* ("the biggest murder scene of all"). As noted earlier, the concept includes the spectacle and its spectators, the narrative and its mise-en-scène and may thus be taken as a cipher for visual representation and spectation.

Let us think then, for the sake of my discussion, of phenotext—the symbolic modality—as the "male" gaze in cinema. Such a designation is persuasive since, as Laura Mulvey and other film scholars have shown, classical cinema installs an objectifying "male" gaze that produces a transcendental masculine subject who comes into being by virtue of staging femininity as *difference*.[33] The scopic regime of classical cinema, where the woman becomes the object of our gaze, fulfills our desire of taking visual possession of the woman. In *Malina* the spectator's desire for visual possession is fulfilled with maniacal force. Huppert's character is present in all 757 shots in the film, and, as Seiderer has shown, 161 shots are close-ups of her face.[34] For all this overwhelming offer of plenitude, Schroeter inserts elements of genotext that radically interrupt the "cinematic phenotext." To counteract his camera's objectifying male gaze, he instrumentalized many of the cinematic techniques that can be designated "cinematic genotext." He used disjunctive editing that denies a sense of causality and thus works against linear narrative. Into ambient sound, he cut counterpuntal sound (music, singing voices), thwarting notions of realism. Perhaps Schroeter's most effective strategy to disrupt the objectifying gaze lies in his direction of Isabelle Huppert. Resembling Brechtian *Gestik*-acting, Huppert's over-the-top acting and manneristic gestures *quote* the woman's part. Such quotation may be said to short-circuit scopophilia by preventing a portrait of the woman as a biologically and psychologically coherent character.

However, Schroeter solved his central problem—to find a visual equivalent for the woman's imagined alter ego—in a way that can be seen as a prime example for the seeming paradox that experimental cinema, so-called avant-garde works of art, is often as conservative as conventional art. Casting Mathieu Carrière in the role of Malina, Schroeter gave the woman's alter ego a body, and moved him from the woman's interior space to the mise-en-scène. This choice has decisive consequences for the spectator's understanding of the woman's portrait. Now that her male alter ego is visible, Malina ceases to be the woman's own creation, and he is no longer an index of her analytical abilities.

A more obvious consequence of giving the woman's alter ego a physical body is that Huppert and Carrière are now *visually* opposed. This opposition results in stereotypically gendered images.

When we see the woman in the frame by herself, Schroeter's direction of Huppert relies on predominantly non-verbal strategies to appeal to the spectator. For example, the character's emotional highs and lows (her experiences of desire and loss), her inability to write, her death wish and so on, are conveyed through intensely stylized gestures and postures. Her frenzied body language and speech patterns may be said to function as ellipses that can be read as a refusal to make sense, constructing a visual syntax that implies schizophrenia. In these scenes, the viewer can experience her portrayal as nearly pure genotext. A consequence of such excess is, as Ulrike Sieglohr points out, that exaggerated femininity in Schroeter's opera films denaturalizes the female performers' biological gender.[35]

As I have discussed, in the film *Malina*, femininity is frequently shown as *constructed*, and gendered subjectivity is clearly marked as an artifact of cultural production. However, when Malina is in the frame with his alter ego, his measured, calm and rational appearance and movements mediate this impression and push the spectator toward a gender-specific interpretation. In these scenes, the viewer experiences the portrayal of the woman less as a cultural construct, than as an embodiment of "female malady" based on *difference*. Even though Carrière is far from a hyper-masculinized figure, his appearance in the frame with Huppert causes her biological gender to reemerge as part of a traditionally accepted binary economy of gender.

The cinematographer's challenge then was to represent a dynamic conflict that is not seen directly, but is registered as *effects*. Schroeter ultimately fails when he stages the physical appearance of the woman's male alter ego. In the novel, we experience the complex dance *Ich* performs in the rhythms of the semiotic and symbolic modalities of language. The visualization of masculinity in the film, on the other hand, performs an erasure of the woman's potential to disrupt the symbolic order. She no longer signifies, as her alter ego takes over her narration. I will return to this issue in a moment.

As I mentioned earlier, Jelinek blames Schroeter for the failure. It seems to me that Jelinek is right when she said that he did not understand her reading of Bachmann's trajectory. An important sign that marks Bachmann's psycholinguistic trajectory is that Malina's female alter ego is named *Ich*. The opening pages to the novel highlight this nomination. Here, Bachmann's narrator gives her lover the name "Ivan," his two sons, the names "Béla" and "András," her alter ego, "Malina," and herself "Ich." She uses the pronoun *Ich* as a *name*.[36] This, I believe, is most significant. Perhaps Jelinek chose to rename *Ich* "the *Woman*" (*die Frau*) in the screenplay in order to render more overt the political and social dimension of the character. Whatever her reasons, her choice may, in fact, have had a deleterious effect, causing Schroeter to misunderstand Jelinek's interpretation of the female character. By not keeping *Ich* as the woman's name in her screenplay, a vital part of the authorial "reading lesson" is effaced.[37]

In our notes about *Ich's* thoughts and actions, we are obliged to disregard the grammatical rule of subject-verb agreement. Relating anything whatsoever about the character named *Ich*, we use a third person pronoun ("I smokes;" "I writes letters;" "I is lost in her Ungargassenland;" "I loves Ivan" etc.). This practice upsets the ontological status of the subject. Cause and effect are put into question. Resembling a Brechtian alienation effect, *Ich* may be said to stand as a *Verfremdungseffekt* that prevents facile identification of the reader with the protagonist. As I have stated elsewhere, "[t]he semiotic ruptures that are created by the subject-verb disagreement disrupt our notions of the unified speaking subject, alienating us from Malina's (and our own) desire for symbolic control and providing us with an opportunity to expand our understanding of the nature of our own linguistic exile."[38]

Since, in the film, Malina is no longer an abstract notion of the struggle in language but a visible, masculine body, the split character can no longer function as a political indictment but results, as I have discussed, in a stereotypical image of "the hysterical woman." It appears, then, that Schroeter's attempt to solve the problem of a speaking subject in process, on trial (Kristeva), of a *self without guarantee* (Bachmann's *Ich ohne Gewähr*),[39] resulted in a representation of female pathology, and the novel's *Ich* is engendered as a voluntary victim of patriarchal machinations in the film. In the novel, both the historical and psycholinguistic—or, to speak in Kristeva's language—the intra- and translinguistic relations, are performed brilliantly by the character named *Ich*.

Perhaps there is no completely satisfying solution for a cinematographer who is caught up in the symbolic. Cinema demands spectacle. In the economy of *Schaulust* (scopophilia), the woman's alter ego cannot be represented as an absence. What remains is the heavy-handed *manner* in which *Ich*/Malina was framed (in both senses of the word)—seven hundred and fifty seven times. Is this what the viewer has learned about the ways the feminine is en-gendered in the symbolic? *Ich* called it Murder.

NOTES

1. I presented earlier versions of this essay at the Ingeborg Bachmann Symposium, "If We Had the Word," in October 1996 at State University of New York, Binghamton, and at "Austrian Writers Confront the Past, 1945-2000," a conference held at the University of Pennsylvania, Philadelphia, PA, April 12-14, 2002. I am indebted to a number of generous colleagues for their careful reading of earlier versions of this article. Many thanks to Gisela Brinker-Gabler, Mary Webster, and Markus Zisselsberger, and I thank Chantal Rodais especially for her insightful suggestions relating to Lacan's work.

2. For example, see Karsten Witte, "Ein gnadenloses Märchen. Schroeter's Film *Malina* nach Ingeborg Bachmann's Roman," *Frankfurter Rundschau*, 17 January 1991, 8; Dorothee Römhild, "Von kritischer Selbstreflexion zur stereotypischen Frauendarstellung: Ingeborg Bachmann's Roman *Malina* und seine filmische Rezeption," *The Germanic Review* 68, no. 4 (1993): 167-75; Alice Schwarzer, "Die Hölle ist die Hölle," *Die Zeit*, 18 January 1991, 42.

3. The term comes from the title of Ute Seiderer's excellent study, *Film als Psychogramm. Bewußtseinsräume und Vorstellungsbilder in Werner Schroeters "Malina"* (München: diskurs film Verlag, 1994). It should be noted that Seiderer does not use the term critically.

4. Like many, I am critical of the film's concretization of the novel's metaphors of fire that culminates in a veritable firework toward the end of the film, casting the woman, as many reviewers have complained, into a pyromaniac. Regrettably, Schroeter's fireworks are not simply a question of aesthetics. They are predicated on reading the novel's protagonist as Ingeborg Bachmann's self-portrait. As if anticipating such interpretive nonsense, Heinrich Böll had already sounded a warning after Bachmann's death in 1973: "Ingeborg Bachmann, who had gone to sleep with a burning cigarette. Those of us, who have known her, know that this was not happenstance or a simple misbehavior, and yet, [we also know] that it should not be set up as an image and most of all that it may not be symbolically linked to her life and *oeuvre* . . . I think of her as a girl (Ich denke an sie wie an ein Mädchen)." *Der Spiegel* 27, no. 43 (1973): 206.

5. Elfriede Jelinek, *Isabelle Huppert in* Malina: *Ein Filmbuch*

(Frankfurt am Main: Suhrkamp, 1991).

6. Ingeborg Gleichauf, *Mord ist keine Kunst* (Hamburg: Verlag Dr. Kovac, 1995). Regrettably, the work is unavailable; I gather from the abstract that Gleichauf faults Jelinek's screenplay for a reductive reading of Bachmann's novel, and sees Jelinek as responsible for "an exaggeration of a perspective" that ignores "the conflict between the sexes." Gleichauf praises Schroeter's film adaptation as returning the novel's polyvalence. wysiwyg://16/http://www.verlagdrkovac.de/3-86064-263-4.htm.

7. Even a cursory glance at the film's production history goes some way toward explaining how this could have happened. Jelinek created a first version of the screenplay in summer 1989. It was published two years later by Suhrkamp, along with stills from the film. In May 1990, the raw version of the screenplay was used to create a German-French working cut. The film was then shot in French, and, after the editing process, synchronized back into German. Ute Seiderer writes: "During the resynchronization of the film from French into German some words and syntax had to be changed; special problems of synchronization . . . made this necessary . . . one must assume that changes in dialogues and cuts and so on were intended by the director" (15-18).

8. Bethman also relates that "[Jelinek] had tried to write the script the way she thought Bachmann would have written it now, after twenty years of feminism." See, "My Characters Live Only Insofar as They Speak": Interview with Elfriede Jelinek," in *Women in German Yearbook* 17, ed. Patricia Herminghouse and Susanne Zantop (Lincoln: University of Nebraska Press, 2000), 73-74.

9. Jelinek, *Ein Filmbuch*, 75.

10. Schroeter began his career as the director of a series of experimental shorts in 8mm that celebrate Maria Callas. His experimental film, *Eika Katapa* (1969)—a depiction of 19th century opera scenes—gave him an international following. He followed this film with *Regno di Napoli* (*Kingdom of Naples*, 1978), and *The Death of Maria Malibran* (*Der Tod der Maria Malibran*), an experimental portrait of the 19th century opera singer. In 1980, his three-hour epic, *Palermo or Wolfsburg* won the Golden Bear at the Berlinale. More recently, Schroeter made a film about Marianne Hoppe (*Die Königin—The Queen*—1999), and yet another film with Isabelle

Huppert in which opera figures prominently, *Deux* (*Two*, 2003).

11. For a detailed discussion of Schroeter's aesthetic, see Ulrike Sieglohr's fine essay, "Why drag the Diva into it? Werner Schroeter's Gay Representation of Femininity," in *Triangulated Visions: Women in Recent German Cinema*, ed. Ingeborg Majer O'Sickey and Ingeborg von Zadow (Albany: State University of New York Press, 1998), 163-172.

12. See especially, Elfriede Jelinek, "Was geschah nachdem Nora ihren Mann verlassen hatte" ("What happended after Nora left her husband") and "Clara S., musikalische Tragödie" ("Clara S., a musical tragedy"), *Theaterstücke* (Reinbek bei Hamburg: Rowohlt, 1992), where femininity is represented as artifice produced by culture.

13. Anke Roeder, "Überschreitungen, Ein Gespräch mit Elfriede Jelinek"(1996). http://ourworld.compuserve.com/homepages/elfriede/INTERVW.HTM.

14. Werner Schroeter, quoted in Seiderer, fn. 49, 24.

15. Sieglohr, 165-166.

16. Sollers, quoted by Julia Kristeva, "Ellipsis on Dread and the Specular Seduction," *Narrative, Apparatus, Ideology*, ed. Phillip Rosen (New York: Columbia University Press, 1986), 237.

17. Emile Benveniste, *Problems in General Linguistics*, trans. Mary Elizabeth Meek (Coral Gables, FL: Miami University Press, 1971), 224.

18. The other two texts in the trilogy, *Der Fall Franza* (*The Book of Franza*) and *Requiem for Fanny Goldmann*, are fragments.

19. Ingeborg Bachmann, "Malina," *Werke*, 4 vols., ed. Christine Koschel, Inge von Weidenbaum and Clemens Münster (München: Piper, 1978), 3:288, my translation. Philip Boehm's translation of "Todesraten" as "Death Stales" does not capture the sense of "installments" (Ingeborg Bachmann, *Malina*, trans. Philip Boehm [New York: Holmes & Meier, 1990], 190. Hereafter cited as *Malina*).

20. Ingeborg Bachmann, *Werke*, 3:276/*Malina*, 182.

21. Bachmann, *Werke* 3:235 /*Malina*, 154.

22. See also Ingeborg Bachmann, *Wir müssen wahre Sätze finden. Gespräche und Interviews*, ed. Christine Koschel and Inge von Weidenbaum (München: Piper, 1983). Here, Bachmann makes the

historical connection explicit: "Fascism doesn't begin with the terrorism about which one can read in every newspaper. It begins in the relationship between one man and one woman. Fascism is the first thing in the relationship between one man and one woman and I have tried to say in this chapter [in *Malina*] that in this society there is always war" (144).

23. According to Jacques Lacan, the mirror stage is that period in an individual's life (between six and eighteen months) when he/she has stopped to think of him-/herself as coextensive with the world. This self-recognition-misrecognition is the fiction upon which the ego is founded. Cf. Jacques Lacan, "The Mirror Stage as Formative of the Function of the I as Revealed in Psychoanalytic Experience," *Écrits: A Selection*, trans. Alan Sheridan (New York: Norton, 1971), 1-7.

24. Lacan, *Écrits*, 2.

25. Benveniste, 224.

26. Julia Kristeva, "Revolution in Poetic Language," *The Kristeva Reader*, ed. Toril Moi (New York: Columbia University Press, 1986), 91-92 (Kristeva's emphasis).

27. Kristeva, "Revolution in Poetic Language," 125-126.

28. Mathematics for instance is nearly all genotext, while some music is pure phenotext.

29. Kristeva, "Revolution in Poetic Language," 92ff.

30. Bachmann, *Malina*, 5.

31. The penultimate sentences in the novel are spoken by Malina. He reports to the person who telephoned that the address and phone number are correct, but that there is "no woman," and ends the conversation with "My name? Malina." In the film, Malina simply stops with "My name?" and hangs up.

32. For Jane Marcus' remarks, see Ingeborg Majer O'Sickey, "Mystery Stories: The Speaking Subject in Exile," *Women's Writing in Exile*, ed. Mary Lynn Broe and Angela Ingram (Chapel Hill: University of North Carolina Press, 1989), 388 and fn. 25, pg. 392.

33. Laura Mulvey, "Visual Pleasure and Narrative Cinema," *Narrative, Apparatus, Ideology*, ed. Philip Rosen (New York: Columbia University Press, 1986), 198-209.

34. Seiderer, 101.

35. Sieglohr, 164.

36. *Werke* 3:11-12 / *Malina*, 1-2.

37. For a detailed description of this "reading lesson," see Ingeborg Majer O'Sickey, "Rereading Ingeborg Bachmann's *Malina*: Toward a Transformative Feminist Reading Praxis," *Modern Austrian Literature* 28, no. 1 (1995): 55-73.

38. Ingeborg Majer O'Sickey, "Mystery Stories: The Speaking Subject in Exile," 387-388.

39. Ingeborg Bachmann, "Das schreibende Ich" ("The Writing Self"), *Frankfurter Vorlesungen*, *Werke*, 4:218.

9 / Living and Lost in Language: Translation and Interpretation in Ingeborg Bachmann's "Simultan"

Gisela Brinker-Gabler

> In what language am I, suis-je, bin ich, when I am inmost?
> —Georg Steiner, *After Babel: Aspects of Language and Translation* (1975)
>
> The answer to the question "*What* does language communicate" is therefore "All language communicates itself."
> —Walter Benjamin, "On Language as Such and on the Language of Man" (1955)
>
> Ask not: "What goes on in us when we are certain that..."—but: How is the 'certainty that this is the case' manifested in human action."
> —Ludwig Wittgenstein, *Philosophical Investigations* (1953)

Writing in the M/other Tongue

After having settled permanently in Rome, Italy, later in life Ingeborg Bachmann was often asked why she lived in Rome and not in her home country, Austria. In 1953 she had left Vienna, and had not returned to Austria for good. In a statement that was broadcasted by the ORF in 1969, she explained: "But I am [more] in Vienna, when I am in Rome, because without this distance I could not imagine it [Vienna] for my work."[1] For an author, to live in a country whose language is different from the language in which she creates her work, can be a difficult experience. In Bachmann's case things were even more complicated, for her mother tongue, Austrian-German, is already an "other" tongue that links her, the Austrian writer, to an "other" culture, nation, and location: Germany. In an interview of 1965 she remarked: "For myself I have experienced the difficulty for a long time in the fact that I write in German, and that I am then put into a relationship with Germany only because of this language."² The Austrian Bachmann recognizes a relation to Germany due to the German language but also an estrangement based on her different "wealth of experience, wealth of feeling from another area."³ The "other area" for her is not so much a geographical category. In an early interview of 1955, in which she emphasized as most important for a writer the "effort with language" ("Bemühung um die Sprache"), she remarks:

> Austrians have participated in so many cultures and developed a different feeling of the world than the Germans. Their sublime serenity comes from there; but also their sadness and some uncanny traits—which sometimes appear reasonable, sometimes insane, and are due to tragic experiences.⁴

This particularity does not create for her, however, the option of a regional literature. The contemporary Austrian writer, according to Bachmann, will be positioned in the Austrian tradition, which is very European, but "for him there will be only German literature."⁵

As a resident of Rome, Bachmann lived in distance and in touch with her m/other tongue. Her everyday language was Italian; German continued to be her language as a writer, a "strenuous and schizophrenic way to live,"⁶ she acknowledged in 1969. In fact she lived in a threefold *in-between*, the interstice of Austrian-German, her native tongue or *accent*, as I may call it, and German as well as Italian. In an interview of 1972 with the German writer Barbara Bronnen, Bachmann clarified that Italy for her was not an exile: "I was born at the Italian border. To be integrated: that depends on language and whether one is accepted."⁷ Although not truly alienated by language, and therefore not living in exile, it seems to be appropriate to look at Bachmann as an expatriate, someone who had to leave her country in order to live, and to create her *work in progress* on Austrian post-World War II culture and history.

In her story "Simultan," which is the subject of this essay, the protagonist Nadja, an interpreter born in Vienna, left her home country to live in Rome. I did not mention Bachmann's own situation in the beginning of this essay in order to pursue biographical similarities, but to sketch out some problems with mother and other tongues that affect multilingual subjects and that also are relevant to this story. My reading is focused on the question of language in the many facets that are offered and intertwined in this story, intersecting in creative and sociopolitical forms: the creation of multilingual spaces by global expansion, and geographical mobility, and its effect on multilingual subjects, the deterioration of language as communication, the loss of one's mother tongue, language as sacrifice or relation, and the possibility of a "universal" or an utopian language.

The Flexible Wo/man

Living and working in an international, multilingual environment characterizes the life of Nadja, the protagonist in "Simultan," the titular story of Bachmann's collection of stories published in 1972. Flexible and mobile, exciting and international, her life style presents itself as highly attractive, negating an existence constrained by *one* place, by family, and social responsibilities or the agony of the everyday with the absence of imagination and adventure. In his book, *The Corrosion of Character*, Richard Sennett describes flexibility as the central category of the New Capitalism that shapes Western society based on the dramatic change of temporality, characterized by ever increasing fast-paced innovations and changes in the market place.[8] As a lifestyle by choice, flexibility exposes dynamism as the self-indulgence of "postmodern" man. As Jost Schneider points out, Nadja can be understood as a "prototype of the 'flexible' man" described by Sennett.[9] She embodies change, dynamism, easy adjustment, and youthfulness. But there is also hard work to perform under tremendous time pressure, forced performance that continues into her private life, and produces an everyday masquerade. The problematic of flexibility, described convincingly by Sennett, presents itself not only in the first story of Bachmann's collection; it is also present in the final story with its female protagonist Elisabeth Matrei, a famous international photographer from Vienna, who lives in Paris. Contrasting figures to Nadja and Elisabeth—two women and two stories with manifold connections—are the protagonists of two additional *Simultan* stories, Beatrix and Miranda. Both still live in their hometown of Vienna. They resist mobility as well as their everyday world that seems to be inadequate for them, without being able, however, to bring about a change in their lives.

All stories of the collection have in common that they do not give easy answers by simply presenting the dark side of flexibility and the New Capitalism or sham existence. In other words, they do not allow an ideology critique that, from an outside perspective, uncovers the deception behind an illusionary world and life style. In the case of flexibility, for example, the ugly side could be described as the destruction of security, of relation and solidarity, the pressure of tempo and assimilation, the loss of choice and lasting values. Clearly, there is recognition of the price of flexibility in the stories of Nadja and Elisabeth. More important, however, is a noticeable ambivalence in Bachmann's storytelling that does not erase or neutralize subjective and objective realities, does not resolve in sober dialectics or playful deference of possibilities.

Living in Transit

Nadja, who left Vienna at the age of nineteen, holds several diplomas, and enjoys a free and independent life style, just as she had always wanted. She appears confident and self-assured, a radically individualized subject who believes to be autonomous and free: "She would never have tolerated staying at home, not with her independent spirit, it's an incredibly demanding job, but I enjoy it nevertheless, no, marry? never, she certainly would never marry."[10]

Ludwig Frankel, whom Nadja meets in Rome at a conference, was also born in Vienna. Like her he enjoys a cosmopolitan life style. Having emigrated as a boy, he now works with the F.A.O. (Food and Agriculture Organization), and has traveled widely. Frankel cannot imagine returning to Vienna although his wife and children still live there. With his children he spends a few weeks of vacation every year.

Nadja and Frankel embark on a journey to the Italian coast, a vacation trip, an escape from their daily routine, and a romantic adventure. For both of them the journey will become a journey within, confronting them with their past, hi/stories that remain unsaid, questions that were not asked. The word "simultan" or "simultaneous" unfolds here in yet another aspect, a compulsive retrospection that according to André Acimen is for exiles almost a "matter of instinct":

> With their memories perpetually on overload, exiles see one place but they're also seeing—or looking for—another behind it. Everything bears two faces, everything is shifty because everything is mobile, the point being that exile, like love, is not just a condition of pain, it's a condition of deceit.[11]

Nadja and Frankel are involved in a simultaneous game, mixed up with other partners and relationships that intrude silently, confusing their encounter with each other and their self-definition. Nadja remembers Jean Pierre, her French lover, who had tried to force her into an "alien life," to marry her, live with her in a small apartment with lots of children. It was "natural for him to hit her occasionally" (*TPL*, 22). Frankel reflects on his family situation in Vienna, job frustrations, and later becomes obsessed with the Cernia, a beautiful seawater fish that escapes his harpoon. Their romantic adventure will turn into a dangerous journey that will bring forth Nadja's incoherence and distress, and confront her with a traumatic experience. Frankel, who, when meeting Nadja, had felt a spontaneous happiness, will realize that in fact happiness had left his life for good. Devoted to his career under daily pressure, he has lost all his energy, "gone the joy, forever" (*TPL*, 15).

The Multilingual Life

The story "Simultan" unfolds as textual web of several languages. The main language, German, is often interrupted by words, phrases or complete sentences of other languages, everyday phrases in ordinary speech. As the text changes from one language to the other, it also shifts from indirect to direct speech, from interior monologue to narrated monologue (*erlebte Rede*), third person, and authorial narration, which gives the text an oral or conversational quality. The presence of various languages in the verbal fabric of the story as well as the various modes of narration and perspectives create a kind of hybrid text. Textual hybridism in the story is linked to the reality of its protagonists, in particular Nadja, who constantly changes places and languages. This is her job and also affects her private life. There is no clean-cut line between work and "life," between one language and the others. Therefore, the mixture of languages and conversational styles serves a purpose of literary realism. But there seems to be more at stake in those shifts in languages and perspectives. Safeguarding the text as an unattainable point of arrival, they allow a problematic of language to emerge throughout the story in many facets.

According to the flow of language, the story is divided into two parts. In the first part, everything that is said in English, French, and German or otherwise produces "surface noise" (*TPL*, ix), as Mark Anderson calls it in his introduction to *Three Paths to the Lake*, a mixture of platitudes and phrases, mostly small talk characteristic of the international conference and business world. Clearly there is a "bond" between Nadja and Frankel, the small talk of the flexible wo/man that serves at the same time as a guard. They are careful not to reveal too much about themselves, and to exchange only some details of their nomadic lives. Their trip up to the cliffs of Maratea turns for Nadja into a climactic event confronting her with the abyss of language, and revealing her multifaceted "destruction." In the second part of the story the superficiality of language is replaced with a search for dialogue, a meaningful relation to life and language.

Nadja has lived flexibility to an extreme, constantly traveling into other countries and languages as an interpreter. Such multilingualism can be a liberating, joyful experience. It allows her to indulge in cosmopolitanism (another form of elitism): to demonstrate one's right to stay, wherever one chooses, to know how to complain, to demand the ultimate in service, to pretend indifference. Traveling into other languages also permits an escape from the mother tongue, that is, a getaway from limitations, censorship, discipline, the "law of the father." It offers most of all the possibility of a separation from both the individual and the collective past.

But there is also a problematic side to linguistic nomadism. Moving constantly from one place and one language into others produces spatial and linguistic fragmentation. Where does one belong? But does "belonging" matter? Who is the "I" who speaks, like Nadja, English, French, German, Italian, Russian, or Slovenian? Who is the "I," constantly uprooted? Is there an "I" at all? Elisabeth in the final story of *Three Paths to the Lake*, meets in Josef Trotta, an exile from

Austria, the diasporic subject in the state of disintegration, whose "languages had also made him go to pieces" (*TPL,* 178).

Returning into the Mother Tongue

Since she left Vienna, Nadja has not spoken German. She has exiled herself from this language, and uses it only when necessary for the purpose of translation. Rejecting contact with the mother tongue cuts off the past, and might be a life-saving strategy, if there is some profoundly detested experience. On the other hand, not to live in the mother tongue constitutes a specific loss, as Julia Kristeva suggests in *Strangers to Ourselves:* "Not speaking one's mother tongue. Living with resonances and reasoning that are cut off from the body's nocturnal memory, from the bittersweet slumber of childhood."[12] To cut off the mother tongue cuts off one's childhood, and whatever past there was in that language.

It is by and through her encounter with Frankel that Nadja, with ironic and nostalgic undertones, reflects on the loss she may have suffered through her separation from her own language world, "a missing taste, an intonation gone flat, that ghostly feeling of home, though she was no longer at home anywhere" (*TPL,* 2). At first she believes that nothing is easier than being together with someone from the same country, same language, same mode of speaking, "Austrian *parlando,*" as Jean Améry called it, someone knowing what can be said and where the limits are. On the other hand, sameness might be more threatening than difference, might even prohibit communication. Nadja wonders, "how much they really had to say to one another, given that they had only this city in common and a similar way of talking, the same intonation" (*TPL,* 2). As always, there is ambivalence present. She is "constantly changing" (*TPL,* 25), Frankel observes.

Nadja begins to accepts Frankel's caring attitude, who sometimes treats her like a child that needs loving care, for example, when drying her with a towel after her shower, holding her tight at night to help her fall asleep. This is all the more surprising since she has an anxiety to be at someone's mercy and made it clear from the start that she wanted to sleep in her own room. As the story moves on, Nadja realizes herself that with the return of her mother tongue, something is changing, that a new light has been cast on her life: "It [the answer, GBG] finally came to her because she had not been searching in French but in her own language and because she was able to talk to a man who gave language back to her" (*TPL*, 7). She tells Frankel honestly about the pressures of her job, and her deep-seated rejection of the conference life. As an interpreter she is under constant stress to "master" languages as codes in order to allow for code switching within seconds. She describes her work in the translator booth, two in a booth to allow a quick switch after twenty minutes. She thinks of herself as a "strange mechanism" (*TPL*, 13), automatically reproducing words and sentences. She has become a word-machine. Immersed in other voices, she herself is living and lost "in translation." Not in control of but controlled by the languages, she faithfully reproduces and lives in fear to get buried under the masses of words.

The story offers precise criticism of the international conference world. Nadja has become quite cynical about its language games, and the male dominated working environment. Quite disturbing is a particular pattern of procedure that has become visible to her:

> [E]ach conference seems to be just another sequel in an infinite indagine...they're always searching for the reason for something that happened long ago, for something terrible, and they can't get through because it so happens that the same path has been trampled by so many, because others have intentionally covered their tracks, because everyone tells only half-truths to protect themselves and then you sift through mountains of inconsistencies and misconceptions, and you find nothing, you'd have to have a revelation to grasp what was going on. (*TPL*, 25)

Ironically, Nadja's typical outline of the conferences that are her daily life will become the blueprint of her own journey back deep into language beyond its surface noise. Searching "for the reason for something that happened long ago," she needs a "revelation," or, to use Walter Benjamin's term, an "illumination" ("Erleuchtung").

By supreme effort Nadja fulfills her interpreter's tasks in the realm of artificial international languages. What happens, if one becomes multilingual like Nadja? How does one's world open up with the pluralization of language? Does it open up at all? Does one live on the borders, or to use Anzaldua's term, in a borderland between various languages, places and histories?[13]

At the beginning of the story, Nadja seems to have accepted her linguistic schizophrenia. It allowed her to escape from her mother tongue with all the restrictions it carried in respect to her past and her self, and to explore her own "others," her multiple subjectivities. She does not, however, really live in the various language worlds, but in the space between them. For Nadja this interstice is a space of containment, a void, a vacuum from which no voice can emerge or no question can be asked. Immersed in functionalized code switching, Nadja has become "language-less," on a continuous journey without taking roots, without "halt." Finally, her adventurous passage into the mother tongue will confront her with something from which she had turned away because it is painful and an accusation.

The Ineffable

The trip to the Italian coast seems to be risky for Nadja right from the beginning. Departing from Rome, she leaves behind what she considers her real identity, her cosmopolitan "self." She keeps tightening her sandal straps, treading on ever more dangerous ground. To compensate for her insecurity and dependency on Frankel, she attempts to demonstrate her brilliant sense of orientation. But her sense of orientation will fail her, too. They cannot find the hotel where she had been before. They get lost. There is no map with directions into the past.

Later, Nadja's journey with Frankel becomes more dangerous. The trip "home" into the mother tongue will bring about an encounter with the uncanny, the "unhomely" ("Unheimliche"). Frankel takes her up to the cliffs at Maratea in his car on a steep road, with one bridge after another. On the last part of the trip, a stony path to the top, Nadja, with her slippery sandals, without a *halt* so to speak, is confronted all of the sudden with "a colossal figure of stone wrapped in a long stone cape, its arm outspread. Her tongue was tied" (*TPL*, 28). What she first sees from behind turns out to be the Christ of Maratea she had seen earlier on a postcard in the hotel. Already before the disturbing encounter, riding in the car with Frankel on the steep road, "at his mercy" (*TPL*, 28), a numbness had started to take hold of her, beginning in her hands, and a feeling of emptiness had begun to fill her: "it could have been the onset of speechlessness, or it was something establishing its presence within her, a fatal disease" (*TPL*, 28). The trip up to the cliff brings to mind Bachmann's radio play *The Good God of Manhattan*. The female figure, Jennifer, struck by a disease called love, relocates with Jan from one floor of the hotel to the next, higher and higher, up to the top, where she will be murdered by the good God, the keeper of the (phallologocentric) world order, the representative of the Father-Law. In *Malina* the I-figure speaks about a disease, a virus, that wherever it strikes makes the world a dangerous place. This disease, as Barbara Agnese convincingly points out, is present right at the beginning of the novel *Malina*; it is "the abstraction, the false integrity, in which a person lives, who already was destroyed and does not want to acknowledge her destruction, cannot understand it yet."[14] Nadja's confrontation with the gigantic figure that looms against the background of the sky, leads her to the recognition of destruction. The shock of point zero—the damning presence of the "insane colossus," and with it "all heavy laden stories of all those weary times" (*TPL*, 29)—is the impossibility of language. In Bachmann's work this always is the moment of the greatest danger, but also the moment indispensable to a revelation.

Nadja's illusionary integrity, hinted at metaphorically with the image of the slippery sandals, is falling apart, facing her with "annihilation," and her realization that she has lost the ability to cry (*TPL*, 29). Speechless and tearless she identifies with utmost suffering. She becomes the crucified: "She slid slowly off the stone and lay down on the ground with her arms outspread, crucified on this menacing cliff" (*TPL*, 29). Frankel, who in the meantime went up right to the top of the cliff, had an exciting experience. He had seen the "entire gulf." "It had been like nothing he'd ever seen before." (*TPL*, 32) After all, menacing or exciting, there are two ways of experiencing the top of the cliff. How to connect those two experiences, how to weave languages and histories together? Is there a new narrative possible?

The Limits of Language

Although Frankel and Nadja share the mother tongue, a linguistic and cultural identity, at the beginning they keep playing the language-games of their everyday professional world. Bachmann's novel *Malina* comes to mind again, in particular, the failure of language between Ivan and the I-figure, and the inability of the I-figure to ask Ivan a single question about anything that is important to her.[15] Frankel has no question for Nadja, although several times she mentions that she had been through bad times: "all he knew about her was something about a shock, and that she'd often had a tough time of it, but who cares" (*TPL*, 12). Nadja, however, will ask a question that definitely matters to her. Significantly, this happens *after* the trip to the cliffs, and the moment when a past returns to encumber the present. She wondered, "whether he was thinking of someone else and if his train of thought led to a multitude of faces, bodies, the broken and battered, the murdered, the said and the unsaid" (*TPL*, 31). Looking at him with "real longing" and with a sense of great urgency, she asks him what he is thinking, a serious attempt of connection with him. A moment of intimacy emerges in a specific Viennese scenario reminiscent for example of Schnitzler's episodes, which always carry the hint of deepest sadness and melancholy in the face of the impossibility of relation. The subject is split and traumatized precisely by this question, which asks about the role it is playing in the desire of the other. The very moment Nadja asks this question, she imagines Frankel to be her former lover, whom she never dared to ask, and, who had hit her occasionally. Frankel, hesitating at first, tells her again about the beautiful seawater fish, the Cernia, a name that alludes to the female "other." The Cernia fish has become his absolute object (of desire), and precisely for that reason he has to sacrifice it. He keeps hunting it, and almost caught it by shooting a harpoon into its neck. His words show an immediate effect on Nadja: she feels hit right there. A dead set of sexual relationships reemerges, indicative of a society imbued with systematic violence: one is the perpetrator or the victim. After the trip to Maratea, which radically put Nadja's existence into question, a process of awakening unfolds that brings forth recognition and traumatized truth.

The Foreignness of Language

The story becomes more cryptic toward the end. The episodes unfolding on the final pages evoke even more than before the artistic form of an assemblage, which can be read from more than one perspective or unlocked with a changing key without any closure.[16] The final pages present three successive moments or three parts of one moment of awakening. The story does not offer or promise an interpretation of these scenes, as they desire a "relation" provided by the reader.

The last day of their vacation Nadja spends at the shore, climbing up the rocks, close to crying, later jumping where she can, risking to fall every moment. Finally, she embraces life with a new perspective: life has to be lived, although a moment later she corrects herself: life has to be accepted as a gift, "I don't have to live at all, I can" (TPL, 33). A transition has taken place: from the fall into silence to the miracle of existence. When Nadja looks toward the horizon, however, a deferral seems to happen. Up on the cliff of Maratea she sees a small figure with extended arms, "not nailed to the cross, but preparing for a grandiose flight, poised for flight or a plunge into the depths" (TPL, 33). In her illuminating reading of Bachmann's poem "Borrowed Time," Sabine Gölz points out: "What 'comes into view on the horizon' is the inevitably restricted economy of any one interpretive framework, however complex, and however eager to dissimulate its limits."[17] The miracle of existence experienced at the beginning of the episode turns into the alternative of flight or fall. How will the limits of the either/or be overcome?

In the final scene of the story, in the hotel lobby, Nadja listens to the screaming voice of a TV commentator of a bicycle race. She hears his inarticulate cry when the victor crosses the finish line, and the roar from the roadside crowd turns into the staccato cries of the victor's name that is spread twice across the page (TPL, 36):

A
     dor
          ni
A
     dor
          ni

Like opening one window after the other on a computer screen, the scene brings forth many images, and links many threads of the story. An important autobiographical statement by Bachmann comes to mind. In an interview she once explained how the marching in of Hitler's troops into Austria destroyed her childhood. For the first time she had felt the fear of death, face to face with "hateful staccato," with "monstrous brutality, shouting, singing and marching."[18] The theme of modern flexibility, of tempo, fragmentation, and distorted language presents itself again. It is sports specifically that serves as the dressage and conditioning of body and mind of the flexible man. In addition, the scene offers to Nadja, the interpreter, a double identification, blurring the subject/object boundaries. The broadcaster appears as a kind of simultaneous interpreter, talking faster and faster, correcting himself, getting lost. The young man behind the bar, "staring at the screen in a trance," (*TPL*, 35), also recalls the interpreter Nadja, who is "immersed in the sentences of others, like a sleepwalker" (*TPL*, 8). "She listened with horror and relief and, in these staccato cries, heard all the staccato cries from all the cities and countries she had ever been to. Hate in staccato, joy in staccato" (*TPL*, 35). An overriding of alternatives happens in this very moment: there can be hate *and* joy in staccato language, and she is able to listen with horror *and* relief. Instead of an either/or there is a both/and, a new possibility, that is the friction of the simultaneous presence of both. The space of language has opened up for her, and it is her space and her existence. In this space *all* staccato cries resonate, without bringing forth her "anxiety of destruction" ("Vernichtungsangst"), embedded in the past, and relived at the cliff of Maratea. She smiles at Frankel when he turns toward her, and takes his hand.

Does the story end on a hopeful note, as a calm and smiling Nadja at the very end suggests? But how, then, should we read the third moment in this final sequence of images of almost cinematic quality? Actually, I am referring to the second moment between the two scenes I discussed above, a scene that seems to suggest the failure of Nadja, the translator.

After returning from the shore on this last day of vacation, Nadja tries to translate a sentence from the Bible, just like she often took up dictionaries "to search superstitiously for a word to help her through the day" *(TPL, 34)*. The single sentence chosen at random resists her translation:

> Il miracolo, come sempre, è il risultato della fede e d'una fede audace...
> She couldn't have translated the sentence into any other language, although, she was convinced that she knew what each of the words meant and their usage, but she didn't know what this sentence was really made of. She just couldn't do everything." *(TPL, 34)*

In this moment Nadja finally cries. What now permits her to cry is: her surrender.

The Task of the Translator

Reading the final scenes simultaneously with Benjamin's seminal essay "The Task of the Translator,"[19] allows an interpretation of her surrender not as a failure but an illumination. In the English translation of the title of Benjamin's essay, "task" stands for *Aufgabe*, which in German has the double meaning of "task" *and* "surrender," and in an illuminating fashion brings forth Benjamin's translation theory. At the end of his essay Benjamin turns to Hölderlin's translation, for him the most perfect to find, and then, in the closing paragraph, to the Bible:

> Hölderlin's translations in particular are subject to the enormous danger inherent in all translations: the gates of a language thus expanded and modified may slam shut and enclose the translator in silence. Hölderlin's translations from Sophocles were his last work; *in them meaning plunges from abyss to abyss until it threatens to become lost in the bottomless depths of lan-*

guage. [My emphasis, GBG] There is however, a stop. It is vouchsafed in Holy Writ alone, in which meaning has ceased to be the watershed for the flow of language and the flow of revelation. Where the literal quality of the text takes part directly, without any mediating sense, in true language, in the Truth, or in doctrine, this text is unconditionally translatable.[20]

Hölderlin in his translation shows a heroic attempt towards language that is extended and controlled to an extreme. Such a translation carries with it the continuous danger of flight or fall that compares to Nadja's imagined alternative, "poised for flight or a plunge into the depths" (*TPL*, 33). In contrast to such a totalizing move towards language Nadja will accept a more limited approach. When returning to the beach on the last day, she at first is not just climbing the rocks, but jumps from one to the other, becoming more and more reckless, risking falling. Finally, however, she will take a look back: "it is the sea, not the whole sea, of course, not the whole coast, not the whole gulf…" (*TPL*, 33).

Benjamin suggests in his essay that in the dangerous flow of language, with meaning plunging from abyss to abyss, the only text that provides a halt is Holy Writ. This is so, because there, meaning no longer separates language and revelation, and word-by-word transcription promises a "halten," the halt in the loss of meaning. However, in her translation attempt, Nadja will find no halt in Holy Writ. From the *stability of the word since the beginning of time*, the focus shifts to the connection, the desire for the understanding of how a sentence, the *connection of words*, works: "She knew what each of the words meant and their usage, but she didn't know what this sentence was really made of" (*TPL*, 34). Language no longer is just a code that allows easy code switching. After Maratea, the cliff and the abyss, the mechanism of "word by word" will fail. Words have no fixed meaning. They need a *halt* that is revealed not *through* but *in* the medium of language itself as the final scene suggests. The transgressive moment of this scene can be described as an exposure to the echo-space of language and its reverberations. The primary content of language beyond its utilitarian function becomes manifest. Benjamin referred to this content in an early essay "On Language as such and the Language of Man" as language's communication of communicability itself.[21] Nadja, the interpreter, immersed herself in the utilitarian function of language, unable to hear what yearns to be heard. Finally she reaches that stage, which for George Steiner is one dimension of translingual imagination: "The polyglot mind undercuts the lines of division between languages by reaching inward, to the symbiotic core."[22] What emerges in this moment is the translatability of language.

The Return of Language

The encounter with language's communication of itself provides a new possibility of language's reassurance in life at the very end of the story. Wittgenstein's philosophy of language comes to mind, notably the transition from the early to the late Wittgenstein, which Bachmann addresses in her radio essay "Sagbares und Unsagbares—die Philosophie Ludwig Wittgensteins" ["The Speakable and the Unspeakable. Wittgenstein's Philosophy"].[23] The early Wittgenstein, in his *Tractatus logico-philosophicus*, presents the world as a totality of facts that can be described. His philosophy, however, aims at solving the problem of the Unspeakable, the limits of description. The mystical, which manifests itself but cannot be said, is this limit and at the same time the prerequisite of description: that there is a relation between language and reality, the logical form. Later, Wittgenstein turns away from the problem of the Unspeakable, and at the same time from the world as the totality of facts, governed by true propositions. The concept of language as a system based on a model theory of propositions that allows a clear distinction of true and false is replaced in his *Philosophical Investigations* by a concept of language as multiple practices, the language games that are connected only by some "family relationship." The emphasis no longer is on the exception, the mystical. Therefore, totality, which as "the whole" is based on exception, is replaced by the "not whole," "non totality," language as lived practice.

In the final scene, the footstep into reality, the flow of language of the everyday returns. Nadja now responds with a new receptivity. She listens differently, and experiences language in a different way. In the beginning of the story Nadja is deranged by language, a result of her desperate attempt to distance herself from her own language and history. Being in-between languages for her has become a barrier that prevents relations with others. It constructs and produces isolation. Nadja's "illumination" is her insight into the relation of languages and language as relation. Having taken Frankel's hand already, she turns around because "the most important thing having just occurred to her, and she called it out to the boy who had seen Adorni triumph. Auguri!" (*TPL*, 36), which is a congratulation and means "all the best." Reemerging from the fall into silence "a human voice"[24] resounds. A new form of life, the understanding of relation has become manifest in this word of "human action." Wittgenstein writes in the *Philosophical Investigations*: "Ask not: 'What goes on in us when we are certain that…'—but: How is the 'certainty that this is the case' manifested in human action."[25]

Not the Whole Sea…

Nadja, the *interpreter*, and Nadja, the becoming *translator* at the end of the story figure allegorically two different styles of *translation* and two different modes of reading. The first one is a word-by-word interpretation, believing that the whole is created word by word. This style of interpreting is based on the stability of the "original" which can be uncovered and recoded by the practice of interpretation. After the experience of the "foreignness" of language the possibility of *translation* emerges based on the effort with language, which provides precisely the *direction* toward a new language where difference and articulation take place. This brings to mind a passage from Bachmann's "Frankfurt Lectures," which refers to literary works:

> Creations shimmering and with blind spots. Fragments of realized hope for the whole language, the whole expression for the changing human subject and the changing world.[26]

Walter Benjamin introduces in his essay "The Task of the Translator" a translation theory based on a longing for language-supplementation. The natural languages complement one another in their intentions. They all intend one and the same thing, "pure language" or the "greater language." Translation in the Benjaminian sense is a *direction*, a commitment toward building the "greater language" in a continuous process of supplementation. Like Benjamin's language in process of supplementation, Bachmann's utopian language makes all existing languages "foreign," and all writing "broken fragments."

To return once more to the story "Simultan": how is Nadja's transition from interpreter to translator possible? In Nadja lives subliminally the Wittgensteinian "instinctive rebellion" against language to which Barbara Agnese refers:

> People are deeply embedded in philosophical, that is to say grammatical confusion. In order to liberate them, one needs to tear them away from the unbelievable multiplicity of connections in which they are trapped. One must so to speak rearrange their entire language. Yet this language developed in this way because people had an inclination—and still do—to think *like this*. This is why the process of tearing away occurs only to those who live with an instinctive rebellion against language. It does not happen to those who according to their entire instinct live in *the* herd, which has taken this language to be its *actual* form of expression.[27]

For Wittgenstein, "*actual* form of expression" is present in ordinary speech, in the "pre-fabricated" sentences we all use.[28] With its continuous departure from the "*actual* form of expression," Wittgenstein's clarifying work on language also offers a *direction* that will benefit language as practice by and large.

In Nadja an "instinctive rebellion against language" is present all along in the story. And it is part of her translingual imagination that provides her with precision and vigilance for the peculiar. At one point in the story Frankel muses about the possibility of a universal language. He can "easily envisage" (*TPL*, 23) such a language that would provide transparency and communication. Nadja's witty response, however, undermines the universal, or global, with the matchless local: "but how then would you say, 'Würstel mit Kren,' or: 'Sie geschlenkertes Krokodil'?" (*TPL*, 23) It is significant that Nadja here returns to her mother tongue, specifically to this particular cadence in a language that is never quite German but not anything else either.

NOTES

1. "Drei Statements." FS-Sendedatum: 29. Mai 1969. ORF Wien. Aufnahmeort: Rom. Aus einer grösseren Sendung unter dem Titel: Zu Gast bei Ingeborg Bachmann. Ingeborg Bachmann, *Wir müssen wahre Sätze finden. Gespräche und Interviews* (München: Piper, 1983; 1991), 65 (all quotes from this volume are in my translation). Hereafter cited as *GuI*.
2. Josef-Hermann Sauter's Interview (September 15, 1965), *GuI*, 63.
3. Ibid.,
4. Interview (1955), *GuI* , 12.
5. Ibid., 12.
6. "Drei Statements," *GuI*, 65.
7. Barbara Bronnen's Interview (October 7, 1992), *GuI*, 121.
8. Richard Sennett, *The Corrosion of Character: The Personal Consequences of Work in the New Capitalism* (New York: Norton, 1998).
9. Jost Schneider, "*Simultan* und Erzählfragmente aus dem Umfeld," *Bachmann Handbuch. Leben, Werk und Wirkung*, ed. Monika Albrecht and Dirk Göttsche (Stuttgart: J. B. Metzler, 2002), 159-171; 161. See this essay also for an extensive bibliography on the story "Simultan." For a more recent interpretation see Erika Greber, "Simultan," *Werke von Ingeborg Bachmann*, ed. Mathias Mayer (Stuttgart: Reclam, 2002), 176-195.
10. Ingeborg Bachmann, *Three Paths to the Lake*, trans. Mary Fran Gilbert, introduction by Mark Anderson (New York: Holmes & Meyer, 1989), 4. Hereafter cited as TPL. Bachmann published her story collection with the title *Simultan. Erzählungen* (München: Piper, 1972).
11. André Aciman, *Letters of Transit. Reflections On Exile, Identity, Language, and Loss* (New York: W.W. Norton & Comp., 1999), 13.
12. Julia Kristeva, *Strangers To Ourselves*, trans. Leon S. Roudiez (New York: Columbia University Press, 1991), 13.

13. Gloria Anzaldúa, *Borderlands. La Frontera. The New Mestiza* (San Francisco: aunt lute books, 1987).

14. Barbara Agnese, *Der Engel der Literatur. Zum philosophischen Vermächtnis Ingeborg Bachmanns* (Wien: Passagen Verlag, 1996), 134 (my translation).

15. See on the language games in *Malina*, Majorie Perloff, *Wittgenstein's Ladder. Poetic Language and the Strangeness of the Ordinary* (Chicago: The University of Chicago Press, 1996), 145-180.

16. I refer to reading "with a changing key" ("mit wechselndem Schlüssel") in my essay on Nelly Sachs, which explores the multiperspectival layers that constitute "Fremde" in her poetry: *German Quarterly* 65 (Winter 1992), 35-41.

17. Sabine Gölz, *The Split Scene of Reading. Nietzsche/Derrida/Kafka/Bachmann* (Atlantic Highlands, N.J.: Humanities Press, 1998), 202.

18. Gerda Bödefeld's Interview (December 24, 1971), *GuI*, 111.

19. Walter Benjamin, "The Task of the Translator," *Selected Writings, vol. 1, 1913-1926,* ed. Marcus Bullock and Michael W. Jennings (Cambridge, MA: Harvard University Press, 1996), 253-263.

20. Ibid., 262 (my emphasis).

21. Walter Benjamin, "On Language as Such and the Language of Man," *Selected Writings,* ibid., 63.

22. George Steiner, *Extraterritorial: Papers on Literature and the Language Revolution* (New York: Atheneum, 1971), 119.

23. Ingeborg Bachmann, "Sagbares und Unsagbares—die Philosophie Ludwig Wittgensteins," *Werke*, vol. 4, ed. Christine Koschel, Inge von Weidenbaum, and Clemens Münster (München: Piper, 1978), 103-127.

24. Bachmann, "Musik und Dichtung," *Werke*, 4:62 (my translation).

25. Ludwig Wittgenstein, *Philosophical Investigations*, ed. G. E. M. Anscombe and R. Rhees, trans. G. E. M. Anscombe (Oxford: Basil Blackwell, 1953), II, xi, 225.

26. Bachmann, *Werke*, 4:268 (my translation).

27. Agnese, *Der Engel*, 62. See also Agnese's essay in this volume.

28. Bachmann, *GuI*, 84 (Ekkehart Rudolph's Interview, March 23, 1971).

10 / The Woman Who Rode Away: Ingeborg Bachmann and Postcoloniality

Sara Lennox

Towards the beginning of "Three Paths to the Lake," the final story of Ingeborg Bachmann's 1972 collection *Simultan*,[1] Elisabeth Matrei, the story's protagonist, stranded in a London hotel without a ticket for a flight back home to Austria, discovers herself to be surrounded by postcolonial peoples: "Room service consisted of Indians, Filipinos, and Africans, once there had been an old Englishman, and all the guests, too, were from Asia and Africa, she rode in the large elevators in the midst of silent masses, the only white person...." Dismayed that "her old London had disappeared, everything she had once enjoyed," Elisabeth complains that the postcolonials do not even speak English properly: "the guests and employees communicated in an English limited to a handful of expressions, and using one more than the allotted number meant not being understood. It wasn't a living language that was spoken, it was a kind of Esperanto. ...." A well-traveled cosmopolitan, Elisabeth adapts herself to her circumstances: "she quickly forgot her English, using that confounded Esperanto," but she is surprised by her own discomfort in the postcolonial metropolis. "She had never felt apprehension in Asia or Africa and had enjoyed being alone and leaving the others when she traveled with a group, being 'the woman who rode away,' but not here. In this place everything was so monotonous, the people were all completely mindless, nothing was right..." ("Paths," 130, trans. modified).

As the editors of the four-volume *"Todesarten"-Projekt* point out in their commentary to "Three Paths to the Lake," "The Woman Who Rode Away" is the title of a 1925 short story by D. H. Lawrence.[2] Notorious at least since 1970, when Kate Millett denounced its sexism in *Sexual Politics*,[3] Lawrence's story explores the consequences of the decision of a white American woman living in Mexico to leave her European husband and ride away in search of the "secret haunts of [the] timeless, mysterious, marvelous Indians of the mountains" who still maintain "their own savage customs and religion."⁴ "She is weary of the white man's God," she tells the Indians she encounters in the mountains. "She would like to serve the gods of the Chilchui."⁵ As Lawrence presents them, this group of Indians, latter-day descendants of the Aztecs, believe that whites have stolen the Indians' power over their god, the sun, but, as one member of the tribe explains, "when a white woman sacrifices herself to our gods, then our gods will begin to make the world again, and the white man's gods will fall to pieces."⁶ Held captive by the Indians for months, the woman scarcely minds, musing that "Her kind of womanhood, intensely personal and individual, was to be obliterated again, and the great primeval symbols were to tower once again over the fallen individual independence of woman."⁷ The story ends on the day of the winter solstice as the woman, laid naked and spread-eagled upon a sacrificial altar in a deep cave, awaits the moment when the last rays of the setting sun enter the cave and the blind old priest plunges his flint knife into her heart.

Why does Elisabeth Matrei turn to the title of D. H. Lawrence's story to characterize her prior experience in the Third World, and what does Bachmann's allusion to Lawrence's text tell us about race, gender, sexuality, and postcoloniality in her writing? In this paper I want to maintain that, here, as elsewhere in her writing, Bachmann employs a reference to another author's text as an ironic device to establish the larger discursive context within which her character functions and thereby to tell her readers something about the character that the character herself does not know. Though Lawrence's tale of a dissatisfied wife's quests for obliteration might on first examination seem to have little relationship to the self-reflections of Elisabeth, a world-renowned photojournalist, I will argue here that the allusion to Lawrence's story can in fact be used as a kind of key to unlock several levels of meaning in Bachmann's story. I want here first to explore what relevance Lawrence's tale might possess for Bachmann's character, portrayed as utterly the opposite of the figure Lawrence represents, and I will show that Elisabeth, like Lawrence, moves within a discursive universe premised upon the binary opposition between a universalizing Western modernity and an Otherness comprising everything the West is not. I then want to show how Elisabeth's distress about current events and her nostalgic attachment to the old Austro-Hungarian empire rests on another version of that binary paradigm, contrasting Elisabeth's longing for a long-lost Austrian home to the postmodern rootlessness of Franz Joseph Eugen Trotta, a figure in the story, borrowed from Joseph Roth's *Radetzkymarsch* (*The Radetzky March*) and *Kapuzinergruft* (*The Emperor's Tomb*). Finally, I want to investigate what those fatal binaries might reveal about the causes of Elisabeth's personal and sexual malaise, so dire that she declares: "it would be best if women and men kept their distance and had nothing to do with each other until both had found their way out of the tangle and confusion, the discrepancy inherent in all relationships" ("Paths," 175)—a quotation that, as the editors of the *"Todesarten"-Projekt* tell us, is also borrowed from D.H. Lawrence.[8]

In *Primitive Passions: Men, Women, and the Quest for Ecstasy*, Marianna Torgovnick identifies "The Woman Who Rode Away" and Lawrence's other late texts set in Mexico and New Mexico as examples of what she terms primitivism.[9] "The West," she argues, "has been engaged, almost continuously, in defining itself against a series of 'primitive' Others in its midst and without." "The primitive," she continues, "is the sign and symbol of desires the West has sought to repress—desires for direct correspondence between experience and language, direct correspondence between individual feelings and the collective life force. It is the sign and symbol of desire for a full and sated sense of the universe."[10] In an earlier book, *Going Primitive*, Torgovnick connects the primitive to "going home": "The metaphor of finding a home or being at home recurs over and over as a structuring pattern within Western primitivism. . . . Whatever form the primitive's hominess takes, its strangeness salves our estrangement from ourselves and our culture."[11] The primitive, Torgovnick concludes, thus becomes the solution to the "transcendental homelessness" Georg Lukács had considered to be the condition of the modern Western mind.[12]

However, in a postmodern and postcolonial era we now recognize that, though the quest for a return to origins, fullness of being, full presence, and "home" may be a founding myth of Western thought—in Novalis's words, "Philosophy is actually homesickness—the urge to be everywhere at home"[13]—it is also only that, a myth. As Iain Chambers puts it, "We can never go home, return to the primal scene, the forgotten moment of our beginnings, and authenticity, for there is always something else inbetween. We cannot return to a bygone unity, for we can only know the past, memory, the unconscious, through its effects, that is, when it is brought into language...."[14] And, moreover, we now know as well that the belief in such an imaginary unity, whether located in an archaic past or in Other primitive peoples and places, is fundamentally an imperialist gesture that disregards the actual heterogeneity of that which is not modern or Western and places all of history and all the rest of the world at our own Western disposal. Or, as Chambers observes: "In absolute difference the rhetoric of alterity locates a pure otherness awaiting our words, like the 'empty' wilderness—from the African to the American West—waiting to be settled and domesticated and brought into the redemptive time of our history."[15]

Precisely this frame of reference explains Elisabeth Matrei. In many ways she can be regarded as the epitome of modernity. She is emancipated in the most literal sense: she is groomed by famous male photographers for her profession as a photojournalist and insists on assuming the position of men even on the most dangerous Third World assignments: "I can't accept my being spared and not the men. It's not like that anymore with other things, all that changed long ago!" ("Paths," 141). At the end of the story, she accepts an assignment a male photographer is unable to carry out and is preparing to fly to Saigon to photograph the Vietnam War. (One recalls Bachmann's statement about *Malina*: "And when in this book *Malina*, for example, I say not a word about the Vietnam War, not a word about all the many catastrophic conditions of our society, then I know how to say something in another way—or I hope that I know how to say it."[16] As a photojournalist, Elisabeth is committed to what a recent volume on *Modernity and the Hegemony of Vision* has termed "ocularcentrism," "a distinctly modern historical form" that is "allied with all the forces of our advanced technologies. The power to make visible is the power to control."[17] (The photographs accompanying the accounts of explorers and anthropologists are one obvious example of how vision and technology have combined to document and control the world's Others, as the authors of *Reading 'National Geographic,'*[18] among many others, have pointed out.) Enlightenment is evidently the process of making visible what is obscured, subjecting it to the clear light of reason, and Elisabeth is convinced that photojournalism performs precisely this task, producing an enlightened understanding of world events like the Algerian War and the Suez Crisis: "people had to be made aware of what was going on there, they needed to see those pictures to 'wake up' to reality" ("Paths," 140-41). Via her success at taking on the power of the male gaze, Elisabeth is able to assume the stance of the universal, disembodied (i.e. male) Enlightenment subject. However, as Meyda Yegenoglu emphasizes:

> Since the universal is conceived of on the basis of one and access to it is restricted, the only possible way for women to enter into this privileged space and enjoy its benefits is through *imitating the male gesture*. In other words, they are allowed to enjoy the benefits of universality only if they assume a male position. The strange paradox here is that women's acceptance of a share in the universalistic simultaneously implies a denial of their difference. There is then no affirmative entry to the universal for women as women.[19]

That is to say, Elisabeth's very assumption of universal subject status means precisely that she will be unable to attend to or even articulate her own female concerns: "She never said a word about the things that really upset her, because they weren't fit to be put in any words at all" ("Paths," 172)—a point I will explore in greater detail below. This analysis can help us, I think, to explain Elisabeth's discomfort in the new postcolonial London. Despite—or perhaps even because of—her avowed support for Third World liberation struggles, Elisabeth occupies a position paradigmatically that of the liberal Western subject who regards the model of progress and development advocated by the West as world-historical—a view that, as Leela Gandhi puts it, regards "'history' as the grand narrative through which Eurocentrism is totalised as the proper account of all humanity."[20] Within the liberal version of this narrative, the West's Others either become (like) Europeans or remain in their proper place. "Propelling itself forward in pursuit of linear redemption," Chambers maintains, "ever newer, ever brighter, ever better, and constantly forgetting itself in order to overcome itself, Western modernity underwrites an alterity located elsewhere in backwardness, in a black cloth of darkness, to both underline and justify its movement."[21] To be sure, that backward, primitive alterity can become readily also conceptualized as object of desire, as Torgovnick emphasizes. But what this Western subject cannot tolerate are Others who refuse the site of alterity allocated to them. Rey Chow, for instance, argues that a neo-Orientalist anxiety reveals itself in the desire—very much like that of "the woman who rode away" to retrieve and preserve the pure, authentic native. However, Chow continues, under the conditions of globalization, like those Elisabeth encounters in London, the native is no longer available as "pure, unadulterated object," but is rather "contaminated by the West, dangerously un-Otherable."[22] In effect, the Empire talks or "writes back," as the title of a famous anthology would have it.[23] Chambers summarizes precisely the situation Elisabeth encounters in London:

> So, a linguistic and literary context such as "English," which has historically stood in Britain, or at least in metropolitan London, for a specific cultural, historical, and national identity, comes to be re-written, re-routed, and re-sited. Inhabiting English, other stories, memories, and identities cause metropolitan authority to stumble. For they talk back to it, take the language elsewhere, and then return with it to interrupt the nation-narration at its very "centre."[24]

As Chambers details, the disruptions to the dominant paradigm of Western modernity occasioned by the emergence of the postcolonial subject are profound:

> The proprietary rights of language, history and truth are no longer able to hide in the metaphysical mimicry of universal knowledge or national identity. Such accounts are now exposed through a radical historicity as partial and partisan. . . . Such journeys among the uneven and unexplained effects of these "contact zones" that have now expanded to compose much of metropolitan culture throughout the world, challenge the myth of modernism as a homogeneous movement and moment, restricted to a centralised economic power and a particular geopolitical population and place. The predator of progress, establishing the ratio of the West, today encounters transmutation and travesty in the very languages it assumed were its own.[25]

Indeed, the woman who rode away has reason to be concerned—her entire belief system has just been undermined.

Elisabeth's is not, however, the only relationship to the new postcolonial culture represented in "Three Paths to the Lake." Though one of the great loves of Elisabeth's life, Franz Joseph Trotta, is also her philosophical and political antagonist in Bachmann's story, and the challenge he poses to her positions makes it possible to bring this critique of Elisabeth back home to a post-imperial Austria. The "home" in the small Austrian city to which Elisabeth returns on a visit to her father stands for the same sort of solace, familiarity, and *Geborgenheit* that Torgovnick ascertained to be the fundamental structure of the Western desire for the primitive, and the lake she cannot reach via any of the three hiking paths, since the new Autobahn built for German tourists has cut off access to it, is a metonymic representation of the oceanic dissolution that Westerners hope the primitive will allow them to achieve. In contrast to the Esperanto of London, Elisabeth is soothed by the "familiar tones" ("Paths," 131, trans. modified) of Austria and "that old civil-servant German" of her father, "always appropriate to himself, his idiom and his mood" ("Paths," 177). Elisabeth conceives the roots of the Austria she loves to derive from the old Austro-Hungarian empire, "this gigantic, pointless empire which was more loved than hated" ("Paths," 170, trans. modified). Like her father, she believes that Austria was most profoundly transformed, not by National Socialism, but by the dissolution of the empire, "that the year 1938 had not been a turning point: the split had occurred much earlier and everything that followed had been a consequence of this older split, and that his world—which he had hardly experienced after all—was destroyed for good in 1914. . . ." ("Paths," 179). From the perspective of the present, Elisabeth conceives her brother and herself to be condemned to estrangement because the Empire is gone: "But what made them strangers wherever they went was their sensitivity, because they came from the periphery and thus their thoughts, feelings and actions were hopelessly bound to this ghostly empire of gigantic dimensions. The right passports didn't exist for them, for it was a country which didn't issue passports" ("Paths," 122-23).

From a postcolonial perspective, it is possible to recognize this apparently benign nostalgia as in fact a desire for the restoration of the good old days of empire, and it is Trotta, originally a Slovenian, now a French citizen, who both embodies the post-imperial condition and reveals what is most problematic about Elisabeth's stance. Trotta acknowledges his position as "a real exile, one of the lost ones" ("Paths," 139); rather than longing for the purity of an originary mother tongue, Trotta speaks all languages of his exile equally well; unconvinced that humanity is infinitely improvable, Trotta ridicules Elisabeth's "fresh, strong faith" that her photographs will make "people . . . see reason" ("Paths," 143); arguing that it is shameful to photograph human suffering for the amusement of newspaper readers, Trotta forces Elisabeth to recognize how her profession is implicated in the injustices she believes she is combating. Most importantly, a member of a subordinate group in rebellion against the old empire rather than of its ruling elite, that is, one of the Empire's Others, Trotta disrupts Elisabeth's affection for an innocent Austria upon which Germany preyed. Intimating that Austrians' behavior after 1938 may be rooted in their imperial past, Trotta observes that, though the German soldiers in Hitler's army were only following orders, Austrian soldiers were genuinely depraved: "the enjoyment they got out of every kind of brutality imaginable was written clearly all over their ugly faces" ("Paths," 151). Though Elisabeth, like other Western subjects, longs and strives in many ways to return to an originary home, Trotta represents the position of Joseph Roth, who affirmed the diaspora, asserted, "A human being is not a tree," and argued, "Wandering is not a curse but a blessing."[26] Though Elisabeth continues to conceive her rootlessness as estrangement and exile, Trotta forces her to understand that home never was what she imagined it to be and that she cannot in any case go home again, "because he made her conscious of so many things, because of his origins and because he . . . had made an exile of her: long after his death he slowly pulled her down with him to ruin, alienating her from the miracles and allowing her to recognize this alienation as her destiny" ("Paths," 139). In conjunction with the Lawrence citation, Trotta's response to Elisabeth suggests a reading of this story that would locate Elisabeth, much in contrast to what she believes to be her intentions, within a discursive paradigm that permits only one monolinear history, the history of the victors, and leaves no discursive space, no language even, for the conquered and colonized to tell their different story.

Finally, Elisabeth's conception of herself as "the woman who rode away" has multiple consequences for the construction of her own femininity. In many ways, "Three Paths to the Lake" is a refiguring of the constellation of characters in *Malina*, though Elisabeth combines in one person cool, rational, masculine Malina and the distraught unnamed female "I" who can find no language to tell her own story. As I have already suggested, the universalistic, disembodied subject position Elisabeth assumes brings her fame and even some fortune but no happiness at all. At many points in her life, she merely moves through the paces of her female role without any interior engagement: as a young woman "she had gone to bed unemotionally, only, as she had believed, to do a man a favor" ("Paths," 138); after age forty, "Her increasing success with men was directly related to her increasing indifference to them . . ." ("Paths," 174). In effect, like the "I" of *Malina*, she is "really" a woman only when she is "really," passionately, in love, and then she performs femininity according to a script men have passed down (the performer in her father's play, as in *Malina*), loving only men, themselves tellingly from the old Empire who treat her badly and abandon her inexplicably, leaving her sobbing alone by the telephone. But "Three Paths to the Lake" is *Malina* with a difference: whereas the "I" of *Malina* acts almost exclusively within the private realm, here Elisabeth shows that the gender paradigm to which she conforms—disembodied universal subject versus woman as man's object—is also inadequate to deal with a postmodern and postcolonial public realm except from the perspective of the dominant order, that is, one diametrically opposed to what Elisabeth believes to be her own quest for justice. One might then inquire whether the quotation she borrows from Lawrence to characterize gender relations and her hopes for their future rectification may be likewise intended to critique her standpoint as a *woman* as profoundly as the allusion to "The Woman Who Rode Away" indicts her as a neocolonialist. Elisabeth muses of romantic heterosexual love: "Perhaps one day something else might come along but only then, and it would be strong and mysterious and have real greatness, something to which each could once again submit" ("Paths," 175). Here sexuality is postulated to be the alternative to her public, masculinist role—but perhaps here, too, she is subjecting herself to a mystical concept of love in the same way that the woman who rode away subjects herself to the flint knife in the icy cave; perhaps here she is once more trapped in fatal binaries that will destroy her as surely as the Good God destroyed Jennifer in the radio play, "Der gute Gott von Manhattan" ("The Good God of Manhattan").

In a somewhat related context, as she interviews prestigious gynecologists to formulate the text for a photo-reportage on abortion and is appalled that the doctors understand nothing at all about what really concerns their women patients "with their problems and their men and their inability to say one single true word about their lives," Elisabeth rages: "Why doesn't someone ask me for a change, why not ask someone who thinks independently and dares to live, what have you done to me and so many others, you with your insane empathy with every kind of problem, hasn't it ever occurred to anyone that you kill people when you deprive them of the power of speech and with it the power to experience and think" ("Paths," 173). Not simply from the perspective of postcoloniality, but also from the perspective of gender relations, Elisabeth's conception of herself as the woman who rode away suggests that she has accommodated herself to, or is the discursive product of, conceptions about gender relations that are virtually assured not to meet her needs as a person *or* as a woman. And this, finally, may explain Bachmann's own peculiar comment about women's emancipation in a 1971 interview (that is, shortly before she published *Simultan*): "Perhaps that's quite remarkable for you that precisely a woman who always earned her own money, who paid for her own university study, always lived alone, that she says that she doesn't care at all about women's emancipation. I've always found the pseudo-modern woman with her tortured efficiency and energy completely strange and incomprehensible."[27] At the end of the same interview, Bachmann remarks that, as she wrote *Malina*, she had the feeling, "that I'm writing against something. Against a persistent terrorism. After all, people don't really die from illnesses. They die from what's been done to them."[28] It may be that Elisabeth, precisely such an emancipated, pseudo-modern woman, is also a victim of the system that has made her a professional success, and that, as Bachmann's use of literary allusions in this story may demonstrate, she is also incapable of saying a single true word about her life. In "Three Paths to the Lake," Elisabeth's reflections may record not just the bloody struggles that accompany movements for national liberation and decolonization, but also, and unbeknownst to her, the story of her "Todesart"—her "Way of Death."

NOTES

1. Published in English under the title *Three Paths to the Lake: Stories by Ingeborg Bachmann*, trans. Mary Fran Gilbert (New York: Holmes & Meier, 1972). The short story of the same title included there is hereafter cited as "Paths."
2. Monika Albrecht and Dirk Göttsche, critical commentary, *"Todesarten"-Projekt*, by Ingeborg Bachmann, ed. Albrecht and Göttsche, 4 vols in 5 vols (München: Piper, 1995), 4:630.
3. Kate Millett, *Sexual Politics* (London: Sphere Books Limited, 1971), 285-93.
4. D. H. Lawrence, "The Woman Who Rode Away," *Shorter Stories*, ed. Stephen Gill (London: J.M. Dent, 1996), 347.
5. Ibid., 360.
6. Ibid., 372.
7. Ibid., 371.
8. Albrecht/Göttsche, 4:633.
9. Marianna Torgovnick, *Primitive Passions: Men, Women, and the Quest for Ecstasy* (Chicago: University of Chicago Press, 1996).
10. Ibid., 8.
11. Marianna Torgovnick, *Going Primitive: Savage Intellects, Modern Lives* (Chicago: University of Chicago Press, 1990), 185.
12. Georg Lukács, *The Theory of the Novel*, trans. Anna Bostock (Cambridge: MIT Press, 1971), 41.
13. Novalis, *Philosophical Writings*, ed. and trans. Margaret Mahony Stoljar (Albany: State University of New York Press, 1997), 135.
14. Iain Chambers, *Border Dialogues: Journeys in Postmodernity* (London: Routledge, 1990), 104.
15. Iain Chambers, "Signs of Silence, Lines of Listening," *The Post-Colonial Question: Common Skies, Divided Horizons*, ed. Iain Chambers and Lidia Curti (London: Routledge, 1996), 57-8.
16. Ingeborg Bachmann, *Wir müssen wahre Sätze finden. Gespräche und Interviews*, ed. Christine Koschel and Inge von Weidenbaum (München: Piper, 1983), 90-91.
17. David Michael Levin, ed., *Modernity and the Hegemony of Vision* (Berkeley: University of California Press, 1993), 2-3, 7.
18. Jane L. Collins and Catherine A. Lutz, *Reading 'National Geographic'* (Chicago: University of Chicago Press, 1993).

19. Meyda Yegenoglu, *Colonials Fantasies: Towards a Feminist Reading of Orientalism* (Cambridge: Cambridge University Press, 1998), 105.

20. Leela Gandhi, *Postcolonial Theory* (Edinburgh: Edinburgh University Press, 1998), 171.

21. Chambers, "Signs of Silence," 57.

22. Rey Chow, *Writing Diaspora: Tactics of Intervention in Contemporary Cultural Studies* (Bloomington: Indiana University Press, 1993), 12, cited in Gandhi, 127.

23. B. Ashcroft, G. Griffiths, and H. Tiffin, ed., *The Empire Writes Back: Theory and Practice in Postcolonial Literatures* (London: Routledge, 1989).

24. Chambers, "Signs of Silence," 49.

25. Ibid., 50, 57.

26. Joseph Roth, "Der Segen des ewigen Juden," *Werke 3: Das journalistische Werk*, ed. Klaus Westermann (Köln: Kiepenheuer und Witsch, 1991), 532, cited in Ute Gerhard, *Nomadische Bewegungen und die Symbolik der Krise: Flucht und Wanderung in der Weimarer Republik* (Wiesbaden: Westdeutscher Verlag, 1998), 6.

27. *Gespräche und Interviews*, 109.

28. Ibid., 110.

11 / The Significance of Remembrance as a Motif and Structural Dimension in the Work of Ingeborg Bachmann

Andrea Stoll

For decades, the significance of remembrance in the work of Ingeborg Bachmann has been underestimated.[1] Primarily, it has been its vast evocation in her novel *Malina* (1971) that has guided the view of research to the work of an author who, for a long time, has been considered the prototype of "poets hostile towards the period and history who were particularly numerous in modernity."[2]

Whoever looks into the coordination of the loss of language, the experience of history and remembrance that are significant for the novel *Malina*, will discover the aesthetic context of the fifties. The historically founded doubt of speech signals the starting point for an understanding of Bachmann's writing.

> We engaged with language, have experienced what speechlessness and silence are— our . . . purest conditions!—and . . . have returned with language that we will resume as long as our life is our continuation.[3]

Remembrance and experience of history cannot be separated from one another in the works of Bachmann. The experience of National Socialism constitutes, according to the author, the key moment of her first experience of pain—it remains present in her writing as a fundamental pattern and thus becomes the synonym *per se* for having to remember. Again and again, from the poems of the fifties to the late works of the *Todesarten*-cycle, the motif of remembrance stands at the center of textual connections. The historically conditioned pattern of experience becomes an aesthetic category that links subjective and collective forms of remembrance on the content level, and can be found on the level of textual composition in the structure of metaphor, motif and reception in the lyric as much as in the modus of narrative technique in her prose. The tensions of the lyrical structure point to an unsolved aesthetic problematic in numerous poems of *Borrowed Time*.[4] Innovative poetic formulas and a traditional poetic figurative expression stand in opposition to each other on sharply contrasting pictorial levels. Intellectually sharpened social criticism clashes with pictures of utmost emotionality.

Bachmann's poems make the loss of language the subject of discussion in terms of a larger part of historical experience. The desire to fall silent implies the hope for a new poetic purification process that, by "finding back" ("Rückkopplung") to the "purest condition of language,"[5] wishes to overcome its historical abuse. The conflict between a traditional aesthetic demand ("Radiance"/"Beauty") and a socio-critical consciousness that is strikingly often made a subject of discussion, opens a view for the conditions of the "highly charged connection of poetic tradition and historical experience"[6] immediately after World War II.

The collection of poems, *Borrowed Time*, highlights the devaluation of language as a central metaphor in its social as well as in its poetic function. With the appeal of silence ("Psalm," *Songs*, 57-59) directed towards the reader, though, Bachmann refuses its followers a misused instrument of dominance. The reduction of an impartial use of language becomes the precondition for an ethical innovation that seeks to link the reader's social sense of responsibility with a critical behavior towards language.

The starting point for poetic speech is the knowledge of the damage inflicted upon cultural tradition by the National Socialistic regime ("Early Noon," *Songs*, 36-39). In the renunciation of traditional poetic conceptions ("Psalm"), lyrical speech gains a place where the aesthetic problematic of a historically founded doubt of language is openly revealed. The hope for an aesthetic innovation is preceded by the readiness for silence. Silence and falling silent thus describe the collective- (reader) as well as subjective poetic (lyrical I) consequence of a destructive historical experience. Above all, this relation to the reader, evident in numerous poems of the first collection, serves as the interpretation and proof of identity of a poetic speech which, in terms of the theme of the loss of language, wishes to overcome precisely this deprivation.

Here, it turns out to be particularly revealing that the phenomenon of a communicative relation to the reader is limited to the first collection of poems. The second collection, *Invocation of the*

Great Bear, shows quite differently disposed structural moments. Its very high proportion of not easily reconstructable motifs of mythos and fairy-tale justifies in equal manner a stronger monologic alignment, just as the previously discussed problematic of poetic speech. In contrast, in her first collection of poems, Bachmann attempts to link the subjectivity of her poetic consciousness with the historical experience of her contemporaries. Against the backdrop of an all-encompassing loss of language and values, the poetic postulate of truth ("Wood and Shavings," *Songs*, 28-31) solely gains in the dialogic alignment of its socio-critical potential. In the confession of the experience and preservation of pain, a moment of resistance manifests itself against the attitude of suppression of post-war society.

For the most part, the motif of remembrance, recognizable in numerous poems, is not disclosed *expressis verbis*, but rather through the refusal to suppress and forget that is expressed in appeals to the reader. Bachmann's first lyrical collection, on the other hand, makes the meaning of remembrance a few years after the end of the War the exact subject of discussion. This is done in a manner similar to its first demonstration in the theoretical discourse in the sixties by Alexander and Margarete Mitscherlich's groundbreaking examination of the post-war debate about "Die Unfähigkeit zu trauern" ("The Inability to Mourn").[7]

The poems identify the collective slander of the past[8] in its essential aspects. On the one hand, they make the "striking emotional frigidity" of the post-war period a subject of discussion, which makes an insight into the "overpowering burden of guilt"[9] impossible:

> Time works wonders. But if it arrives inconveniently
> with the knocking of guilt: we're not at home.
> ("Autumn Maneuver," *Songs*, 21)

On the other hand, the poems depict in forceful pictures the psychic process of a collective "de-realization."[10]

> On Good Friday a hand hangs on display
> in the firmament, two fingers missing,
> and it cannot swear that all of it,

> all of it didn't happen, nor that
> it ever will. It dives into red clouds,
> whisks off the new murderers
> and goes free.
>> ("Psalm," *Songs*, 57)

In a third and last aspect, they unmask the "powerful collective efforts of the German reconstruction in its sham character."[11]

> Let's take a trip! Let us stroll under cypresses
> or even under palms . . .
> to see at reduced rates sunsets . . .
> Let us forget
> the unanswered letters to yesterday!
>> ("Autumn Maneuver," *Songs*, 21)

> Seven years later,
> inside a mortuary,
> the hangmen of yesterday
> drain the golden cup.
> Your eyes lower in shame.
>> ("Early Noon," *Songs*, 37)

As a literary motif, remembrance encompasses both the level of a collective historical experience as well as the level of a subjective consciousness of memory. Beyond that, a poetic meta-level is revealed that makes the far-reaching destruction of German culture through National Socialism clear to the reader through the montage of cultural and literal pieces of mismatch.[12]

For an interpretation of the collection of poems, *Borrowed Time*, the level of collective remembrance is of central significance. Metaphors such as "of the chaff of scorn," "in time's autumn maneuver" ("Autumn Maneuver," *Songs*, 21), "Amid the afterbirth of terror" ("Psalm," *Songs*, 57), etc. can be as little decoded as the final lines of the following poems without knowing about the historical context:

> Our Godhead,
> History, has ordered for us a grave

> from which there is no resurrection.
> ("Message," *Songs*, 47)
>
> ... at the fountain
> resisting the curled allure
> that once made us weak,
> my hair bristles.
> ("Wood and Shavings," *Songs*, 31)
>
> When water churns the mill wheel again,
> who will dare to remember the night?
> ("Night Flight," *Songs*, 55)
>
> We share bread with the rain;
> Bread, a debt, a house.
> ("Salt and Bread," *Songs*, 65)

The level of subjective memory stands in strongest relation to the motifs of truth and language. It is only in the connection of a search for truth and a critical awareness of language that remembrance gains its poetic function.

> Intoxicated by paper on the conveyer belt,
> I no longer recognize the branches,
> or the moss, dyed in darker tints,
> or the word, carved into the bark
> impudent and true . . .
> But in wood,
> as long as it is still green, and with gall,
> as long as it is still bitter, I am
> willing to write what happened at the start!
> ("Wood and Shavings," *Songs*, 29)

With the persistence on the "beginning," a moment of resistance can be detected that would be incomprehensible without knowing the historical context. The resistance of the lyrical I against the attitude of suppression of post-war society ("I do not say, this was yesterday") refers in an equal manner to the social as well as poetical preconditions of a new beginning. From the struggle for historical truth,[13] the function of memory of poetic speech becomes comprehensible. Subjective (lyrical I) and collective (reader) forms of remembrance in *Borrowed Time* aim at "a deeply moving cathartic reliving."[14] The connection of both moments proves to be a significant structural characteristic of the first collection of poems.

The significance of remembrance as a motif and composition principle of the first prose collection *The Thirtieth Year*[15] is not to be separated from the representation of the modern problematic of identity. For all the figures of the prose texts, remembrance becomes the moment of the reflection of the "I": in their attachment to experiences that lie far back in the past, the ruptures of their identity are revealed. Here, the problematic which has been made the subject of discussion in the collection of stories corresponds to Bachmann's poetological reflections in her *Frankfurt Lectures* that were developed parallel to it. In both, Bachmann makes the significance of the process of remembrance the subject for an "I without guarantee": "The first change which the I has experienced is that it is no longer *within* the narrative/history but rather that the narrative/history, as of late, resides *in* the 'I.'"[16]

The "I without guarantee" leads necessarily to a prose without guarantee that can no longer ensure the traditional elements of a narrative order. In the play with the limits of genre, the memory process becomes the decisive moment of the prose composition. It allows the fragmentation of that which is to be narrated: progressive actions in batches and a retrospective that is intermittently employed dissociate the narrative course. The varied play with remembrance as a moment of narrating is a confession of the fragmentation of narrative technique. In the memory processes of the figures, fragments of a subjective experience of reality are formed; as a moment of narrative technique, the memory processes reflect the psychological condition of the protagonists.

Whereas the protagonists' process of remembrance, which is linked to crisis situations ("The Thirtieth Year" and "Wildermuth"), corresponds to the subjective *gestus* of a heterogeneous narrative method, the theme of various forms of memory is very much in the context of a traditional narrative technique. The textual presentation of remembrance and forms of memory alone does not, therefore, have any repercussions for the narrative method; it is only the integration of associative particles of remembrance and episodes in the narrative process itself that leads to a dissolving of a narrating that is oriented towards fable and plot.

Almost all figures of the collection appear limited in their individual form; yet it is precisely this lack of sound individual structures that lets the prototypical emerge from the greater part of the protagonists' consciousness. Life- and reality-connections of the figures insist on revocation; their relation to their own proper life story is just as questionable as their relation to cultural values and social structures of their society.

In the prose texts of *The Thirtieth Year,* a subversive force is added to the motif of remembrance. The subjective memory process of the protagonist leads in the stories "The Thirtieth Year" and in "Wildermuth" to the destruction of existing connections of life. Yet whereas the destruction in "The Thirtieth Year" lays the foundation for the precondition of a beginning reconstruction of identity under altered objectives, the breakdown of Judge Wildermuth destroys both his personal and social existence. In both cases, the employed memory process demands of the protagonists the revelation of long-suppressed experiences. Corresponding to the premises of psychoanalytic theory, the ability to integrate events, suppressed up to this point, becomes the precondition for further existence. Also, the theme of remembrances in the context of a larger, collective scope of reference allows formulating conclusions about the psychic and social structure of the remembering figures. In the comparison of two diverging forms of remembrance, the different handling of suppression and the ability to forget become decisive for the opposing forms of existence: the arbitrary handling of National Socialistic culprits with the will to remember and the ability to forget is confronted with the compulsive-traumatic remembrance of the victims in "Among Murderers and Madmen." In his inevitable connection to that which has once been experienced, the "Jew" Mahler becomes the representative of a traumatic historical experience that has left manifold traces in Bachmann's work from the poems of *Borrowed Time* to the nightmare sequence of the novel *Malina.*

The central motifs of Bachmann's work—reflection on language and search for truth, absolute desire for love and historically motivated social critique—first develop their opposing potentials in the context of subjective and collective forms of remembrance. It is only the inability to forget their utopian claim, which reveals itself retrospectively, that turns the figures into outsiders who refuse to cooperate with social rules just as they shrink back from a final confession of the utopian extent of their desire. Only in the female water figure in "Undine" does the paradigm of a placeless desire experience its symbolic conversion. In Undine, the tendencies of the other narrative figures are radicalized, and the scope and failure of an absolute desire lead to an open declaration in favor of an extra-social existence. Detached from any historical frame of reference, the figure of Undine is also a carrier of traumatic potential of experience, which, unlike "Among Murderers and Madmen," no longer refers to a temporal-historical background but immediately to the structures of interpersonal relationships. In its theme of a destructive gender polarity, the text of "Undine" doubtlessly anticipates motifs of the late prose. The choice of the female narrative perspective lends a dimension to the open declaration in favor of the destruction of the *status quo* that is different from the literary-historically familiar model of an opposing male hero. In the choice of narrative perspective, but also in the composition of a textual form that points furthest beyond the limits of genre, "Undine" takes up an exceptional position in Bachmann's prose that likewise indicates the dissolution of the identity of figures as well as the heterogeneity of textual levels contained in the novel *Malina*.

With her novel *Malina*, Bachmann once and for all goes beyond those forms of a contemporary problematic of identity and narration that turn the narrating subject into an unchallenged starting point of epic models despite all the shocks of self-awareness. Different from the prose collection, *The Thirtieth Year*, and also different from her later collection of stories, *Simultan*,[17] in Bachmann's novel, in the figures of the "I" and Malina, two narrative styles drift apart in which two contrary concepts of identity stand for two opposing forms of remembrance. Clear indications of the significance of remembrance for the course of the narrative can already be found in the introduction that precedes the three main chapters of the novel. Repeatedly, the narrating "I" states the obvious connection of its narrative intention with its powers of memory:

> I must talk. I will talk. There's nothing more to disturb my reminiscing. . . . However, if my memory only entails the usual

recollections, remote, decrepit, abandoned, then I'm still far away, very far away from the silent reminiscence where nothing more can upset me.[18]

The highlighted position of the motif of remembrance in the introduction conflicts with the unusual dramaturgical indication for the "unity of time" (today) and the "unity of place" ("Ungargasse" in Vienna) (*Malina*, 2/3.) In this way, the introduction identifies the conflict between outer action and "inner happening" as significant for the structure and compositional style of the novel; this proves decisive for its narrative technique as well as for the realization of characters.

It is "the work of remembrance of the 'I' figure [that] must necessarily lead to the interior."[19] Analogous to the ambivalent development of the plot, the conception of the figures of the novel also reveals itself as ambiguous. The central figures "I," Malina and Ivan can be understood as independent protagonists on the exterior level of the plot. However, on the stratum of inward happenings, the "I" and Malina, in particular, appear as opposed characters of a single dissolved narrative figure.[20] The introduction in that magnetic field (*Malina*, 4) of the "Ungargasse," in which the alleged relationship triangle between Ivan, the female "I" and Malina develops, is followed by the female "I's" remembrance of her first encounters with the title figure. In an introductory stocktaking of this relationship, the narrating "I" emphasizes the different nature of their existence. Differentiated and isolated from the "bright story" of Malina, the female existence stands for the "unavoidable dark tale" that needs clarification (*Malina*, 8/9).

At the same time, the clearly formulated will for narrative enlightenment (*Malina*, 9) is confronted with the obvious interference in the remembrance of that "dark tale" which will have a lasting affect on the course of the narrative.

I don't want to talk, it all upsets me, in my remembering. (*Malina*, 11)

The conflict between remembrance and narrative intention discussed in the introduction of *Malina* provides the model for the novel's formal composition. All three chapters of the novel unite a number of heterogeneous levels of text, genre, and style whose compository connection is linked, in the sense of a *Leitmotif*, with the course of a disturbed process of remembrance. Already in the first chapter, the Ivan-imaginations and Ivan-happenings of "Happy with Ivan" are interlarded with repeated indications of a traumatic experience that shows an undiminished effect as a blockade in the female "I's" ability to remember:

> because Ivan must first wash my eyes with his own, removing the images which landed on my retina before his arrival. Nonetheless after many cleansings a gloomy, fearsome picture reemerges, practically inextinguishable, whereupon Ivan rushes to cover it with some bright image to stop my evil eye and make me lose this horrible look – which I know how I acquired but do not remember, I do not remember . . . (You still can't, not yet, there's so much upsetting you . . .). (*Malina*, 15)

The mode of a realistic narrative style, indicated by the autobiographical experience of the "first slap" on the "Glanbrücke," is immediately interrupted again. It is the "discreet remembrance" of the "I" that demands a different narrative and breaks through the chronology, hierarchy, order, unity and perspective of an epic report.[21] The theme of a far-reaching distraught state of the "I" corresponds to the structure of a dissociated course of narrative that manifests itself in the succession of the various textual levels. In the stream-of-consciousness sections such as in the telephone dialogues and the encounters of the "I" with Ivan, the Jellinek letters and conversations, the utopian fragments of the "beautiful book," the interviews and letters, the scenes of conversation at the "Wolfgangssee," the resumption of the Malina dialogue, the novel provides many manifestations of the motif of a traumatic defeat. The composed play with different genres and textual forms turns into the paradigm of the confusion of the "I." In particular, the change of the various textual levels prismatically illuminates those reactions, emotions and behaviors of the "I" which place it in strongest contrast to social conventions and connections.

> When I stand in front of a familiar door in Vienna, perhaps because I am invited, it occurs to me at the last moment it might be the wrong door, or day or hour, and I turn around and drive back to the Ungargasse, too quickly tired, too much in doubt. (*Malina*, 165)

Refusal and withdrawal of the "I" from the environment of social action do not appear at all as the autonomous gesture of a critical refusal. The retreat of the "I" at the end of the novel becomes much more an expression of a compulsive movement that is most strongly linked to the disrupted remembrance discussed at the beginning. The inability of the female "I" to communicate socially is the outward sign of an interior distraught state that refers back to a far-reaching dissociation in the narrative consciousness of the "I." "Beginning" and "ending" of the interference of narration and remembrance are inseparably linked (*Malina*, 10/11). Immediately before the end, the female "I" takes up a motif once again ("Nous allons à l'Esprit!") that can be considered as the key to the problematic of the "I" and the narrative of the novel (*Malina*, 222).

> I might ask about the most impossible things. Who invented writing? What is writing? Is it property? Who first demanded expropriation? Allons-nous à l'Esprit? Are we of a lower race? Should we get mixed up in politics, do nothing more and simply be brutal? Are we accursed? (*Malina*, 81)

The reflection on writing discussed here doubtlessly goes beyond its significance as the medium of human communication. The question of the female "I" in terms of writing, its associates and the practice of exclusion, implicates the question of the significance of the symbolic in the language of the work of art.[22]

Analogous to the presentation of problems of poststructuralist thinking, writing appears in the context of reflection on the writing of the novel as an instrument of power of Western culture. In the symbolic order of the historically traditional use of language, each speaker encounters the "foreign countenance of an order of the other"[23] that dramatically illuminates the boundaries of the "I"-awareness. As a result, the perspective of a female narrator aggravates the reflected problematic.

The "system causing principle of the 'I,'" "the pure method" of ratio that "is given priority to any content"[24] cannot be claimed by the female "I." Within the scope of the novel's composition, it is Malina that represents the system of ratio. Both, the "I" and Malina function only as the female and male part of a split figure which, with their division, make the boundaries of the characters a subject of discussion.[25] In their mutual conversations about the problematic of remembrance and narrative reflection of the "I," Malina discloses his identity as "the other" (*Malina*, 89) who, as the rational-systematic antipode, conflicts with the ambitions of the female "I."[26] From the very beginning, the novel's concept of remembrance is linked to the Malina figure. The initially noted "contradiction between the will and the refusal to narrate"[27] manifests itself in the polarized conception of the figures. Malina's superior reaction towards the disrupted remembrance at the beginning of the novel (*Malina*, 11) already makes it clear that both figures stand for opposed terms of remembrance. Malina's function within the process of remembrance of the "I" is that of an analytical reconstruction which, from an emotionally indifferent position, attempts to fixate conceptually the dissociated process of remembrance in the consciousness of the "I." Malina's role as an analytical partner for dialogue of the traumatically distraught "I" becomes obvious in the opening of the second chapter of the novel: "Malina shall ask about everything" (*Malina*, 113). The layout of the chapter is structured on the basis of the constant alteration between the nightmare sequences of the "I" and the analytical dialogues with Malina, which aim at the clarification of the nocturnal pictures.

> Malina shall know everything. But I decide: they shall be the dreams of this night. (*Malina*, 113)

In the conversations of the dream chapter Malina clearly reveals himself as the "superior figure" (*GuI*, 95)[28] of the novel. It is Malina who tries to grasp the great themes of the nocturnal picture sequences. The central motifs of the nightmare sequences circle around sexuality, destruction and the death of the female existence. The *"voiceless"* scream (*Malina*, 127) becomes the central metaphor of the second chapter of the novel. In the vision of a ripped-out tongue (*Malina*, 115), the trauma of a forcefully disturbed ability to express oneself is symbolized by way of a mutilation of the identity of the female "I," and leaves it behind in its distraught state. Also, the third chapter of the novel, "Last Things," circles around the female's disturbed ability of articulation. Ever more clearly does the "I" link the blockade of its ability to remember to its opposite Malina: "There is a disturbance in my memory; I shatter against every memory" (*Malina*, 172).

> It's Malina who isn't letting me talk (*Malina*, 175).

In the dialogues between the "I" and Malina, the male part gains noticeably in significance. As a result of this, the tone of conversation changes. Admonitions become quiet threats that increasingly push the "I" onto the defensive. Malina's attacks against the female "I" aim at the basic characteristics of identity; living space, styles of articulation and work ethics of the female "I" are increasingly dominated by Malina. Malina's penetrating glance aims especially at those weaknesses of the "I" that stand in the way of his disciplined way of life and pertinent argumentation.

> I am the first perfect extravagance, ecstatic and incapable of putting the world to any reasonable use, and I may show up at the masked ball of society, or stay away like someone who has been detained, or has forgotten to make a mask, or can no longer find his costume out of carelessness, and so one day will no longer be invited. (*Malina*, 165)

In the third part of the novel, Malina succeeds in regaining apparently lost terrain. Malina reverses his extensive suppression of the Ivan-love in the first chapter.

> Malina: . . . and someday you'll know whether it was a good thing to forget me, or whether it isn't better to pay attention to me again. Except you'll probably never have a choice, already you don't have one. (*Malina*, 187)

The controversial dialogue between Malina and the woman reveals itself as an open battle in which the ability of memory and articulation of the "I" becomes ever more the focus of the confrontation.

The antipodean constellation of figures does not only stand for two opposed forms of memory; Malina's distanced, analytical attempt to remember increasingly reveals itself as a concept of narration that is opposed to the fragmentary narrative style of the novel.[29] His systematic behavior all the more highlights the contradictory narrative stance of the female "I." The increasing resistance of the "I" to Malina's efforts to achieve an "unemotional, but consequently conceptual and discursive mediation of the 'ways of dying'-problematic"[30] elucidates the extent of the existential threat, which arises for the female "I" from the increasing dominance of its male counterpart:

> I don't understand Malina...We will never understand each other, we're as different as day and night, he is inhuman with his whispering, his silences and the questions he omits. (*Malina*, 211)

Only in the very last chapter of the novel does the narrative reflective-function of the polarized conception of the figures openly come to light. The conflict between the contrary poles of a dissolved narrative figure represents the conflict of two manners of memory and narration which determines the poetological center of the novel.

> For me this is one of the oldest, yet almost buried memories as well: that I have always known of having to write this book—already very early on while I was still writing poems. That I continually searched for this protagonist. That I knew: it will be masculine. That I can only narrate from a male perspective. But I often wondered: why anyway? I did not understand it, even in my narratives, why I had to take the male "I" so often. It was for me like finding my own person; not to deny the female "I" and nevertheless to place the emphasis on the male "I" . . . [31]

With the dissolution of the traditional narrative figure, *Malina* also complicates the rupture in the experience of the subject. The subjective narrative outlook of an "I" falls apart into two opposed forms of consciousness. The beginning "deconstruction of the

'I'"[32] goes doubtlessly beyond those forms of a contemporary problematic of identity and narration that turn the narrating subject into the unchallenged starting point of epic models despite all the shocks of the "I"-awareness. Still different from the prose collection *The Thirtieth Year*, two narrative styles diverge in her novel in the figures of the "I" and Malina, in which two contrary terms of identity stand for two opposed forms of memory.

Malina radicalizes the contemporary problematic of identity from the perspective of a writing woman; this is already of constitutive significance for Bachmann's first prose collection. For the female "I" as author of the novel, memory becomes likewise the moment of the "I"—as well as the moment of narrative reflection. The insisting reference to its disturbed ability to remember corresponds to the consciousness of a disturbed sense of identity which lets the disparate parts of its personality diverge irreconcilably. The artistic claim of the female "I," made a subject of discussion many times, fails. It neither succeeds in completing the utopian fragments of the "beautiful book" nor in collecting the "dark tale" of the *Todesarten*-manuscripts in a publication (*Malina*, 190). Again and again, it is the lasting disturbance of its ability to remember that interrupts the aptitude of the "I" to look back in a way that would provide a sense of identity, and thus refuses[33] the narrating subject the hermeneutically structured retrospective. In the destruction of an epically rounded-off mediation of the past, the continuation of linguistic- and identity-critical narrative styles of Austrian modernity are revealed.[34]

Bachmann also insists on empty spaces of subjective experience of the past.[35] The contrast in the conduct of memory and language of the figures becomes thus the model of disparate narrative styles. The model of an "analytical-discursive" narration represented by Malina stands in radical contrast to the "imaginative-coding" narrative style of the female "I."[36] Different from its "erratic monologues," the "last dialogues" (*Malina*, 162) with Malina seek to decipher the memories and distraught state of the "I." The conversations again and again vary the concept of gender polarity in its effect on the understanding of language, writing and narration of the "I."

> I: You understand, my inflammatory letters, my inflammatory appeals, my inflammatory stance, this entire fire I have put on paper with my burned hand —I'm afraid it could all become a charred piece of paper. . .
>
> Malina: The ancients used to say of someone dumb that he had no heart. They placed the seat of intelligence in the heart. You don't have to hang your heart on every single thing and have all your speeches blaze and all your letters.
>
> I: But how many people just have a head, nothing more than a head and no heart at all? (*Malina*, 161)

The dispute over rationalism and emotion in its function for the speaking and writing of the "I" is a barely coded dialogue about the preconditions for poetic production; it illuminates the conflict between the traumatic zones of the experience of the "I" and the aspect of distance that precedes poetic style in the traditional understanding of art. Malina's function as a distanced conversation partner (i.e. his interventions, comments on and valuations of the traumatic potential of experience) does not only serve an analytic evaluation. Malina's influence also proves increasingly powerful in the question of poetic style; he obstructs and prevents the emotional speech of the "I."

> Malina interrupts me, he is protecting me, but I think that his wanting to protect me is preventing me from telling. It's Malina who isn't letting me talk. (*Malina*, 175)

Yet Malina goes even further. His symbolic attack upon the articulate ability of the "I" is only the preliminary stage of his last and final destruction.

> I can't say anything more, because Malina takes two pieces of paper, crushes them and throws them in my face. (*Malina*, 191)

Unmistakably, Malina threatens at last the awareness of identity and self of the female narrative figure:

What you want doesn't count anymore. In the proper place you will have nothing more to want. There you will be yourself so much you'll be able to give up your self. (*Malina*, 208)

Doubtlessly, the diffusion of identity and "I" of the narrative figure stand for the "thematic self-reflection of modern narration."[37] Furthermore, the narrative moment of memory gains, against the backdrop of its genesis in Bachmann's work, an aesthetic relevance as a continuous reflective moment in the writing process of the author. Malina's objectivizing narrative outlook is lacking any authentic relation to life. His attempts to systematize the discontinuously flashing process of memory of the "I" aim at the chronological presentation of remembrance of an epically ordered retrospect. In contrast, the narrative model of the female "I" is based on the fragmentary and unsystematic representation of a process of memory and awareness, the course of which is determined solely by the shocks of an "inner happening."

In view of the ruptures, empty spaces and traumatic fixations in the awareness of the "I," a course of narration constitutes itself, the disparate narrative outlook and articulate forms of which mirror the dissociation of contemporary experience from reality. Numerous intertextual references,[38] but also the play with various genres and textual forms link the conflict of narrative styles that is tied to the figures "I" and Malina to an overall composition of the novel whose heterogeneous construction refuses all interpretative attempts. Only seemingly does death leave the Malina-part of the "I's" existence behind as the victor. The recordings of the narrating "I"—the novel itself—document the contradictions and resistance against a traditional epic retrospect. Above all other motifs, it is the motif of remembrance that lays the foundation for the fragmentation of the narrative. In the confrontation between the female "I's" traumatically disturbed ability to remember and to narrate and Malina's systematical-rational style, the question of the *how* of contemporary narration culminates.

[Translated by Nicole Franke]

NOTES

1. Cf. Andrea Stoll, *Erinnerung als ästhetische Kategorie des Widerstandes im Werk Ingeborg Bachmanns* (Frankfurt am Main: Peter Lang, 1991).
2. Ulrich Thiem, "Die Bildsprache der Lyrik Ingeborg Bachmanns" (diss., University of Köln, 1972), 51.
3. Ingeborg Bachmann, "Musik und Dichtung" ("Music and Poesy"), *Werke*, 4 vols, ed. Christine Koschel, Inge von Weidenbaum, and Clemens Münster (München: Piper, 1978), 4:60.
4. All citations of Bachmann's poems refer to Ingborg Bachmann, *Songs in Flight: The Collected Poems of Ingeborg Bachmann*, trans. Peter Filkins (New York: Marsilio, 1994). Hereafter cited as *Songs*.
5. Peter Fehl, "Sprachskepsis und Sprachhoffnung im Werk Ingeborg Bachmanns" (diss., University of Mainz, 1970), 98.
6. Hans Höller, *Ingeborg Bachmann. Das Werk. Von den frühesten Gedichten bis zum "Todesarten"-Zyklus* (Frankfurt am Main: Athenäum, 1987), 27.
7. Cf. Alexander Mitscherlich and Margarete Mitscherlich, *Die Unfähigkeit zu trauern. Grundlagen kollektiven Verhaltens* (München: Piper, 1977).
8. Cf. ibid., 40.
9. Ibid.
10. Ibid.
11. Ibid.
12. Cf. ibid., 20.
13. Ibid., 57.
14. Ibid.
15, Ingeborg Bachmann, *The Thirtieth Year. Stories*, trans. Michael Bullock (New York: Holmes & Meier, 1987).
16. Bachmann, *Werke*, 4:230: "Die erste Veränderung, die das Ich erfahren hat, ist, dass es sich nicht mehr *in* der Geschichte aufhält, sondern dass sich neuerdings die Geschichte *im* Ich aufhält."
17. Published in English translation under the title *Three Paths to the Lake*, trans. Mary Fran Gilbert (New York: Holmes & Meier, 1989).

18. Ingeborg Bachmann, *Malina*, trans. Philip Boehm (New York: Holmes & Meier, 1990), 9. Hereafter cited as *Malina*.
19. Sigrid Weigel, "'Ein Ende mit der Schrift. Ein anderer Anfang.' Zur Entwicklung von Ingeborg Bachmanns Schreibweise," *Ingeborg Bachmann. Sonderband Text und Kritik* (München: Edition Text und Kritik, 1984), 78.
20. Ellen Summerfield, *Die Auflösung der Figur in Ingeborg Bachmanns Roman Malina* (Bonn: Bouvier, 1976), 2.
21. Sigrid Weigel, "Ingeborg Bachmann—Was folgt auf das Schreiben? Zu ihrem 10. Todestag am 17. Oktober, *Frankfurter Rundschau*, 15 October 1983.
22. Cf. Weigel, "Ein Ende mit der Schrift," 76; cf. Höller, *Ingeborg Bachmann*, 240.
23. Manfred Frank, *Was ist Neostrukturalismus?* (Frankfurt am Main: Suhrkamp, 1984), 384. Cf. also Jacques Derrida, *Grammatologie* (Frankfurt am Main: Suhrkamp, 1974), 168.
24. Theodor W. Adorno, *Negative Dialektik*, in *Gesammelte Schriften*, 20 vols., ed. Rolf Tiedemann (Frankfurt am Main: Suhrkamp, 1970), 6:36.
25. Weigel, "Was folgt auf das Schreiben?," 3.
26. Cf. Summerfield, *Die Auflösung der Figur*, 49.
27. Dirk Göttsche, *Die Produktivität der Sprachkrise in der modernen Prosa* (Frankfurt am Main: Athenäum, 1987), 197.
28. Ingeborg Bachmann, *Wir müssen wahre Sätze finden. Gespräche und Interviews*, ed. Christine Koschel and Inge von Weidenbaum (München: Piper, 1983), 95.
29. Cf. Göttsche, *Die Produktivität der Sprachkrise*, 199.
30. Ibid., 198.
31. Bachmann, *Gespräche und Interviews*, 99f.
32. Ibid., 202
33. Wolfgang Düsing, *Erinnerung und Identität. Untersuchungen zu einem Erzählproblem bei Musil, Döblin und Doderer* (München: W. Fink, 1982), 16.
34. Cf. ibid., 15.
35. Cf. Ibid., 17
36. Göttsche, *Die Produktivität der Sprachkrise*, 200.
37. Ibid., 208.

38. Cf. Annette Klaubert, *Symbolische Strukturen bei Ingeborg Bachmann. Malina im Kontext der Kurzgeschichten* (Bern: Peter Lang, 1983).

12 / "Beneath the Rubble": Correspondences in the Writing of Ingeborg Bachmann and Inge Müller[1]

Karen Remmler

Like Sigmund Freud before him, Walter Benjamin once described memory as the medium in which "dead cities are buried (*verschüttet*)."[2] This approach to remembering requires an archeological bent in recovering past experience. If the meticulous sifting-through of buried cities is both the medium and means for making sense out of the past, what kind of tools does one need to distinguish between the ruins of natural disasters and those wrought by human hand? In his collection of essays, *The Natural History of Destruction*, W. G. Sebald wonders why the memories of the nights of destruction during the Allied bombing of German cities like Hamburg or Dresden have not appeared in a form that he can trust: "I repeat, I do not doubt that there were and are memories of those nights of destruction; I simply do not believe they were a significant factor in the public consciousness of the new Federal Republic in any sense except as encouraging the will to reconstruction."[3] Sebald's query comes at a time when public debate in Germany about the form and place for the remembrance of the devastation of the bombing is at its peak. It is no longer tabu to talk about the trauma experienced by German civilians during Allied bombardments of their cities and towns. Sebald wonders about the absence of literary renditions of these memories in the then Federal Republic, but what of the literary renditions in the other states implicated in World War II and its atrocities, the German Democratic Republic (GDR) and Austria? Sebald overlooks the work of two premiere postwar poets of these respective nations, Inge Müller and Ingeborg Bachmann.

If we return to the metaphor of burial as an apt trope for locating the remembrance of the bombing attacks and the subsequent destruction of cities, we can begin to trace its recovery in Bachmann's *Todesarten* (Ways of Dying) and Inge Müller's poetry. Each writer locates the nexus of unsanctioned personal remembering and the collectivized public memory that derides it through images of burial. These images are often associated with a covering up (*ver-schütten*) that is both a way of preserving the experience of trauma and of exposing its roots. One need only think of the many scenes in *Der Fall Franza* (*The Book of Franza*) in which the main protagonist experiences the sensation of being buried alive or feels distraught at the site of un-burial as in the case of the Egyptian mummies. In order to explore this notion of live burial as metaphor and cipher for a memory against the grain of a sanctioned public memory in the GDR and in Austria, it is helpful to recall Benjamin's notion of insightful remembrance (*Eingedenken*) as a method for sifting through rubble, not to rebuild (the reconstruction that Sebald refers to in his essay), but rather to see the rubble of the past as it gathers in vast piles in the present. *Eingedenken* is not so much a cognitive or historical memory, but a stance toward remembrance that sharpens the senses of sight and insight. In his dialectical method of understanding how the past can be experienced not as "dead time," but as living memory, Benjamin calls for a perception of the past's presence in the present. There is "the increasing concentration (integration) of reality, such that everything (in its time) can acquire a higher grade of actuality than it had in the moment of its existing."[4] As Ulrich Baer has shown us in his recent study of trauma, atrocity remembered is not simply a reliving of the event that caused the trauma, but a creation of that which might have happened.[5] Just as the Messiah's footprint may alight upon any threshold at any time, so too the meaning of the past reveals itself in a flash (Benjamin's dialectical image) to those with a presence of mind. The writings of Bachmann and Müller share these rare moments of recognition, among other correspondences, in their particular mediation of trauma through the trope of burial.

This essay explores the correspondences between the textual representation of the medium and means of remembrance and experiences of live burial in selected writings of the former GDR writer Inge Müller (1925-1966) and the Austrian writer Ingeborg Bachmann (1926-1973).[6] Both came of age as writers within a social and national context in which traumatic subjective experiences associated with civilian suffering and culpability were neither accepted nor perceived in those forms of collectivized memory readily available in the public sphere. Trauma is seen here in its elementary form: "an overwhelming experience of sudden, or disastrous events, in which the response to the event occurs in the often delayed and uncontrolled repetitive occurrence of hallucinations and other intrusive phenomena."[7] In their book, *Testimony*, Dori Laub and Shoshana Felman emphasize that a witness account of a traumatic experience serves as an echo and a confirmation that the victims of a trauma are not alone and do not succumb to confusion between the connection of personal experience and history.[8] In their writings, Müller and Bachmann portray the experience of trauma via the metaphor of live burial (*Verschütten*). This does not only refer to the emergence of a direct visceral experience, but also to fragments of repressed history rendered inaccessible through the silence of a societal collective. Bachmann's writing about the aftereffects of the traumas of World War II, represented by the protagonist's structures of memory in *The Book of Franza*, has an apparent affinity with "the writing of the disaster" (Maurice Blanchot)[9] in Inge Müller's poetry. "The disaster, not experienced. It is what escapes the very possibility of experience—it is the limit of writing. This must be repeated: the disaster de-scribes. Which does not mean that the disaster, as the force of writing, is excluded from it, is beyond the pale of writing or extra-textual."[10] By de-scribing disaster and re-invoking its presence in the present, Bachmann and Müller unearth the silenced recollections of the war. Their writing transmits the traces of the incommensurability between personal trauma and official history, and the asynchronicity between national narratives that bring closure and the unclocked appearance of individual recollections of trauma. The trauma of the war "at home" and the inability to speak about it in public are displayed in Bachmann's texts through the failed attempts of her protagonist to mourn the victims of the Shoah without eliding their experiences into her own stories of victimization. In Bachmann's texts, this dilemma remains unresolved. Traumatic experience is either projected outwards, that is, toward the figure that in the public sphere most represents the image of the victim—i.e., the Jews, the Papua, the pariah—or becomes internalized as forms of hysteria and self-destruction. Müller's poems, in contrast, do not mediate phenomena of repression per se, but of an actual experience of live burial that in retrospective, poetological rendering becomes a cipher for the ineffability of trauma.

I would like to introduce Inge Müller's work here in order to suggest a new way of reading the writings of both authors. The artistic processing of trauma associated with the experience of fascism and war in the writings of Bachmann and Müller, present two projects of memory that run contrary to postwar public memory and official historical accounts of the war. The significant differences between the experiences of the two writers during the war should not be disregarded. In fact, the structural similarities of the national contexts in which they came of age do not elide the more immediate rendering of experience in Müller's work. Even as live burial serves as a point of comparison, the relationship of the metaphor to reality cannot be compared without differentiation. Even though the metaphor of live burial has a central meaning in the works of both writers, and they articulate a similar critique of the sanctioned memory structures in the representative societies, their connection to the experienced trauma is fundamentally different. To investigate the denial (and recovery) of civilian trauma in the works of Müller and Bachmann, we must first contrast the political models from which the "interior settings" ("inwendige Schauplätze")[11] draw: the "sacrificial land" Austria and the "victorious state of history," the GDR.

From their respective socio-political vantage points, the texts of both writers recall not only the traumatic experience of the victims murdered in World War II by the Nazis and their active and passive accomplices, but also the silencing of the trauma by civilians, who did not fall victim to the Nazis or die on the battle fields. The absence of a collective public forum for expressing painful recollections of civilians in both countries led to a void of memory referred to by both writers. Whereas Bachmann's writings recall the presence of fascistic ideology in postwar Austria and its effect on everyday language and on the relationship between men and women, for example, Müller's writing expresses the correspondence between fascistic and Stalinist thinking and practices without effacing their differences. Müller's experience of being buried alive for three days beneath rubble lends her writing a visceral immediacy that Bachmann's writing renders more reflectively. There, the suffering of a dominated female figure symbolizes the detrimental side effects of living in a social context that represses the dialectical relationship between personal trauma and collective, national history.

Both authors cover not only the disaster of the war but also the after-effects of German fascism and the silence that takes place behind the scenes in the "interior settings" of experience. "And the threat does not take place in war, nor in times of the raw cruelty through the dominance of survival, but before and after, that is in peace times, and I had now a true notion, . . . that peace would be more difficult for us."[12] In recognizing the ongoing existence of trauma in the supposed time of peace, Bachmann does not merely repeat the continuing forms of trauma: "I have always demanded something beyond historicity, and I always wanted my grounding."[13] This grounding both within and through the forgotten moments of the dialectical relationship between individual remembrance and history is found within the depths of language shaped by repressed experience. Bachmann's texts imply that the recollections of World War II are displaced by civilians into a repressive discourse, a discourse which does not only infiltrate everyday speech, but also psychic space. However, that which leads to disruption when exposed can make the cause of the destruction visible. Bachmann's writing of disaster echoes Benjamin's note on Brecht's *Fatzer*: "To bottom out means here always: to get to the bottom of things."[14] Utterly grounded by devastation, one gets to the core of things, a recognition that Müller formulates in her poems, as we shall see.

Bachmann and Müller name the wounds inflicted in the wake of a repressive collectivized national history. While official historical accounts try to make individual suffering relative in the name of collective history, Müller and Bachmann write specifically about the connection between their own history and the publicly denied history. They anticipated the complexity of a phenomenon that has been only recently publicly addressed. The war trauma of Germans and Austrians was mostly silenced in postwar times in the interest of fabricating less culpable national histories (Austria = "sacrificial land," GDR = "antifascist state"). The question of the guilt of the "silent majority" was not raised, at least, in the public sphere. Had this question been asked, it would have meant that this majority, guilty by their silence, would have had to acknowledge their share in the guilt. This would have had not only moral but also political and financial consequences, as we now see in the discussion for reparations for forced laborers and Swiss Banks' harboring of German Jewish property. A language to address this question—be it through art or politics—was not missing, but rather the political (and moral) will to recognize and accept the responsibility and the guilt. This is true for both countries. Where there is a consciousness of guilt, a language for it can develop and transform guilt into responsibility. If this consciousness is suppressed, language-voids develop that become filled with clichés and phrases (*Gerede*). Bachmann and Müller counter these clichés in their texts by citing them out of kilter and contrasting them with historical and social realities that encompass the absented civilian trauma. The public lacked a language to speak in one breath of the suffering of the victims of National Socialism and the suffering of the civilians, at least in the public realm. Simultaneously, civilians could, by association with the national myths of being on the "right side," free themselves from participating in their own grief, as well as their guilt, even as they commemorated the victims of National Socialism through routinized rituals.

When the trauma was expressed, it was often in the form of identification with the victims of the Shoah. Austria as the victim and the GDR as the victor developed similar ideological mechanisms to establish the official recollections of the war. In the GDR, the Stalinist anti-Semitism of the early 1950s was hushed with the ideology of a consequent antifascist state. The "overwhelming identification with the antifascist struggle and the opposition to Hitler" led to a silencing of the National Socialist structures of behavior, personal attitudes and educational principles which continued after the war in daily life.[15] In Austria, the decision of the Allies to declare the Austrians victims of Nazi occupation enabled the Austrians to deny their responsibilities for the cruelties until the Waldheim-Affair in 1986 led to public debate about Austria's responsibilities in World War II.

In both cases, the social constellations based on national myths led to the denial of guilt and responsibility. However, neither of the two countries honored their own fallen soldiers or civilians with a grand display of monuments or memorial walls. Even though the GDR celebrated their Communist heroes and resistance fighters and Austria their national patriots, no major national memorial celebration was held. The official GDR saw itself as heir of the "better" Germany and as the "victor of history," despite the Nazi-socialization of the majority under the Third Reich, reflected, for example in Christa Wolf's *Kindheitsmuster* (A Model Childhood). The GDR relied on its status as "victor of history" and simultaneously saw itself as a victim of National Socialism, a status that Bachmann criticizes in her essay fragment "Auf das Opfer darf sich keiner berufen" ("No one may refer to the victim").[16]

Despite its nearly seamless annexation by Hitler's troops in 1938, Austria internalized the decision of the Allies to declare it the first victim of National Socialism. This assumption, and the subsequent political neutrality, neutralized any semblance of responsibility in the body politic. In that regard, the general tendency of many Austrians to claim victim status and the tenets of GDR society that embraced an "innocent" antifascist stance had much in common. Even though historians, intellectuals, and some politicians have, ever since the 1950s, investigated the past, the Waldheim-Affair in the mid-eighties, and the ongoing attacks aimed at "foreigners," serious questions about the processing of the past in Austria remain. Despite the drastic difference between the cultural and political conditions in the GDR and in Austria, both countries built their national identity on a myth that denied the co-responsibility for the crimes in World War II.

Bachmann experienced these myths, and her dissection of them forms the core of her poetological work. Bachmann's writing in the postwar years works against the denial of the "skeletons" in the Austrian closet. The interweaving of personal trauma with collective history absent in Austria's public sphere pervades throughout Bachmann's writing. She writes against the covering-up of pain and suggests that the refusal to express this pain is associated with the inability to name the source of loss. The structure of remembrance in Bachmann's *Todesarten* offers an alternative to the routine grief ritual and the fossilization of subjective experiences of loss in the state's sanctioned collective memory. The expression of a forgotten, repressed history through images of personal trauma in Bachmann's work, therefore, contradicts the social and national forms of memory that strove to mask the sources of this trauma.

Under these circumstances, Bachmann and, as I will show, Müller refuse to participate in the typical postwar discourses devoid of contradiction and loss. Instead, the authors strive to find words to express a "counter-memory" which Charlotte Delbo, author and survivor of Auschwitz and Ravensbrück, calls "deep memory,"[17] and for which Walter Benjamin coined the term *Eingedenken* (insightful remembering). *Eingedenken* is a process of remembrance in which the past is seen as part of the present, and a critical historiography recognizes subjective forms of memory and, therefore, questions the content of official history, the history of the victor. These forms of memory do not recall the past as a unified completed event but, as the recurrence of the trauma *and* the possibility for redemption, bring the past and the present into a dialectical image. *Eingedenken* is not so much a cognitive or historical memory, as a memory of recognition, brought to perception through a presence of mind for the overlooked remnants of the past in the present. Thus, the past is not "dead time," but living memory.

The writing of disaster in Bachmann's and Müller's oeuvre reminds us that 1945 was not the end but the beginning of a new "cold" war that was continued without being declared. The process of remembrance is not without painful consequences, as both authors attest in their own reflections on the historical context in which they came of age. They both insist on looking back, even as they recognize the acute pull of the rhetoric of progress in their respective postwar social and political contexts. Like Benjamin's angel of history, the figures in both writers' works remain hampered by the accumulation of debris even as they name the causes of the destruction.[18]

The similar socio-political structures in which Bachmann and Müller came of age inform their self-understanding as writers. Their biographies are inscribed in their writing not as reflections of an outer reality, but as ciphers of underlying social and cultural repression. The details of Bachmann's biography are well known, and she herself spoke of the elision of a childhood experience of betrayal (a slap from a boy she thought her friend) with the first sight and sounds of Hitler's troops marching into her hometown, Klagenfurt. The experience haunts her for the rest of her life:

> There was a certain moment that destroyed my childhood. The march into Klagenfurt by Hitler's troops. It was so horrible, that on this day my memory began: through pain ex-

perienced too soon in an intensity that I perhaps never experienced again. Of course I did not understand it in the sense in which an adult would understand. But this monstrous brutality which could be felt, this screaming, singing, and marching—the occurrence of my first death fright. A whole army entered our quiet, peaceful Kärnten.[19]

Bachmann describes this trauma as something that continues during peace time:

> It is still with me today and at age eighteen I saw the second destruction of the world, the army camp, the retreat, the advance, the partisan war, the low-flying aircraft, the hunger, the commerce, the red-white-red flags, the Donau waltz after the war with the war, the profiteering, the brutality of the early peace, and the morality of war and peace.[20]

The loss of childhood, the shock of history, and the image of ruins form the experience of a whole generation of Germans and Austrians who, like Bachmann and Müller, were born during the 1920s and who grew up during World War II.

Inge Müller was born in Berlin in 1925 and spent most of her life there. The many-layered history of Berlin as the site of war and postwar division is the source of her historical experience, the place where she was buried alive, and from whose destruction she never fully recovered. It is the location of the primal scene of her adult life. After spending a year on a work detail in Steiermark (Austria) during the war, she was sent back to Berlin to support an anti-aircraft position. During a bomb attack by Soviet artillery, shortly before the end of the war in April 1945, Inge Müller was buried alive for three days under the rubble of an apartment building. This experience forms the structural and figurative framework of her poetry. A few weeks after being rescued from the ruins and the darkness, Müller discovered the bodies of her parents beneath a burned door. The trauma is doubly severe; she discovers that someone had cut off her mother's ring finger to steal the wedding ring attached to it while she is off trying to find a cart to take her parents' corpses to a mass grave. This experience will form the basis for much of her poetry in the aftermath of the war. Her memory of live burial and of the desecration of her mother's body is not so much mirrored as it is transformed into a metaphor of archeological remembering. Like Benjamin's metaphorical rememberer who sifts through layers of buried fragments, the daughter in Müller's mourning poem, "Trümmer 45" ("Rubble 45"), records the fragmentation, and leaves them unfettered from their origin rather than integrating them into a unified history.

Müller's experience during the war resulted in a recurrent trauma. She committed suicide in 1966. The ruins beneath which she lay for three days in Berlin toward the end of the war remained with her, reminders of the ruins wrought by the aftermath of war, as much as by war itself. In her short, sparse poem "Rubble 45," it is the bare bones of trauma which she describes. It is not the failure of memory that leads to the repetition of the sensation of live burial, but the difficulty of bearing the weight of the rubble in a public sphere that refuses to acknowledge them.

Rubble 45

There I found myself
And wrapped myself in a cloth:
One bone for mama
One bone for papa
One for the book.[21]

The lyrical "I" presents her parents with bones. The bones recall her origin—she returns a remnant of herself to her progenitors—yet the origin is a mere bare bone left after the intact bodies of the dead have rotted away. The bones are instruments of writing, and, through poetological displacement recall the missing ring finger of her mother. The loss becomes readable "in the book" and can be deciphered as a remnant of a former existence. The notion of unearthing one's self in order to expose loss is a common trope in Bachmann's poetry as well. The lyrical "I" in Bachmann's poem "Strömung" ("Stream") takes a piece of herself from the earth, as one would remove bones after the flesh has rotted away, leaving the bare bones of memory: "So far in life and so close to death, / that I shall litigate no more, / From the earth I rip my par."[22]

The sparseness of Müller's poems reminds one of the figures of Giacometti that were produced during World War II. The figures, in their apparent lack of excess, do not recall the destruction in the camps, nor of the death itself, but the overflow of death and despair in the spaces they inhabit. Similarly, Müller's "I" recalls the fragmentary remnants of a life; in the poem, the daughter herself becomes a ruin. Her ancestral connection is recorded through the cipher of the bone wrapped in a cloth as a type of sacred gift. She returns a part of herself to her dead parents, thus creating a space for them in the realm of the living. The poet fulfills the role of the witness in a society that prefers not to see the bodies, nor to recognize the presence of the dead.

Like the allusions to fairy tales in the works of Bachmann, Müller's line: "And wrapped myself into a cloth" recalls Grimm's fairy tale "Von dem Machandelboom" ("The Juniper-Tree"). In that fairy tale, the dead brother speaks through a bird, and the bird asks the sister to wrap her brother's bones in a cloth: "My sister, Marlenichen, / find all my bones, / wrap them in a silk cloth. . . ."[23] Like the bones in the cloth, Müller documents the mutilation that takes place during war, but also the hope that the dead will not be forgotten nor used by the living toward the purpose of legitimization of collectivized public memory. Thus, the ritual of wrapping a bone (the missing finger, as well as the imagined sacrifice of her own bones by the daughter) is a motif for representing the undoing of the improper burial of the dead "I" in the throes of war. While the severed finger is a lived experience for Müller, it is a significant intertextual coincidence with the portrayal of the missing ring finger in Bachmann's *Malina* in the description of the cemetery of the murdered daughters.[24] Therefore, the poem extends beyond the biographic topology of Inge Müller's life to the question of remains in the aftermath of the bombing and of the Shoah. The rubble of 1945 also consisted of the ashes of Auschwitz and other concentration camps. The poem does not recall the death of the victims of the Shoah. The symbolic returning of the bones of the dead to the dead does, however, suggest that a marking of the absence of the bones of the victims is not elided by the recalling of individual German trauma.

The image of the I-figure retrieving her own bones and returning them to those who perished beneath the rubble implies that the dead parents took the place of their daughter in the cellar. The dual trauma of being buried alive and then having to bury her own parents becomes the main motif in Müller's writings. Müller uses images of live burial as metaphors for the contradictory desire to forget the trauma but also to name it: "The truth is quiet and unbearable."[25]

Let us turn to Müller's trilogy of live burial, "Unterm Schutt" ("Beneath the Rubble").

> Beneath the Rubble I
>
> Under the howl of the iron pipes I slept
> In the grip of the earth
> The child Moses drifting in the basket
> Amongst reeds and surf
> And woke up when somewhere in the heart of the continents
> Smoke rose from the open sea
> Hotter than a thousand suns
> Colder than a marbled heart
> Carried by sixteen feet I walked in the middle
> The first step against the dust.
>
>
> Beneath the Rubble II
>
> And then suddenly the heaven crumbled
> I laughed and was blind
> And was a child again
> In Mother's womb wild and mute
> With arms and legs flailing unpracticed
> Grabbing and running.
> Images all around
> No ground no roof
> That which is—disappeared
> I am before I was
> One breath hours
> The others! A moment as bright as the sea
> Someone's knocking—

Hand me the globe!
To hold on to myself
Bridges and poles
A million hands I need
You won't take me, death, I will make myself heavy
Until they come and dig
Until they have me
You will leave empty-handed.

Beneath the Rubble III

When I fetched water a house fell on me
We bore the house
The forgotten dog and I.
Don't ask me how
I do not remember
Ask the dog how.[26]

In the first poem of Müller's rubble trilogy, the divide between life and death becomes permeable; a threshold opens up with the recognition that catastrophe is present for the living *and* the dead. The catastrophe of being buried alive becomes the point of departure not only to uncover other atrocities, but to overcome them and to survive the unbearable task of recording them. The poem is dialectical in its attempt to record an unnatural disaster. The images of doom allude to man-made destruction, such as the dropping of the atomic bomb ("a thousand suns"), and maintain the separation from natural disaster, thus avoiding the integration of atrocity into the "natural history of destruction" of which Sebald has written. There is no record of retribution or of deserved suffering here, but rather a plea to acknowledge the trauma of the bombing, not to mythologize it or use it to legitimize the forgetting of the crime of extermination.

The sound of howling with which the trilogy ends and begins points to another crucial source of interpretation beyond the mirroring of experience and poetics. The sound of the iron pipes are both the sound of domestic comfort—the sound of heating pipes—but also the thunder of artillery in war. The common, everyday sound is transformed into its opposite—the horror of destruction on the home front. The domestic act of fetching water is juxtaposed with the transformation of the heavens into fiery hell. The shock of the disaster initially puts the lyrical "I" to sleep. She enters a state of suspended reality, and the boundary between the wakefulness of life and the oblivion of death is the threshold where the "I" returns to non-symbolic speech. Her voice on the other side of speech is smothered. The "I" survives in this state of suspension because she enters the twilight in which the living and the dead, the past and the present, coexist. The darkness of the crypt becomes the darkness of the womb. When the "I" awakens, she enters a new world as a Moses figure. This figure is both reminiscent of the biblical Moses who brings his people forth from slavery, thus ending his own state of limbo as a child drifting down the Nile, and figurative for a moment of salvation yet to be manifested. Müller's Moses floats down the Nile river which, again, by intertextual coincidence, is the same river that Franza, in Bachmann's *The Book of Franza*, hopes will heal and save her from her traumatic memories. Similarly, the "I" beneath the rubble of a nation destroyed for rendering destruction, becomes, in the face of danger, the chronicler of the disaster in its mythical and legendary guises.

Trapped in the space of destruction, the "I" in Müller's poem reverts to a place in which she both preserves the semblance of the world in geological terms and retreats to a space where she has no means to speak of the world in its physical, earthly incarnation. In the "grip of the earth," she is simultaneously transported away from the war and directly into it. The war is evident in the experience of thirst and hunger, but it is the experience of awakening "unearthed" that creates the space for remembering. Like Coleridge's "Ancient Mariner," the "I" imagines salvation even as hope fades away. Yet, the actual awakening and unearthing—the contact with the outside world that knocks and drags her out of her crypt/womb beneath the rubble—isolates the "I." She is "somewhere" undefined, without orientation and homeless and in search of re-orientation ("Hand me the globe!"). On the other hand, she is in the heart of the continent, not unlike the protagonist in Joseph Conrad's *Heart of Darkness*. The marbled heart of the earth is Berlin, the same location that Bachmann described in the early sixties, as she was working on *The Book of Franza*, as a place for "coincidences" and chance encounters in the disorientation of the aftermath of war and atrocity. Like Bachmann's "I" in the poem "Böhmen liegt am Meer" ("Bohemia Lies by the Sea"), Müller's "I" is also "[u]nderground—that means the ocean, there I'll find Bohemia / again. / From my ruins, I wake up in peace. / From deep down I know, and am not lost."[27] The journey in Müller's poem is one in the realm of the apocalypse, in the center of the earth and in the core of the disaster. Like the figure in Bachmann's poem, the "I" reawakens with a renewed sense of displacement from that which has kept her from the means of remembrance.

In the second poem, "Beneath the Rubble II," the "I" becomes the fetus in the womb, a fetus not only torn from the place of its possible death but from its original refuge. The "I" describes the experience of being buried alive not as an Antigone trauma, but as the sensation of being in the womb. She is standing at the beginning of life. The disaster represents a return to the source and a return to complete helplessness. The structures which bury the "I"—the house—become the symbol of the womb but also of imprisonment, detainment, and paralysis. In the womb each breath takes an hour. Life is precious and the experience of trauma does not take place in chronological time. The place of burial, the earth, is at once crypt and refuge and contains the hope of rebirth, which finds a metaphoric echo in Franza's experience of being buried alive by the mud of the Nile.

In the state of disaster, the "I" in Müller's poem reverts to the state of pre-symbolic speech—a speechlessness in the face of the ineffable. In the ever-present state of emergency in which the "I" finds herself, she regresses to a time before speech, a speech that she never really recovers despite the return to life. The reawakening or the rebirth carries with it the destruction of the semblance of safety and of being at home. No longer at home in the world and literally without home, the "I" is also reduced to speechlessness. The location in which to speak of the trauma is absent; we are left with a void. Unable to speak of the experience of the trauma, the "I" leaves the remembering to the dog, itself a figure that cannot speak, even as it is the mythical border-crosser between life and death. The dog is the witness, even as it is a creature unable to speak of the experience. Even as the lyrical "I" is saved, she remains in the realm of the dead for she cannot speak of what she has seen. We return to the beginning of the trilogy, to the sound of the bark, the howl, the undecipherable, and the animal-like sound of the iron pipes and the war artillery. The speechlessness represents the absence of a place where it is possible to speak about the loss and the pain even though the "I" triumphs over death. Despite the loneliness caused by being buried alive, the poem expresses the desire to be witness and chronicler of the disaster. The figure in the poem does not give up hope even though she cannot put the experience of being buried alive into words. The "I" in the poem becomes "the place holder of the human voice" from which Bachmann writes in her "Frankfurter Vorlesungen" ("Frankfurt Lectures").[28] Like the dog that lies at the feet of Dürer's allegory of Melancholia, the dog in Müller's poem, forgotten among the living, symbolizes the unspoken memories that are audible only at the threshold where the living and the dead coexist.[29]

Müller's three poems are examples of the poetological correspondence to which I referred in the beginning of this essay. In *The Book of Franza*, the connection between personal trauma and world history is represented through metaphors of live burial in ways similar to Müller's poems. Like "Beneath the Rubble I, II and III," *The Book of Franza* presents the experience of trauma as the unspoken experience of the war and its aftermath. As I have written in my book, *Waking the Dead. Correspondences between Walter Benjamin's Concept of Remembrance and Ingeborg Bachmann's 'Ways of Dying,'* the desire to bury one's own by remembering the trauma of the bombing in World War II, often gets displaced into a commemoration of the victims of the Shoah.[30] In *The Book of Franza*, for example, the protagonist identifies with victims of atrocity and oppression, in order to get to the bottom of her trauma. Gravesites and metaphors of live burial play a major role in unearthing the trauma from which the protagonist slowly dies.

While traveling with her brother in Egypt, the female protagonist Franza asks him to cover her with the mud of the Nile in the hope that this will heal her: "She had buried her feet into the mud and asked [Martin] to pack her in mud. You will see, she said with feverish excitement, I will be healed by the mud of the Nile."[31] In hope of rebirth and healing and to flee the memory of her treatment by her husband Jordan, Franza has Martin cover her completely in the mud. While Franza experiences the feeling of being buried alive as the mud hardens and "petrifies" her, Martin is distracted by the passing of the presidential ship, representative of the development of a new order in Egypt. While Martin is busy with the official course of history, Franza realizes that she is paralyzed and is suffocating.[32] The stories, "which make up the whole history," remain silenced because the public memory drowns them out. The thinking that supports the order of power and makes it possible that the water of the Nile washes away (instead of converging) many stories in the name of technology takes no notice of the silent. Martin is simply distracted from the official history by his sister's small story, not illuminated by it.[33] Once Martin notices her distress and frees her from the encaked mud, Franza jumps into the Nile, the same water in which the ship, the symbol of world history, passed by. Franza experiences a simulated live burial reminiscent of Antigone's punishment for her disregard for the new order.[34] In *The Book of Franza*, Franza's painful experience of simulated live burial embodies the "dialectical image" that produces a "flash of recognition" (Benjamin). Franza consciously experiences the break between her personal story and world history, symbolized by the passing of the presidential ship whose passengers visit the construction of the Assuan Dam, a symbol of progress and power.

Despite the proximity of the metaphor, the difference between the experience of being buried alive and its poetic reflection remains. Franza has insight into the source of the trauma, a flash which Benjamin calls a "dialectical image." Even if Franza understands her situation, this understanding will not be incorporated into world history but into her body. In the moment of danger, the ability to speak the trauma comes into reach. The piles of debris beneath which collectivized history has buried personal trauma prevents the insight that this trauma is part of a larger history. It is the presence and the recognition of the pain of trauma that characterizes Bachmann's and Müller's work. The separation between subjective and collectivized forms of remembrance remains fictitious and a delusion, like the second skin of which Delbo writes: "Auschwitz is so deeply etched on my memory, that I cannot forget one moment of it. I live next to it (Auschwitz). Auschwitz is there, unalterable, precise, but enveloped in the skin of memory, an impermeable skin that isolates it from my present self."[35] Similarly, the simulated burial, which Franza hopes to be a cure and perceives as a second, stronger skin, becomes an illusion.

The writings of Müller and Bachmann convey the memorial depth needed to speak of the trauma experienced by German civilians in the bombing attacks, even as they struggle with the impossibility of finding a language that does not replace one form of atrocity with another. Remembering the victims of the Shoah without speaking for them or *with* them remains a dilemma that will not end, even with the passage of time. Since the public memory of the GDR and post-war Austria did not permit an adequate commemoration of the victims of the Shoah, nor a space for the trauma of the German civilian, the writings of the two authors serve as witness of the discrepancy between the subjectively experienced trauma and its silence in the official myth of non-culpability. As Camus said in his Nobel Price speech (1957), the task of the writer is not to serve the victors of history, but those who are the subjects and the victims of history.[36] Bachmann and Müller bear witness. Both question the collective monumentalized history of their respective nations and write as subjects caught in the crossfire between the debilitating unspoken trauma of individual Germans in the war and the repressive public memory that lacks spaces within which to speak of this trauma. The metaphors of live burial which Bachmann and Müller rely upon are the assemblages of their social and cultural discourses and experiences. While Bachmann's writing reflects this metaphor to portray repressive structures of misremembering in her society, Müller's experience of being buried alive has lent directness to her writing; thus, she seems to forgo reflective commentary. The experience of silence and denial of respective national responsibility and the inability to speak of personal suffering may provide insight into the reasons why little was said of the bombings in the immediate aftermath of the war. And perhaps this inability was also part of an unconscious realization that speaking of German and Austrian wartime trauma among civilians would do injury to the dead victims of the Shoah.

NOTES

1. This essay is a revision of the English translation of my essay "*Unterm Schutt*: Eingedenken in den Werken von Ingeborg Bachmann und Inge Müller," *"Über die Zeit schreiben": Literatur- und kulturwissenschaftliche Essays zu Ingeborg Bachmanns Todesarten-Projekt*, ed. Monika Albrecht and Dirk Göttsche (Würzburg: Königshausen & Neumann, 1998), 119-134. I am grateful to Monika Albrecht and the publisher, Königshausen & Neumann, for permission to publish this article in English.

2. Walter Benjamin, *Gesammelte Schriften*, ed. Rolf Tiedemann and Hermann Schweppenhäuser (Frankfurt am Main: Suhrkamp, 1980), IV/1:400.

3. W. G. Sebald, *The Natural History of Destruction*, trans. Anthea Bell (New York: Random House, 2003).

4. Walter Benjamin, *The Arcades Project*, trans. Howard Eiland and Kevin McLaughlin (Cambridge, Mass: Belknap Press, 1999), 329.

5. Ulrich Baer, *Spectral Evidence: The Photography of Trauma* (Cambridge, Mass: MIT Press, 2002).

6. See Ines Geipel, *"Dann fiel auf einmal der Himmel um." Inge Müller. Eine Biographie* (Berlin: Henschel, 2002), 215-16. Geipel briefly alludes to the similarities between the poets' tragic lives, but does not develop the relationship beyond the biographical similarities.

7. Cathy Caruth, "Unclaimed Experience. Trauma, Narrative, and History," *Yale French Studies* 79 (1991): 181.

8. Shoshana Felman and Dori Laub, *Testimony. Crisis of Witnessing in Literature, Psychoanalysis, and History* (New York and London: Routledge, 1992).

9. Maurice Blanchot, *The Writing of the Disaster*, trans. Ann Smock (Lincoln: University of Nebraska Press, 1986).

10. Ibid., 7.

11. Ingeborg Bachmann, *The Book of Franza*, in *The Book of Franza and Requiem for Fanny Goldmann* trans. Peter Filkins (Evanston, Ill.: Northwestern University Press, 1999), 4, and *Der Fall Franza*, in *Werke*, 4 vols., ed. Christine Koschel, Inge von Weidenbaum and Clemens Münster (München: Piper, 1978), 3:342.

12. Ingeborg Bachmann, "Ein Ort für Zufälle" ("A Place for Coincidences"), *Todesarten-Projekt. Kritische Ausgabe.* 4 vols. in 5 vols., ed. Monika Albrecht and Dirk Göttsche (München: Piper, 1995), 1:176. For Bachmann, peace times are not necessarily the end of war, but the continuation of war under different circumstances: "Order has returned, peace is again so secured that it could be threatened daily. Then, when it was beyond danger, in the Maydays, in its wildly wonderful, and screaming Maydays, I had the premonition that with peace and the new order something was upon us that would be more difficult to maintain than the war and the chaos, that lay in wait in the occupation and the subordination, in the fantastic arrangement of the war" (179).

13. Ibid., 173.

14. Walter Benjamin. *Gesammelte Schriften,* II/2:509.

15. Barbara Heimannsberg. "Kollektive Erinnerungsarbeit und nationale Identität," *Das kollektive Schweigen. Nationalsozialistische Vergangenheit und gebrochene Identität in der Psychotherapie,* ed. Barbara Heimannsberg and Christoph J. Schmidt (Köln: EHP Edition Humanistische Psychologie, 1992), 21f.

16. *Werke,* 4:335.

17. Charlotte Delbo, *Auschwitz and After,* trans. Rosette C. Lamont (New Haven: Yale University Press, 1995), 3.

18. Perhaps it is no coincidence that Müller's texts were published as a whole for the first time after the German unification. In June 1995, a gravestone was placed in her honor at the Pankow cemetery. Two edited volumes of Müller's writing, including her poetry, have been published by Aufbau Verlag: Inge Müller, *Irgendwo; noch einmal möcht ich sehn. Lyrik, Prosa, Tagebücher. Mit Beiträgen zu ihrem Werk,* ed. Ines Geipel (Berlin: Aufbau-Verlag, 1996), and *Daß ich nicht ersticke am Leisesein. Gesammelte Texte,* ed. Sonja Hilzinger (Berlin: Aufbau Verlag, 2002).

19. Ingeborg Bachmann, *Wir müssen wahre Sätze finden. Gespräche und Interviews,* ed. Christine Koschel and Inge von Weidenbaum (München: Piper, 1983), 111.

20. Bachmann, *Todesarten. Kritische Ausgabe,* 1:178-9.

21. Inge Müller, *Dass ich nicht ersticke am Leisesein,* 9. All translations of Müller's poems are my own.

22. English translations of Bachmann's poems are taken from *In the Storm of Roses: Selected Poems by Ingeborg Bachmann*, trans., ed., and intro. Mark Anderson (Princeton: Princeton University Press, 1986), 165.
23. Brüder Grimm, *Kinder- und Hausmärchen*, vol. 1 (Stuttgart: Reclam, 1980), 243. My translation.
24. Bachmann, *Todesarten. Kritische Ausgabe*, 3.1:548. For an in-depth discussion of the missing-finger motif in Bachmann's *Malina*, see Karen Remmler, *Waking the Dead. Correspondences between Walter Benjamin's Concept of Remembrance and Ingeborg Bachmann's "Ways of Dying"* (Riverside: Ariadne Press, 1996), 108f.
25. Inge Müller, *Wenn ich schon sterben muß. Gedichte*, ed. Richard Pietraß (Berlin: Aufbau Verlag, 1985), 83.
26. Müller, *Daß ich nicht ersticke am Leisesein*, 24-26.
27. Bachmann, *Selected Poems*, 177.
28. Bachmann, *Werke*, 4:237.
29. The figure of the dog deserves further investigation. The barking dog as a trope for the presence of unspeakable memory also appears in Bachmann's short story "Das Gebell" ("The Barking"). In this story, the neglected mother of Franza's husband, the psychiatrist, Jordan, hears the barking of her long-dead dog. In western mythology, the figure of the dog is mostly associated with the ability to pass between the realms of the living and the dead. Dogs act as intermediaries between the living and the dead.
30. *Waking the Dead*, 62.
31. *The Book of Franza*, 104.
32. Ibid., 106f.
33. Ibid., 106.
34. Cf. Johanna Bossinade, *Das Beispiel Antigone. Textsemiotische Untersuchungen zur Präsentation der Frauenfigur. Von Sophokles bis Ingeborg Bachmann* (Köln: Böhlau, 1990).
35. Delbo, *Auschwitz and After*, xi.
36. Cf. Albert Camus, "Rede anläßlich der Entgegennahme des Nobelpreises am 10. Dezember 1957 in Stockholm," *Kleine Prosa* (Reinbek: Rowohlt, 1961), 8.

13 / "Every name in history is I"[1]: Bachmann's Anti-Archive

Michael Eng

> The shaft that art directs at society is itself social; it is counterpressure to the force exerted by the *body social*...
>
> With the continuing organization of all cultural spheres the desire grows to assign art its place in society theoretically and practically; this is the aim of innumerable round table conferences and symposia. Once art has been recognized as a social fact, the sociological definition of its context considers itself superior to it and disposes over it.
> —Adorno, *Aesthetic Theory* (1970)

The Situation of the Work of Art

Such then is Adorno's characterization of the dual—and dialectical—nature of art works as simultaneously "autonomous structures and social phenomena,"[2] whose autonomy arises from that very ground against which they seek to resist. Yet these statements also capture Adorno's well-known pessimism about modern culture's ability to recuperate the forces which critique it, to affirm modernism's critique of society's functional self-organization while at the same time appropriating this critique as simply one other category for societal administration. This is how in a time (*our* time) that many have identified as late capitalism, reification—the fragmentation and abstraction of social life, what Fredric Jameson calls the "conquest of culture" by capital[3]—extends to accommodate all such criticism targeted against it. It is a reach, in Adorno's view, so extensive that not even the "hermeticism" of Celan's poetry is able to escape it: rather than read Celan's work negatively as a poetry "without aura" (as Benjamin does with Baudelaire), Adorno contends that reified consciousness, in the form of a literary criticism modeled after the "pseudo-scientific ideology" of communication, emphasizes instead the work's "thematic content and putative informational value."[4]

For Adorno, this challenge to the autonomy of art by reified consciousness thus affects the autonomy of art's "materials," especially poetic language. However, it is modernism's response to the dissolution of the material—modern art's reflection upon, and resistance to its loss of what Adorno calls its self-evidence—that constitutes the second stage of the dialectical relation between art and the social. This is where Adorno's remarks on Hofmannthal's *The Lord Chandos Letter*[5] recalls Ingeborg Bachmann's prior analysis of Hofmannsthal and the question of the justification of literature and literary language in her *Frankfurter Vorlesungen (Frankfurt Lectures*, 1959-60).[6] More the case with Bachmann than with Adorno, however, the engagement with Hofmannsthal approaches the status of Jameson's notion of metacommentary, the (artistic) struggle with both the object of thought as well as one's own process of thinking about the object. Bachmann's reflection on Hofmannsthal's struggle with poetic language (via *Chandos*) becomes then a mode of struggle with her own possibility of speech, a struggle with what I would propose and aim to explain is the historicity of this speech (and of course the speech of historicity).

My hypothesis with respect to the idea of metacommentary in the present context, however, is that the problem of historicity (the relation of language to history) in Bachmann is not only a problem within her work, but also a problem posed by her work, and specifically by the question of the status of her work within the context of reification and culture outlined above. This entails, I would suggest, acknowledging a combination of both the Althusserian sense of overdetermination and Jameson's concept of a political unconscious, a combination, that is, of the sense of multiple determining conditions in history and the *necessary repression* (the necessity of ideological investment and closure, of necessary failure, the necessity of Necessity itself)[7] of any number of these conditions in identifying and attending to a single one, or even a combination of them. As a result, the aesthetic anxiety about the status of literary and poetic language expressed in the *Frankfurter Vorlesungen* becomes also a(n unexpressed) class anxiety, an unease about the effect of one's own position (and not only the effect of one's own language) within the (social) "Whole" ("das Ganze," [4:198]).

Although the example is a simple one, and although, as I will soon discuss, Bachmann is quite adept at mapping out multiple tracts of history (a kind of attention to overdetermination),[8] the issue, as it pertains to what Adorno calls a "self-unconscious historiography,"[9] is not impertinent. In her lectures there are significant allusions to literature's position against the fragmented social horizon (4:198), some in which Bachmann even likens the status of literature in the contemporary setting to a stock exchange (4:186). Yet the engagement with such an image of literature immediately becomes an internal contradiction once the gesture with which Bachmann denounces the instrumental and economic organization of the image is turned on her own remarks advocating the "usefulness" of literature for stirring the sleep of human beings (lest society fall into "bankruptcy") (4:198-99). There is a sense on Bachmann's part that one cannot simply imagine oneself out of one's position. One is always, that is to say, *in language, in history,* in a "historical situation," so to speak (4:196). But the relative autonomy of her position is thus at the same time constituted by the framework of reified consciousness, which her interventions are intended to dismantle, and it becomes a question of what—again, necessarily—*of history* Bachmann's text represses even as it seeks to engage its historical conditions (or contradictions).

However, reification is at work in a parallel manner much more severely and yet also much more transparently in the critical reception of Bachmann's writing, in the field of Bachmann-Studies as it is generally organized (or more appropriately, *Bachmann-Forschung,* since Bachmann's American audience is still in its initial formation, and, more importantly, since the methodological, *wissenschaftliche* demands of philology in the European context are a determining influence on the problem that concerns us here). I think most immediately in this connection of Sigrid Weigel's protests in her important monograph on Bachmann in which she posits an image of Bachmann as someone engaged in the social-political project of *"Denken nach Auschwitz"* ["thinking after Auschwitz"] (directly, as it were, as an *Intellektuelle*) against the autobiographical "mythologeme" of Bachmann as the *"poeta assoluta* of Gruppe 47," the Wittgensteinian-influenced storyteller, the "fallen poet," the feminist of the *Todesarten-Projekt,* the Austrian post-War writer, or a combination of all of these.[10] Although Weigel herself does not employ the concepts of a Marxian analysis, these images whose workings she seeks to disrupt strike me as so many fragmentations brought about by an ideology of reflection and essentialism, in which the philosophical question is reduced to the reproduction and demonstration of the philosophical concept in literary form (literature as philosopheme, as Philippe Lacoue-Labarthe says[11]); the feminist question is reduced to Bachmann's performance of "her" gender as a woman writer, and the questions of trauma and history are reduced to notions about the horror and *a priori* ineffability of the Shoah and the Second World War.

In all of these instances, it seems to me, the wounds inflicted by such ideological and mechanical renderings of Bachmann's text become all the more severe precisely because they themselves are the cause that cuts their analyses off from the ground which they propose to address. I am in agreement with Weigel to the extent that she sees these maneuvers as strategies of containment; yet, I would go even further than she in saying that their confinement does not begin with Bachmann as such, but with a prior, reifying gesture dividing, as Jameson suggests, the private from the public, the individual from the historical, the psychological from the social, and the poetic from the political.[12] As a result, it becomes easier to deal with Bachmann's thought if we could simply isolate and analyze it in terms of creative (i.e., private, individual) facts and not have to consider its relation in totality or to the social whole.[13]

By attending to the problem of the formation of the question of history in Bachmann's work, I believe it will then be possible to begin to imagine a different organization of her writing. Rather than confirming mirror reflections—representations—of history and its "causes" (whether they be class, gender, disaster, etc.) from without, much can be gained in the way of provoking the text to pass into its social-historical ground, I think, by inverting the problem and investigating the "concept of history"[14] *produced by* Bachmann *in her work*.[15] Such a process brings with it the questions of overdetermination and repression raised above, and involves not the reduction of the text to its so-called background or context (historicism), but asking about what the text *does*, so to speak, about what ways it "acts on" the question of history (historical praxis) and therefore acts on our understanding, for example, of what

Foucault calls the archive, the production of those statements within the social imaginary that determine what *can be said*.

This struggle with language has always been acknowledged in Bachmann's text, yet seldom *as also* a struggle with the *event* of history—its taking-place, it might be said, in the taking-place of the text (and vice-versa). No longer is it a question of *"das Ich in der Geschichte"* ("the I in history"), Bachmann says, but of *"die Geschichte im Ich"* ("history in the I")(4:230). "Every name in history is I," Nietzsche tells us. The I which speaks, which is always the I of language and not of people, is always forced in Bachmann to deal with a history that simultaneously addresses and repels it. Conversely, history itself is treated by Bachmann as the thing-in-itself that must always pass through the resistance of language. That is to say, it must always be subject to a process of articulation and yet can never be fully articulated.

In the space that remains, I would like to contribute further to the possibility of reading Bachmann in this manner by returning to several scenes in her later prose work in which the image of the archive is operative and operated upon. I would like specifically to entertain again that question of forgiveness in *Der Fall Franza* (*The Book of Franza*) which the work of Karen Remmler has studied in terms of the problem of history, memory (or remembrance), and *Vergangenheitsbewältigung,* and which Weigel's research has recently and so appropriately placed in relation to other discussions of forgiveness (Derrida's, Kristeva's, and Arendt's, in particular) within contemporary thought.[16] Both Remmler and Weigel do so not coincidentally in terms of Bachmann's relationship to Benjamin, with Weigel emphasizing the process of Bachmann's reading of him. Mine will be a modest addition to their already substantial interventions, with the aim of giving further weight to Bachmann's confrontation with that sense of contradiction between the present and the past which Benjamin names the dialectical image.

Forgiveness and History

It was perhaps one of Bachmann's great misfortunes, we might now say, never to have been read by Benjamin. The imaginary scenario would go beyond wondering what might have taken place had he owned some of her writings in his private library, and instead would concern what he might have made of her meditations on the relation of aesthetic form to the presentation (as in *Darstellung*) of history itself. Bachmann's stance in this sense is less a full, theoretical position than an intervention in history's "presentational moment" ("darstellendes Moment").[17] It is an intervention that concerns, as Christopher Fynsk suggests, and as I will argue, history's "legibility" in the dialectical image. For the moment, it seems important to keep in mind that the interruption and "halting" ("Stocken") that constitutes the following scene from *Der Fall Franza*, and which Weigel reads as a dialectical interruption to the opposition between forgiveness as a private category and justice as a public category, is not a conceptual resolution to this opposition but a presentation in its own right of "the claim of history" itself.[18]

While confronting a doctor who participated in medical experiments on concentration camp prisoners and is now in hiding in Egypt, Franza surprises herself when she utters the words, "Forgive me" ("Verzeihung"). She then immediately recalls reading transcripts of testimony of witnesses in the Nuremberg trials (something required of her while assembling materials for her husband's, Jordan's, psychological study of the period), particularly the testimony of one witness who at one point in being questioned utters the same phrase: "*Excusez-moi si je pleure.*"[19]

> And then witness B, after the earth had gone round once, so that this page could be written on: Forgive me for crying ...
> No other instance of these words, "Forgive me," had occurred in the entire records. From the doctors nothing but sentences and decrees and what must appear legally foolproof, thus: I was in no position to judge that. And: I don't know. And: I had no knowledge of that. And: if you ask me, that cannot be judged in this way. There was constant talk of views and opinions; no silence fell, and never did anything come to a halt. (3:458)[20]

The passage (and especially its reception) becomes instructive on many levels. It speaks to the felt contradictions between the ethical impulse to respect the singularity of the victims of history and the juridico-political necessity which only recognizes information and facts and conducts inquiries into truth (as adequatio, as correspondence). It also—and much more to the point as far as Bachmann is concerned, it seems to me—(re)stages what Bachmann refers to in *Malina* as the punishment of language itself, its cruel law of repetition which condemns the victim to speak *as a victim* each time they seek to speak.[21]

For Weigel, as I have been saying, the scene serves as an accentuation of the "abyss" that she sees as having opened up between Arendt's account of the public utility of the concept of forgiveness in the juridico-political sphere and life of the *Mitwelt* in general, and Kristeva's call for an exclusively ethical preservation of the concept in a private, psycho-analytic, (quasi-)religious employment.[22] According to Weigel, neither Arendt's linear account nor Kristeva's atemporal conception does justice, so to speak, to the confrontation with what Weigel characterizes as "post-Shoah history." Arendt's 1958 treatment of forgiveness in *The Human Condition* has yet to fully answer the challenge posed to it by the book on Eichmann written five years later, in which the irreconcilability of the ethical and juridical meanings of justice makes its appearance. Conversely, Kristeva, by reserving forgiveness for the privacy of the psychoanalytic (and, as Weigel contends, the aesthetic), ends up emptying the concept of any historical content. In Weigel's estimation, Bachmann offers "a theory of forgiveness" that calls for an ethical relation to the past (in the way of Derrida's formulation of "forgiving the unforgivable") *as* "a rupture in political discourse."[23] Franza's personal shock thus becomes the shock of the past interrupting the historicizing discourse of the present.

Remmler, too, will situate the text within contemporary debates about the proper form of memory in the post-war period and Austria's inability to come to terms with its role during the Second World War. The scene thus corresponds for Remmler to Benjamin's opposition between *Andenken* (commemoration) and *Eingedenken* (insightful remembrance, as Remmler translates it). The universalizing discourse of the juridico-political process is a form of *Andenken*, of a memory that monumentalizes and petrifies the past.[24]

Eingedenken, by contrast, is then a kind of negative remembrance, a memory that serves as an index of absence, a language on the order of Mallarmé's poetics.[25] Franza's shock, again, symbolizes both the need for memory and the impossibility of memory in the collective space. The monumentalizing memory of the public sphere constitutes an erasure of the singularity of suffering and victimization, thereby re-inscribing such experiences in the form of a collective forgetting.[26] Not only the suffering of the victims of the *Nazizeit* or Shoah, but all suffering that receives no expression and is therefore re-marginalized, is symbolized in this scene. This is why Franza's identification with the victims of the Shoah rests on her experience of marginalization and suffering at the hands of her husband in the domestic sphere (in addition to his rape of her, he makes her the object of his psychological study). Accompanying this identification are her identifications with the colonized in history (she calls her husband a colonizer), a bound woman in an Egyptian train station, and even, as Lyotard says, "a paradigm of the victim," the animal.[27] Franza's figure functions then as a kind of historicization of the intersection of race, class, and gender and of their overdetermining presence (as absence) in the constitution of the social. They "are," that is to say, insofar as they are (continuously) forgotten.

Finally, there is yet a third aspect of modern experience being presented to us in the scene, the experience, that is, of modernity that characterizes the contradictions pervading the *Todesarten-Projekt* in general. I mean what contemporary Marxist thought calls the problem of mediation.[28] This critique, which arrives to us from Marx, the Frankfurt School, but also Sartre and the Marxian encounter with psychoanalysis,[29] situates the connection between the supposed interiority of the private and the exteriority of the public or the social within the problematic not of relation, for the Marxist presupposition is that they are always already related, but of mediation. If there is a moment of freedom, in other words, within the Marxist hermeneutic, as Jameson calls it, then it is precisely in the moment when what is socially determined[30] and named the private turns back onto the social and historical sphere from which it comes and resists that reification/privatization/colonization of collective experience that sections collective experience into specialized, non-related areas. Here the private, individual experience, which is really an artifact of an experience of alienation from the social (this is the experience of modernity par excellence, according to Benjamin, because it destroys experience as such), in affirming the life given it by the social and the historical, denies any *apolitical* characterization of it, thereby giving the lie to any opposition pitting the so-called freedom of the individual and the creative—the poetic, for example—against the necessity of the socio-political and historical field.³¹

The scene from *Franza* offers us such a denial in its presentation of all the relations that we conventionally perceive as private—the personal story in the psychoanalytic relation, the relation to the family (the domestic), and even and especially Franza's relation to her body—within the implacability of their social formations. In this way, Bachmann really does provoke the simultaneity of the personal and the political for which both Marxist commentary and contemporary feminism has been arguing. As Remmler suggests, we are everywhere reminded in *Franza* of Bachmann's description in the text's preface of the *Schauplätze* (settings) that *das Innen* (the interior) paradoxically requires in order to become present (3:342).³² Thus, any inner experience Franza attempts to claim as her own is exposed immediately and relentlessly to an exteriority that interpolates it *as inner experience*. Franza, it seems, can only internalize her frustration (too tame a word) at having to speak always already in a "being-for-others"; yet, even if her speech could attain the status of "being-in-itself," the only enunciation that would be recognized in a social space saturated by the communicative regime is the reified speech of information and facts. From the perspective of a feminist interrogation of the space allowed Franza's character, any speech attributed to her can only be recognized as gendered speech, the irrational speech of the madwoman, of the hysteric. This shows us however, that if Franza's attempts to inject singularity into the collective social life are met with the generalizing vacuum of the ideological logic of gender-privilege and the economic, then her "fantasies" are no more fantastic necessarily than those of the system. What gives the staging of the entire problematic, with all of its intersections and crossings, additional critical precision though is the "fact" that Franza comes to her position from out of a space of class and racial privilege. Franza is thus "implicated" in the very system that oppresses her and those with whom she identifies. This is the novel's position, rather than Franza's own, and the reason that it gains in criticality instead of being called into question is because it dispels with the ideological belief that there is an exit from history's closure.

There is a danger, nonetheless, in remaining too satisfied with interpretations of the novel's movements directed exclusively at its content, historical or otherwise. Although I think Weigel's and Remmler's readings of the scene are provocative and even necessary when placed in the context of such debates, I am not fully convinced that in attending solely to the content of the scene (as both seem to do, even when they later point out the scene's problematic aspects), there is enough evidence to suggest anything like the offering of either a theory of forgiveness or a strict advocation of memory as *Eingedenken* on Bachmann's part. Or rather, the Wittgensteinian distinction seems to apply here: in focusing so much on what the passage seems to *say*, one loses sight of what the text *does*. Here it becomes important to remind ourselves of the impact the turn to Benjamin (on Bachmann's part, but also on the part of her interpreters) has on the form of reading itself. In Weigel's case, one cannot talk about the turn to Benjamin along the axis of *"das Sich-Zeigende"* (that which shows itself) without also talking about the formal aspect of the literary work and the *darstellendes Moment* mentioned above—a presentational moment not of the past, but of "truth" as the present's confrontation (*Auseinandersetzung*) with the past, of the Then and Now in the dialectical image.[33] In similar fashion, Remmler seems to attend to Franza's reaction as an instance of the dialectical image contained within the scene rather than consider Bachmann's text as such as an attempt to "read" the dialectical image.[34]

I will investigate just what is at stake in Bachmann's relation to the dialectical image in a moment. Let me conclude this section by saying, though, that the impulse to theorization with respect to the text strikes me as a philosophizing gesture, not (or not only) in terms of the formation of a deployable concept, but in terms of a reduction of literary content to the status, again, of a philosopheme and of the literary form—the form of writing—to a vehicle of philosophical communication. The gesture consequently substitutes a juridico-political historicism for a philosophical one, positing the Shoah as the reason or ground represented (if only negatively) *in* the scene and thus failing to ask about the modes of production organizing the scene *as a scene*.

The distinction between the interpretive reading and what I am arguing for as the reading of the text as an interpretive text, as a meditation, that is, on the act of interpretation as such, carries with it substantial ideological (and not just methodological) consequences. In the former method, the text is at best a commentary, the staging of the historical in literary terms. This view, at its most radical, treats the text as a symbolic work and history as a relatively stable category. Treating the scene as an act interpreting its own attempts at interpretation, on the contrary, opens it up to its libidinal investment in the object; it does not seek (only) to represent the historical context or event, but instead *presents itself* as an event of history. The text, having become reflective of its event of "textuality" (as it was once fashionable to say), becomes historical in the fullest sense, and takes on the task of metacommentary, as Jameson describes it, an allegorical writing of (the writing of) history *in time*.[35]

The Dialectical Image

> A historical materialist cannot do without the notion of a present which is not a transition, but in which time stands still and has come to a stop. For this notion defines the present in which he himself is writing history. Historicism gives the "eternal" image of the past; historical materialism supplies a unique experience with the past. The historical materialist leaves it to others to be drained by the whore called "Once upon a time" in historicism's bordello. He remains in control of his powers, man enough to blast open the continuum of history.
> —Benjamin, Thesis XVI, "Theses on the Philosophy of History"

> For the historic index of images doesn't simply say that they belong to a specific time, it says above all that they only enter into legibility (*Lesbarkeit*) at a specific time. And indeed this entering into legibility constitutes a specific critical point of the movement inside them. Every present is determined by those images that are synchronic with it:

every Now is the Now of a specific recognizability (*Erkennbarkeit*). . . . It isn't that the past casts its light on what is present or that what is present casts its light on what is past; rather an image is that in which the Then (*das Gewesene*) and the Now (*das Jetzt*) come together into a constellation like a flash of lightning. In other words, an image is dialectics at a standstill. For while the relation of the present to the past is a purely temporal, continuous one, the relation of the Then to the Now is dialectical: not of a temporal but of an imagistic nature. Only dialectical images are genuinely historical, i.e., not archaic images. The image that is read, that is, the image at the Now of recognizability, bears to the highest degree the stamp of that critical, dangerous impetus that lies at the source of all reading.
—Benjamin, Convolut N, 3.1 [On the Theory of Knowledge, Theory of Progress], *Arcades-Project*

It is perhaps best for me to take a moment to clarify the argument being undertaken here. At issue, I feel, is not whether Bachmann applies Benjamin's reflections on the philosophy of history to the literary sphere or whether Bachmann was interested at all in the problems posed by the tradition of historical materialism, although she does acknowledge this latter aspect.[36] Rather, I think that the question concerns what of the historical materialist problematic Bachmann's text—intentionally or unintentionally, consciously or unconsciously—contains. It is a question, therefore, of how Bachmann's work impacts and adds definition to the problematic of historical materialism as such.

For my part, I view this form of questioning as particularly advantageous in approaching Bachmann's later prose work because a genuinely historical materialist approach, a dialectical criticism, that is to say, does not reduce the text to one organizing principle which the text then "expresses" repetitively. Opposed to those readings, some of which I have already mentioned, that continuously reduce the complexity of Bachmann's writing to the sounding of a single note, a criticism attuned to the constellation of forces recognized by the historical materialist field instead attends to the work's presentation of multiple, determining contradictions and intersections and is as a result rightly suited to accommodate, in a manner of speaking, the intricacies, turns, and contradictions (and frustrations) that texts such as the *Todesarten* present. I began to suggest something of the presentation of such a constellation of historical forces in the previous section of this essay by pointing out, as a few other readers of Bachmann have done, the crossing of economic, class, gender, race, and geo-political categories in *Der Fall Franza*. None of these categories can be seen to be a single, determining cause of history or even history in themselves, and some of them, we have learned, come to oppose and contradict the other. But *Franza* does reveal alternatively the importance of constructing a criticism that can mediate between, say, concerns targeting determinism from the standpoint of modes of production and concerns targeting determinism on the basis of gender bias and the patriarchal order. The combination, rather than the competition, of these forces will be required in order to resist the fragmentation of the social which characterizes our contemporary experience. As Franza asks in *Das Buch Franza*: "My story and the story of all people; together, they surely comprise the sum of history, but where are the points of intersection between these and the whole of history?"[37]

I also began to suggest, however, that attention to overdetermination in terms of the content of the text is incomplete as long as we do not ask how this content then turns upon the form of writing itself. This is to say, then, that what remains equivocal in Bachmann's work—what keeps the question of its historical character in the Benjaminian (and Marxian) sense in suspense—is not only the degree to which her writing addresses history, but also and especially the degree to which it pushes through to and comments upon the situation of its taking-place. Drawing attention to such ambiguity is not to criticize Bachmann outright, though, for it could not be otherwise. On the one hand, as Jameson tells us, any approach to history must confront also that dialectical play between Identity and Difference, between "history" in its writing and History as the relation to finitude, the fact of existence. Because, as I have noted, one is always already "in situation"—which is to say, in language, in the imaginary, and ultimately in ideology—, one never fully reaches Difference as such, the Other is always otherwise. This is why the underlying attraction of the identification Franza undergoes in relation to the victims of the Shoah, of colonization, of domestic abuse, and animal cruelty is in fact the attraction of abstraction,[38] of reification. As a result, Franza's identification comes to resemble the history of Austria's own identification of its experience of the *Anschluß* (Annexation) in 1938 with that of the victims, if not of the Shoah specifically, then of the *Nazizeit* in general. From the perspective of Franza's place as a white woman within Viennese society, her identification with global victimization then is an attempt to separate herself from the perpetrators of the crimes of history and absolve herself of responsibility in the world.[39] As it is with Franza, so it is with Austria. It is in this sense not a turn to history, but a flight from it, an exercise in *mauvais-foi*. In the staging of the inevitability of abstraction (in language) and the temptation of reification, of occluding the fact of abstraction, how, I ask, does it stand with the work itself? How does it stand with the text *as text*?

It is in this manner on the other hand that this alternation between the Same and Other in the text need not be as maddening as it appears to be to many of Bachmann's readers, especially to those who prefer to view Bachmann's writing in an exclusively liberating mode. The ambiguity, I feel, encourages a view of her text as an engagement with the category of aesthetic form and the question of the aesthetic's share in constituting what I called above a concept of history. Prior to all the versions and drafts of the *Franza* novel, prior to all evidence within the content of the work, prior to any preface describing the context of the text, there is an indication in the competing titles: *Der Fall Franza, Das Buch Franza*. Both frame the text within the fact of textuality itself, or as such, and both name an immanent, necessary relation to reading—to legibility—as a result. This becomes the real effect (the effect of the Real?) in Franza's experience, a suffering, in the Lacanian sense, of the signifier that is unconscious not because it denotes an inner experience proper to her, but because it indicates an entrance into language that always precedes her (knowledge), that is always to come, "to arrive." Similarly, "we," as readers, are positioned in a reading of the writing of Franza's reading. It is not a simple case, then, of Franza acting as an allegorical representation of Austria, but of the writing of allegory itself. If there is a necessary relation to legibility posed by the text, if, that is to say, the relation to history is the image of history's entrance into legibility, then there *must be* a condition of ambiguity, of the undetermined, of the unconscious, of the to-be-written/to-be-read conditioning the encounter of the Then and the Now.[40]

Other than the meditation on the essence of language, the related question of the legibility of the dialectical image continues to be the most ignored area in Benjamin's work.[41] This is where we might disagree with Jameson's assessment that it may have been Benjamin's good luck never to have been translated fully into English until now. For the arguments presented in *The Origin of the German Tragic Drama*, linking the form and *Formensprache* (language of forms) of the work of art to the history of the origin (of truth) (and vice-versa), find their completion, so to speak, in the recently completed translation of the *Passagen-Werk* (*Arcades-Project*) and its meditations on the dialectical image. Important for us to remember, though, without launching into a full discussion of his writing on it, is the inextricable relation between the image's historicality and its entrance into recognizability and legibility. Dialectical images are historical not by their content, but by their *becoming* recognizable and legible "at a specific time"—in short, by their becoming images. Not only do dialectical images give themselves to be read, but they indicate "that critical, dangerous impetus that lies at the source of all reading."

Bachmann's text comes at the other side, I believe, of the danger within which Benjamin was writing. This is not to equate their individual experiences, for the task again is to emphasize the experience of the text. This is also not to rule whether the work is or is not a dialectical image, or whether the work contains dialectical images (as some might characterize the scene from *Franza*). That would be a strange exercise indeed. For the dialectical image does not name a stable, recoverable moment (as does an archaic image for Benjamin), and it is first of all historical inasmuch as it becomes *our concern* (an "our" that is always to be determined in the act of reading). It is, as Benjamin tells us, always unique and consequently always exposed to the threat of the "will-never-have-been-read." It is precisely this threat of the missed encounter with the past that addresses "us." No, I would want to say against the notion of a recovery of the past in the dialectical image, that the stakes of the question of Bachmann's reading of Benjamin do not become apparent until we ask about the "claim of history" that appears as a provocation to all reading in the latter's work, and until we ask about the movement of appropriation (of "becoming-our-concern," and therefore of the presentation [*Darstellung*] of history) at work in Bachmann's text.

Conclusion, or: the Postmodern

> This is how one pictures the angel of history. His face is turned toward the past. Where we perceive a chain of events, he sees one single catastrophe which keeps piling wreckage upon wreckage and hurls it in front of his feet. The angel would like to stay, awaken the dead, and make whole what has been smashed.
> —Benjamin, Theses IX, "Theses on the Philosophy of History"

> No one may call on the victim. It is an abuse. No land and no group, no idea, may call on its victims.
> But the difficulty in expressing this.
> —Bachmann, "No one may call on the victim" (Fragment)

Fredric Jameson has suggested on a number of occasions that a newly reunified Germany could benefit from a national reception of Benjamin. His status as a "pre-Nazi era exile" might serve to frame his writing within a literary canon "not tainted by any of its earlier avatars (from the West German Federal Republic, through Hitler, back to Weimar or the Wilhelminian period)."[42] By contrast, Ingeborg Bachmann's fate in the reified arena of German letters still prevents her work from serving as that moment of interruption that the Austrian social imaginary so desperately needs. However, recent debates scrutinizing the seamlessness of Austrian post-war memory, such as those surrounding Rachel Whiteread's *Holocaust-Denkmal*, suggest that there may yet be a space left open for a contribution by Bachmann's "Texte." Such a contribution would actually assist in the most radical sense in the much needed realization of an Austrian national literature fallen into ruin, come undone, or at least become bankrupt by a flight from history. One is tempted to think that only such a shock—the shock, in Benjamin's full sense, of a lack of shock—to the system of letters in the Austrian cultural scene (one that would at the same time call the category of culture itself into question) could stir the collective slumber that Bachmann describes in the *Frankfurter Vorlesungen*.

For those of us working in the Anglo-American reception of Bachmann's text, I believe that much can be gained in maintaining a sense of the specificity of the formation of the image of history in her work. The key, I feel, lies in pursuing what is at stake in precisely this idea of the practice of producing an "image-of" in a way that demands us to thematize the fact of "our" act of reading now (or in anticipation of the Now). Her writing provides us with an image of cultural resistance, of a resistance to the supposed transparency and monumentality of Culture, but confronts us also with the contradictions of ideological/libidinal investment in any desire to engage history as Difference, including her own.

NOTES

I wish to express my thanks to Gisela Brinker-Gabler for encouraging me to pursue my earlier concerns with Bachmann's text in this direction and for directing me to the debates to which this essay attempts to contribute.

1. Friedrich Nietzsche, Letter to Jacob Burckhardt, 6 January 1889. Friedrich Nietzsche, *Nietzsche Briefwechsel. Kritische Gesamtausgabe*, hg. von Giorgio Colli und Mazzino Montinari. Unter Mitarbeit von Helga Anania-Hess. 3. Abt., Bd.5 (Berlin/New York: Walter de Gruyter, 1984), 578. Translated in *Selected Letters of Friedrich Nietzsche*, trans. Christopher Middleton (Chicago: University of Chicago Press, 1969), 347. Cited in Gilles Deleuze and Félix Guattari, *Anti-Oedipus: Capitalism and Schizophrenia*, trans. Robert Hurley, Mark Seem, and Helen R. Lane (Minneapolis: University of Minnesota Press, 1977), 21, where they write: "There is no Nietzsche-theself, professor of philology, who suddenly loses his mind and supposedly identifies with all sorts of strange people; rather, there is the Nietzschean subject who passes through a series of states, and who identifies these states with the names of history: '*every name in history* is I. . . .' "

2. Theodor W. Adorno, *Aesthetic Theory*, trans. Robert Hullot-Kentor (Minneapolis: University of Minnesota Press, 1997), 248.

3. Fredric Jameson, "Interview," interview by Leonard Green, Jonathan Culler, and Richard Klein, *Diacritics* 12, no. 3 (Fall 1982): 77.

4. *Aesthetic Theory*, 321-22.

5. *Aesthetic Theory*, 16.

6. Ingeborg Bachmann, *Frankfurter Vorlesungen: Probleme zeitgenössischer Dichtung*, in *Werke*, ed. Christine Koschel, Inge Weidenbaum, and Clemens Münster (München: Piper, 1978), 4:188-90. Volume and page numbers given in parentheses throughout the text refer to this edition.

7. See, for example, "Architecture and the Critique of Ideology," Fredric Jameson, *The Ideologies of Theory: Essays, 1971-1986. Volume 2: Syntax of History* (Minneapolis: University of Minnesota Press, 1988), 40.

8. Two important texts which contribute to our understanding of Bachmann along these lines are Monika Albrecht, "Colonization and Magical World View in Ingeborg Bachmann's Fragment of a Novel *Das Buch Franza*," trans. Lilian Friedberg and William Tucker, *glossen*, heft 7 (1999): http://www.dickinson.edu/departments/germn/glossen/heft7/albrecht.html, and Sara Lennox, "White Ladies and Dark Continents in Ingeborg Bachmann's *Todesarten*," *The Imperialist Imagination: German Colonialism and Its Legacy*, ed. Sara Lennox, Sara Friedrichsmeyer and Susanne Zantop (Ann Arbor: University of Michigan Press, 1998), 247-263. What is emphasized in these studies is Bachmann's occupation with the intersection of racial- and gender-specific historicization and subject-formation.

9. Adorno, *Aesthetic Theory*, 182-3.

10. Sigrid Weigel, *Ingeborg Bachmann. Hinterlassenschaften unter Wahrung des Briefgeheimnisses* (Wien: Paul Zsolnay Verlag, 1999), 15.

11. Philip Lacoue-Labarthe, "The Unrepresentable," *The Subject of Philosophy*, ed. Thomas Trezise (Minneapolis: University of Minnesota Press, 1993), 116-157.

12. See Fredric Jameson, *The Political Unconscious* (Ithaca, NY: Cornell University Press, 1981), 20.

13. Cf. Jameson's remarks about this attitude in terms of the anti-theoretical and anti-intellectual stance of the Anglo-American tradition in general and, in a manner that will concern us shortly, with respect to Benjamin's thought in particular: Fredric Jameson, "The Theoretical Hesitation: Benjamin's Sociological Predecessor," *Critical Inquiry*, vol. 25, issue 2 (Winter 1999): 267.

14. Jameson, "Architecture and the Critique of Ideology," 39.

15. The difference between a conception of history as an *internal relation* and history as an *external cause* is what informs Adorno's characterization of the modern work of art: "They are the self-unconscious historiography of their epoch . . . . Precisely this makes them incommensurable with historicism, which, instead of following their own historical content, reduces them to their external history" (*Aesthetic Theory*, 182-83). I believe that this notion, when paired with the question of history in Bachmann, as well as with Benjamin's concept of the dialectical image discussed below,

shares the stakes of a constellation Sara Lennox outlines in her essay, "Materialistischer Feminismus und Postmoderne," *Literaturtheorie und Geschichte: Zur Diskussion materialistischer Literaturwissenschaft*, ed. Rüdiger Scholz and Klaus-Michael Bogdal (Opladen: Westdeutscher Verlag, 1996), 53-71.

16. Karen Remmler, *Waking the Dead: Correspondences between Walter Benjamin's Concept of Remembrance and Ingeborg Bachmann's "Ways of Dying"* (Riverside, Calif.: Ariadne Press, 1996). Sigrid Weigel, "Secularization and Sacralization, Normalization and Rupture: Kristeva and Arendt on Forgiveness," trans. Mark Kyburz, *PMLA* 117, no. 2 (March 2002): 320-23.

17. Walter Benjamin, *Ursprung des deutschen Trauerspiels*, cited in Christopher Fynsk, *Language and Relation: ... that there is language* (Stanford: Stanford University Press, 1996), 215-26.

18. Fynsk, *Language and Relation*, 211-226.

19. Ingeborg Bachmann, *Todesarten-Projekt. Kritische Ausgabe*, ed. Monika Albrecht and Dirk Göttsche, 4 vols. in 5 vols. (München: Piper, 1995), 2:49. Cited in Weigel, *Ingeborg Bachmann*, 503.

20. Cited and translated in Weigel, "Secularization and Sacralization," 323. This scene is included in both the originally published text (under the title *Der Fall Franza*) in the Piper-edition of Bachmann's collected works (*Werke*) as well as the critical edition of the *Todesarten Projekt* (under the title *Das Buch Franza*, as Bachmann had later decided to call it). In the course of my essay, I will refer to both versions of the text. I do not wish to ignore the questions of the unity of the text by treating these two editions as the same text, but I have to say that I will also not be overly concerning myself here with their differences. Indeed, I think the fragmentary character of the *Todesarten Projekt* actually contributes to my interest in pursuing the event-character of the text, but when I cite further passages from the project, I will of course acknowledge the edition from which they originate as I have done with the preceding quotation. For an English translation of Bachmann's novel-fragment, see *The Book of Franza* and *Requiem for Fanny Goldman*, trans. Peter Filkins (Evanston, Ill.: Northwestern University Press, 1999).

21. I pursue this with some greater attention in "Among Murderers and Madmen: Ingeborg Bachmann, Fascism, and the Experience of Writing," *How2*, vol.1, no. 6 (Fall 2001): http://www.scc.rutgers.edu/however/v1_6_2001/current/readings/encounters/eng.html

22. Weigel, "Secularization and Sacralization," 320-23. See also Julia Kristeva, "Forgiveness: An Interview," *PMLA* 117, no. 2 (March 2002): 278-295.

23. Weigel, "Secularization and Sacralization," 322-23.

24. Benjamin writes, for example: "Commemoration (*Andenken*) is the secularized version of the adoration of holy relics.... Commemoration is the complement to experience. In commemoration there finds expression the increasing alienation of human beings, who take inventories of their past as of lifeless merchandise. In the nineteenth century allegory abandons the outside world, only to colonize the inner. Relics come from the corpse, commemoration from the dead occurrences of the past which are euphemistically known as experience" (cited in Fredric Jameson, *Marxism and Form* [Princeton: Princeton University Press, 1971], 73).

25. A "negative theology," Benjamin says elsewhere of Mallarmé (Walter Benjamin, "The Work of Art in the Age of Mechanical Reproduction, *Illuminations*, ed. Hannah Arendt, trans. Harry Zohn [New York: Harcourt, Brace and World, 1968], 224).

26. Remmler, *Waking the Dead*, 29-49.

27. Jean-François Lyotard, *The Différend: Phrases in Dispute*, trans. Georges Van Den Abbeele (Minneapolis: University of Minnesota Press, 1988), 28. Phrases that have courted extensive critical attention include Franza's declarations, "Ich bin eine Papua" (3:414), or "Ich bin von niedriger Rasse" (*Todesarten*, 1:257). Cf. Remmler, *Waking the Dead*, 56-69; Weigel, *Ingeborg Bachmann*, 496-508; Albrecht, "Colonization and Magical World View in Ingeborg Bachmann's Fragment of a Novel *Das Buch Franza*." As Albrecht notes, this equation of the feminine with the victim/colonized and the masculine/patriarchal with the oppressor/colonizer was a prevalent theme in the sixties while Bachmann was working on the *Todesarten* but also in the eighties when Bachmann's work was "rediscovered."

28. Cf. Fredric Jameson, *Marxism and Form*.

29. Jameson, *Marxism and Form*, 215. See also Fredric Jameson, "Imaginary and Symbolic in Lacan," *The Ideologies of Theory: Essays, 1971-1986. Volume 1: Situations of Theory* (Minneapolis: University of Minnesota Press, 1988), 75-118.

30. Jameson goes to great lengths in his work to mark a distinction in this respect between a conception of determination based on the Enlightenment sense of materialism, a mechanical determination, and the concept of determination within a Marxist materialism, a determination from modes of production. See for example, "Architecture and the Critique of Ideology," 42.

31. Cf. Jameson, *The Political Unconscious*, 20.

32. Remmler, *Waking the Dead*, 45.

33. Weigel, *Ingeborg Bachmann*, 99-106. Cf. Fynsk, *Language and Relation*, 211-226.

34. Remmler, *Waking the Dead*, 60.

35. Jameson, *Marxism and Form*, 66-83.

36. Bachmann speaks about her current reading in historical materialism in a 1963 interview. See Ingeborg Bachmann, *Wir müssen wahre Sätze finden. Gespräche und Interviews*, ed. Christine Koschel und Inge von Weidenbaum (München, Zürich: Piper, 1983), 42, cited in Albrecht, "Colonization and Magical World View in Ingeborg Bachmann's Fragment of a Novel *Das Buch Franza*."

37. *Todesarten*, 2:270, cited and translated in Albrecht, "Colonization and Magical World View in Ingeborg Bachmann's Fragment of a Novel *Das Buch Franza*."

38. Remmler, *Waking the Dead*, 50-1.

39. Albrecht, "Colonization and Magical World View in Ingeborg Bachmann's Fragment of a Novel *Das Buch Franza*."

40. It is in this sense that I follow Weigel's contention of a turn in Bachmann's conception of language from the utopic to the messianic. See Weigel, *Ingeborg Bachmann*, 482-95.

41. The one exception, and the one upon which these and preceding comments on the legibility of the historical in Bachmann are based, I have already named in Christopher Fynsk's *Language and Relation*.

42. Jameson, "The Theoretical Hesitation: Benjamin's Sociological Predecessor," 267.

Contributors

Karen Achberger is Professor of German at St. Olaf College in Northfield, Minnesota.

Barbara Agnese teaches Comparative Literature at the University of Vienna.

Monika Albrecht is currently Visiting Professor of German at the University of Massachusetts in Amherst.

Gisela Brinker-Gabler is Professor of Comparative Literature at the State University of New York at Binghamton.

Michael Eng teaches philosophy at Pratt Institute in Brooklyn, New York.

Peter Filkins is a writer, poet and translator who teaches at Simon's Rock College of Bard.

Lilian Friedberg received her Ph.D. in Germanic Studies at the University of Illinois, Chicago.

Sabine I. Gölz is Associate Professor in the Department of Cinema and Comparative Literature at the University of Iowa.

Frederick Garber is Distinguished Emeritus Professor of Comparative Literature at the State University of New York at Binghamton.

Sara Lennox is Professor of German Language and Literatures and Director of the Social Thought and Political Economy Program at the University of Massachusetts, Amherst.

Ingeborg Majer O'Sickey is Associate Professor of German at the State University of New York at Binghamton.

Robert Pichl teaches at the Institute for German Language and Literature Studies (Germanistik) at the University of Vienna.

Karen Remmler is Professor of German and Director of the Weissman Center for Leadership at Mt. Holyoke College.

Andrea Stoll received her Ph.D. at the University of Mainz. She is a lecturer at the Institute for German Language and Literature (Germanistik) in Salzburg, Austria, and lives as dramaturgist and free-lance writer in Mainz, Germany.

Markus Zisselsberger is a Ph.D. candidate in Comparative Literature at the State University of New York at Binghamton.

Index

Abbeele, Georges Van Den, 282n
Abjection, 61
Absence, 150, 151, 181, 268; acoustical, 157; place of, 55
Abstraction, 262, 275
Abuse, 171, 275
Achberger, Karen, 6n, 26, 28, 32n, 37, 46n, 143n, 144n, 147n, 164n, 168n
Aciman, André, 205n
Adorno, Theodor W., 133, 145n, 239n, 262, 263, 264, 279n, 280n
Aesthetic, 268
anxiety, 263; form, 267
Agnese, Barbara, 111n, 114n, 196, 204, 206n
Akhmatova, Anna, 43
Albrecht, Monika, 3, 6n, 17n, 111n, 124n, 145n, 163n, 165n, 168n, 169n, 205n, 219n, 259n, 260n, 280n, 281n, 282n, 283n
Algerian War, 211
Alienation, 150, 153, 173, 188, 269
Allegory, 41, 45, 275
Alsop, Stewart, 16n
Alterity, 212
Althusser, Louis, 263
Améry, Jean, 193
Amnesia, 5
Amplification, 64
Analysis, structural, 115
Anania-Hess, Helga, 279n

Anderson, Mark, 31n, 165n, 166n, 192, 206n, 261n
Annexation, 2, 275
Anscombe, G. E. M., 206n
Anti-Lyric, 45
Anti-Rationalism, 93
Anti-Semitism, 246
Anxiety, 263
Anzaldúa, Gloria, 195, 206n
Apollinaire, Guillaume, 47, 83, 86n, 87n, 90n;
biography of, 47-48;
readership of, 48;
techniques of writing in poetry of, 48; *"A la Santé,"* 55-56, 57-60, 61, 63, 71; figure of the chain in, 56; loss of language in, 56-57; masculine gender in, 59; repetition and doubling in, 58; *"Mirabeau Bridge,"* 50-52, 53-54, 60, 64-73, 74, 77-78, 79; amplification in, 64; asymmetry in, 49; concept of bridging in, 53; division/splitting of gendered difference in, 62; Doppelgänger(in) in, 65; masculine gender in, 49, 61; memory in, 63; relocation of subjectivity in, 73; subject position in, 47; time in, 62; uncanny encounter in, 65-66; voice in, 61,62; *"Prison-poem,"* 52-53, 54, 55
Archetype, 40

and the trope of journey, 40
Archive, 266
Arendt, Hannah, 266, 268, 282n; *Human Condition, The*, 268
Art, 263, 276
Articulation, 266
Ashcroft, B., 220n
Atzler, Elke, 167n
Aura, 262
Auschwitz, 251, 257
Austro-Hungarian Empire, 209
Authenticity, 210
Author, 128, 187
Autonomy,
  of art, 263
Avant-garde, 187

Baackmann, Susanne, 141n, 144n-145n, 146n, 167n
Bachmann, Ingeborg
  birth and biography of, 2, 248, 249; critical reception of, 26, 264, 278; dissertation of, 2, 93, 95; and emancipation movement, 138, 217; exile from Austria, 24; Frankfurt Lectures, 1, 96, 107, 133, 158, 161, 203, 226, 256, 263, 278; history in writing of, 245, 246, 247, 263-264, 265, 273; influence of Wittgenstein on, 4, 94, 95, 96, 100, 101-102, 104; life of, 1-2; memory and counter-memory in writing of, 248; trauma and war in writing of, 244, 245, 246, 247, 248; TV documentary about, 1; works of:
  Among Murderers and Madmen, 227, 228;
  "*Autumn Maneuver*," 224;
  "*Bohemia Lies by the Sea*," 27, 255;
  Book of Franza, The, 3, 5, 150, 242, 243, 254, 256-258, 266, 267, 270, 274, 275;
  "*Borrowed/Mortgaged Time*," 2, 36-37, 42, 198, 222, 224, 226, 227;
  "*Bridges, The*," 47, 49, 74-77; bridging in, 79; deconstruction of subject position in, 47-48; deconstructive reading of, 85; naming and its significance in, 78-81; plural subject in, 77; time and space in, 74, 76, 77;
  "*Children's King, A*," 33;
  "*Early Noon*," 18, 222;
  "*Every Day*," 27;
  "*Exile*," 2, 22-24; Autobiographical connection to Bachmann in, 24; language and gender in, 25; neutral gender references in, 24; unspoken in, 24-25, 28; use of male voice in, 24;
  Eyes to Wonder, dedication to Groddeck in, 123;

destruction of feminine concepts of identity in, 119; Goethe's Faust in, 121-122; interpretation of, 115, 116; narrative in, 117-118; subconscious in, 120-121, 122; textual structure in, 118; time and space in, 117; vision in, 119-120, 122, 123;
"Game is Over, The," 33, 34, 35;
Good God of Manhattan, The, 161, 196, 217;
"Great Landscape Near Vienna," 25;
"How Shall I Name Myself?" 43, 44;
"In the Storm of Roses," 39-40;
"Invocation of the Great Bear," 2, 33, 222-223;
"Journey Out," 40;
Ludwig Wittgenstein — On a Recent Chapter in the History of Philosophy, 93, 94, 106-107;
Malina, 3, 4, 22, 127, 132, 133, 196, 197, 216, 227, 228, 251, 268; absence of female in, 150, 157; autobiographical references in, 127; character of Malina in, 129; development of plot and figures in, 229-230, 232, 234; Doppelgänger in, 128; dualistic perspective on gender in, 135; écriture féminine in, 128; father as patriarchal principle in, 157; female experience and writing in, 128; female "I" in, 128-129, 132, 133, 134, 135, 136, 137; gender-specific references in, 127, 128, 130, 235; historical specificity in, 138; history and remembrance in, 221, 222; identity in, 233, 235, 236-237; loss of language, 221, 222; masculinity in, 129, 130, 137; mode of remembrance in, 228-234; music as language in, 151-153, 154, 157, 158, 159, 160; narrative perspective in, 127, 128, 129; silence in, 150, 157; theme of murder in, 154, 155-157; trauma in, 232; writing in, 231
Malina (Schroeter/Jelinek, 1991); Doppelfigur in, 173; film adaptation of, 170-171; gender in, 179; Gestik-acting in, 178, 179; "I" protagonist in, 173, 174, 175, 176, 177; murder of "I" in, 174, 177; naming in, 179-180; portrayal of alter-ego in, 178; split female protagonist in, 170, 171; symbolic and semiotic in, 175; violence of symbolic in, 173; woman as object in, 178

"No Delicacies," 2, 27, 38, 44, 158
No One May Refer to the Victim, 247
"Odysseys, The," 34, 38
"Of a Land, a River and Lakes," 19, 28, 34-35, 36, 39, 40
"On Many Nights I Ask My Mother," 20; against constraints of tradition in, 21-22; melody in, 21, 26; relationship between mother and daughter in, 21; role of gender in, 22, 25; role of mother tongue in, 21, 25; scheme and meter in, 21, 28; unspoken language in, 28
Problems and Pseudo-Problems, 96
"Psalm," 38-39, 40, 41, 222, 224
"Reklame," 161
Requiem for Fanny Goldmann, 3
"Salt and Bread," 40-42; community in, 41
Simultan, 188, 189, 204, 228; characters of Nadja and Elizabeth in, 189, 190; language in, 192, 193, 194, 195, 199, 202-203; linguistic nomadism in, 192; mother tongue in, 193, 194, 197, 204; narration and perspective in, 191, 192, 196, 198; plot elaboration of, 190, 191, 192, 195-196; question of belonging in, 192, 193; split subject and trauma in, 197, 198; textual languages in, 191, 193; theme of exile in, 191; translation in, 194, 195, 200, 202, 203, 204
Speakable and the Unspeakable, The, 93, 95, 96, 97, 102, 202
Speech to the War Blind, 122
Step Towards Gomorrha, A, 130, 131, 132, 133, 134, 138
"Stream," 250
Thirtieth Year, The, 2, 129, 133, 134, 226, 227, 228, 235
Three Paths to the Lake, 3, 118, 123, 138, 192, 193, 208; allusions to D.H. Lawrence in, 208-209; construction of femininity in, 216, 217, 218; home in, 214, 215; male gaze in, 211, 212; theme of postcoloniality in, 209-213, 214-215, 217; Western modernity in, 213
"Truly," 44
Undine Goes, 133, 161, 228
Ways of Dying, 3-5, 129, 157, 161, 173, 208, 210, 221, 235, 241, 247, 264, 269, 274; publication of, 3
Wildermuth, 226, 227
"Wood and Shavings," 223;
"You Words," 44
Baer, Ulrich, 242, 259n

Baker, G. P., 112n
Bareiss, Otto, 140n
Bartsch, Kurt, 143n, 148n, 168n-169n
Bass, Alan, 88n
Baudelaire, Charles, 103, 104, 262; *"Le Gouffre,"* 104, 120
Becker-Cantarino, Barbara, 141n-142n
Bell, Anthea, 259n
Bender, Wolfgang, 32n
Benjamin, Walter, 5, 37, 45, 187, 194, 206n, 241, 242, 245, 248, 250, 259n, 260n, 262, 266, 269, 271, 272-273, 274, 276, 277, 278, 281n, 282n; *Arcades Project*, 276; *Task of the Translator, The*, 200-204; *On Language as Such and the Language of Man*, 202; *Origin of the German Tragic Drama, The*, 276
Beethoven, Ludwig van, 152, 154
Benveniste, Emile, 173, 174, 184n, 185n
Bethman, Brenda, 170, 183n
Blanchot, Maurice, 259n
Bloom, Harold, 88n, 89n
Boa, Elizabeth, 164n
Boehm, Philip, 30n, 142n, 163n, 165n, 184n, 239n
Bogdal, Klaus-Michael, 281n
Border/borders: concept of, 19; limitations of, 27; of speech, 19, 22; speaking across, 19
Borges, Jorge Luis, 35

Bossinade, Johanna, 261n
Bostock, Anna, 219n
Bödefeld, Gerda, 206n
Böll, Heinrich, 182n
Brecht, Bertolt, 168n
Bridge, trope of, 47, 54, 61, 64, 66, 71, 82, 84, 85
Bridging, 47, 85
Brinker-Gabler, Gisela, 6n, 182n, 207n, 279n
Broe, Mary Lynn, 185n
Brokoph-Mauch, Gudrun, 146n
Bronnen, Barbara, 188, 205n
Brusatti, Otto, 165n
Bullock, Marcus, 206n
Bullock, Michael, 144n, 238n
Burial, 241, 242, 243, 244, 256, 258

Caduff, Corina, 164n, 167n
Camus, Albert, 258, 261n
Capitalism, 262
Carrière, Mathieu, 176, 178
Carnap, Rudolf, 93, 96, 100
Caruth, Cathy, 259n
Celan, Paul, 21, 83, 262
Chambers, Iain, 210, 212, 213, 219n, 220n
Chow, Rey, 213, 220n
Cixous, Hélène, 142n, 174
Class, 269, 274
    anxiety, 263
Coleridge, Samuel T., *"Rime of the Ancient Mariner, The,"* 254
Collective memory, 242, 247, 251, 257
Collectivity, 61

Index 291

Colli, Giorgio, 279n
Collins, Jane L., 219n
Commemoration, 256, 258, 268
Coming to terms with the past, 2, 266
Communism, 246
Comparative literature, 50
Conrad, Joseph,
    Heart of Darkness, 254
Consciousness, 262, 264
Cosmopolitanism, 192
Counter-memory, 248
Crisis, 119, 226
Culler, Jonathan, 279n
Culture, 188, 262, 263, 278
Curti, Lidia, 219n
Czeike, Felix, 124n

Daigger, Annette, 146n
Death, 232, 251, 256
Decadence, lyric of, 37
Décaudin, Michel, 87n
Deconstruction, 49, 54, 68, 83
Delbo, Charlotte, 248, 257, 260n, 261n
Deleuze, Gilles, 279n
De Man, Paul, 67, 89n; and Prosopopeia, 67
Denial, 270
Derrida, Jacques, 64, 88n, 119, 239n, 266, 268
Desire, 213, 278
Destruction, 192, 241, 248, 251, 253-254
Devastation, 245
Dialectic of enlightenment, 128

Dialectical, 190, 253, 262n; image, 248, 257, 266, 267, 271, 272, 276; method, 242; play, 274; relationship, 245, 263
Dialogue, 121, 192
Difference, 193, 274, 278
Disappearance, 154
Disaster, 5, 245, 255, 256
Discourse, 116, 118, 121, 150, 153, 245, 268
Dissemination, 49
Dominance, 222, 234
Doppelfigur, 173
Doppelgänger(in), 65, 128, 129, 135, 136, 137, 150, 151, 156
Doubling, 49, 59
Dreams, 176
Dusar, Ingeborg, 123, 124n, 125n, 142n, 146n, 147n
Dürer, Albrecht, *Melancholia*, 256
Düsing, Wolfgang, 239n

Eckert, Andrea, 125n
Eco, Umberto, 124n, 125n
Ego, alter, 172, 175, 176, 177, 179, 181; transcendental, 173
Eichmann, Adolf, 268
Eiland, Howard, 259n
Eliot, T.S., 46n
Enlightenment, 128, 211
Epic, 34, 35; hero, 37, 40
Epistemology, 115
Equality, 130
Ethics, 102, 103
Exile, 24, 41, 188, 191, 215;

language of, 2
Fairy Tales, 33, 133, 251;
    Grimm's, 34, 35;
    subversive readings
    of, in Bachmann's poetry,
    33-34
Fascism, in human relations, 4
Father, as patriarchal
    principle, 157
Federal Republic, 127, 241
Fehl, Peter, 238n
Felman, Shoshana, 243,
    259n; *Testimony*, 243
Femininity, 172; as
    difference, 178; as social
    construct, 172, 179
Feminism, 174, 270
Feminist, 170, 265;
    interrogation, 270;
    perspective, 120-121
Filkins, Peter, 6n, 31n, 46n,
    91n, 163n, 166n, 238n,
    259n, 281n
Fitzgerald, Zelda, 149n; *Save
    Me the Waltz*, 139
Forgetting, 119, 252, 269
Forgiveness, 266, 267, 268,
    271
Foucault, Michel, 266
Fragmentation, 192, 226,
    250, 262, 265, 274
Frank, Manfred, 239n
Franke, Nicole, 123, 139. 237
Frankfurt School, 269
Freud, Sigmund, 157, 165n,
    241
Friedberg, Lilian, 7, 16n, 280n
Friedrichsmeyer, Sara, 280n
Frisch, Max, 144n, 165n;
    Gantenbein, 131, 132
Fynsk, Christopher, 267,
    281n, 283n

Gandhi, Leela, 212, 220n
Garber, Frederick, 6n
Gaze, male, in cinema, 178
GDR, 241, 247
Geipel, Ines, 259n, 260n
Gender, 127, 128, 131, 133,
    137, 138, 179, 209, 269,
    270, 274; construction of,
    172; dualistic thinking in,
    134; equality, 130;
    relations, 216
Genre, 42; phenomenology
    of, 38
Gerhard, Ute, 220n
Gestik-acting, 178-179
Giacometti, Alberto, 251
Gilbert, Mary Fran, 125n,
    205n, 219n, 238n
Gill, Stephen, 219n
Gleichauf, Ingeborg, 183n
Goethe, Johann Wolfgang,
    125n; *Faust Part Two*, 121-122
Goya, Francisco de, *Kronos
    Devours His Children*, 120
Gölz, Sabine, 32n, 86n, 88n,
    91n, 198, 206n
Göttsche, Dirk, 3, 6n, 17n,
    111n, 124n, 145n, 146n-147n, 164n, 165n, 166n,
    168n, 205n, 219n, 239n,
    259n, 260n, 281n

Greber, Erika, 205n
Green, Leonard, 279n
Greuner, Suzanne, 163n, 164n
Griffiths, G., 220n
Grimkowski, Sabine, 169n
Grimm Brothers, 34, 35, 261n; *Juniper Tree, The*, 251
Groddeck, Georg, 121, 125n; *Book of the It*, 123
Guattari, Félix, 279n
Guilt, 223, 246
Gürtler, Christa, 141n

Hacker, P. M. S., 112n
Haller, Gerda, documentary by, 1
Heidegger, Martin, 93, 95, 103, 108, 110n, 111n, 119; *Being and Time*, 93
Heimannsberg, Barbara, 260n
Heinrich, Margareta, 125n
Henze, Hans Werner, 159, 166n
Herder, Johann Gottfried von, 42
Hermand, Jost, 124n
Hermeneutic, marxist, 269
Herminghouse, Patricia, 183n
Heurck, Jan van, 168n
Higonnet, Margaret, 86n
Hilzinger, Sonja, 260n
Historical, 248, 265, 272, 273, 276
Historicity, 263
Historiofictional memoir, 5
History, 4, 5, 39, 40, 43, 188, 221, 224, 245, 246, 247, 248, 249, 250, 256, 257, 258, 263, 264, 265, 266, 267, 269, 271, 272, 273, 274, 275, 276, 277, 278; and its significance, 121, 123; links between poetics and, 38; repressed, 243, 247
Hitler, Adolf, 247, 277
Hofmannsthal, Hugo von, 108, 157-158, 165n; *Difficult Man, The*, 158; *Everyman*, 158; *Lord Chandos Letter, The*, 151, 263; *Salzburg Great Theatre of the World, The*, 158
Holocaust, 2, 277
Home, 210, 243, 255
Homer, 35
Horkheimer, Max, 133, 145n
Horsley, Ritta Jo, 143n, 145n
Hotz, Constanze, 167n
Hölderlin, Johann Christian Friedrich, 39, 43, 200, 201
Höller, Hans, 26, 31n, 141n, 142n, 144n, 148n, 168n, 238n, 239n
Hsu, Linda, 109
Hullot-Kentor, Robert, 279n
Huppert, Isabelle, 170, 171, 178, 183n-184n
Hurley, Robert, 279n
Hübner, Adolf, 113n
Hyde Greet, Anne, 86n
Hysteria, 243

Identification, 132, 174, 269, 274, 275

Identity, 117, 132, 222, 226, 274; subjective, 120
Ideological belief, 271; consequences, 272
Ideology, 4, 262
Imprisonment, 53, 54, 55
Inferiority, 132
Ingram, Angela, 185n
Insightful remembrance, 242, 248, 268
Internalization, 176
Interpretation, 115, 119, 272
Interpreter, 192
Irigaray, Luce, 174

Jameson, Fredric, 262, 263, 265, 269, 272, 274, 276, 277, 279n, 280n, 282n, 283n, 284n
Jelinek, Elfriede, 168n, 170, 171, 172, 179, 182n, 183n, 184n
Jephcott, Edmund, 145n
Jennings, Michael W., 206n
Jordan, Christian, 125n
Jouissance, 177
Journey, 40, 42, 150

Kampits, Peter, 110n
Kerckvoorde, Colette van, 31n
Kienlechner, Toni, 129
Kierkegaard, Søren, 91n
Kilmartin, Terence, 146n
Klaubert, Annette, 166n, 240n
Klein, Richard, 279n
Kohn-Waechter, Gudrun, 142n, 146n, 147n, 148n

Komar, Kathleen L., 148n
Koschel, Christine, 3, 6n, 31n, 86n, 110n, 125n, 126n, 140n, 145n, 163n, 184n, 206n, 219n, 238n, 239n, 259n, 260n, 279n, 283n
Köndgen, Cornelia, 125n
Kraft, Viktor, 96
Kristeva, Julia, 88n, 164n, 174, 175, 180, 184n, 185n, 205n, 266, 268; *Strangers to Ourselves*, 193
Kunze, Barbara, 166n
Kyburz, Mark, 281n

Lacan, Jacques, 174, 182n, 185n, 275
Lacoue-Labarthe, Philip, 265, 280n
Lamont, Rosette C., 260n
Lane, Helen R., 279n
Language, 1, 2, 59, 94, 98, 107, 108, 128, 151, 153, 154, 159, 160, 172, 174, 175, 188, 189, 191, 192, 193, 194, 196, 201, 202, 203, 211, 215, 222, 225, 227, 235, 258, 263, 264, 266, 268, 274, 275, 276; analysis of, 98; and borders, 19; and ideology, 4; and its connection to history, 5; and naming, 43, 44; as instrument of dominance, 222; complexity of, 49; limits of, 26, 29, 103, 106; logical form versus ordinary form

of, 98-100; loss of, 221, 222, 223; misconceptions concerning, 96, 105; of disaster, 5; poetic, 47, 48, 60; pure, 204, 222; role of, 96; shaped by repressed experience, 245; spoken, 116; unspoken of, 18; utopian, 26, 204

Language games, 94, 100, 107, 194, 197; multiplicity of, 105

Language poets, 45

Laub, Dori, 243, 259n; *Testimony*, 243

Law of the Father, 177

Lawrence, D. H., 210, 216, 219n; *Woman Who Rode Away, The*, 208, 209

Lensing, Leo A., 149n

Lennox, Sara, 110n, 111n, 113n, 142n, 280n

Leonhard, Sigrun D., 146n, 148n

Levin, David Michael, 219n; *Modernity and Hegemony of Vision*, 211

Limit, 26, 29, 103, 106, 243

Linguistic schizophrenia, 195; nomadism, 192

Lindemann, Eva U., 164n, 167n

Literary criticism, 262

Literature, 264, 277

Logic, 100, 103; propositions of, 97

Logical form, 98-100; positivism, 96

Logocentric certitude; undermining of, 5

Loss, 53, 54, 61, 68, 84, 189, 193, 221, 222, 223, 247, 248, 250, 263; location of, 55

Lukács, Georg, 210, 219n

Lutz, Catherine A., 219n

Lyotard, Jean-François, 269, 282n

Lyric, 37, 38, 39, 42, 43; allegory and, 41; blend of melos and voice, 39; modern, 42; poetry, 19; speech, 222; voice, 45

Mahler, Gustav, 157, 166n

Mahony Stoljar, Margaret, 219n

Majer O'Sickey, Ingeborg, 6n, 184n, 185n, 186n

Malaise, personal, 210; sexual, 210

Male gaze, 178, 212

Mapping, 264

Marcus, Jane, 177, 185n

Marx, Karl, 269, 274

Marxist thought, 269

Masculinity, 171

Masochistic tendencies, 171

Mayer, Hans, 140n, 141n, 166n-167n

Mayer, Mathias, 205n

McGuinness, Brian, 113n

McLaughlin, Kevin, 259n

Meaning, 171

Meek, Mary Elizabeth, 184n

Melos, 39, 42-43

Memmert, Günter, 124n

Memory, 5, 35, 61, 62, 63,

79, 210, 224, 225, 226, 228, 235, 237, 241, 243, 244, 247, 248, 250, 258, 266, 268, 269, 271, 272, 277; collective, 242, 247, 251, 257; historical, 248
Metacommentary, 263
Metaphor, 36, 47, 68, 242
Metonym, 37
Meyer, Eva, 86n
Middleton, Christopher, 279n
Millett, Kate, 219n; *Sexual Politics*, 208
Mise-en-scène, 177
Misrecognition, 174
Mitscherlich, Alexander and Margarete, 238n; *Inability to Mourn, The*, 223
Modern experience, 269; lyric, 42
Modernism, 38, 137, 209, 211, 221, 235, 262, 263, 269
Moi, Toril, 185n
Moncrieff, Scott C. K., 146n
Monologue, interior, 191; narrated, 191
Montinari, Mazzino, 279n
Monuments, 246
Moore, G.E., 98, 111n
Morality, 108
Morries, Leslie, 6n
Morrison, Tony, 4
Mother tongue, 188, 194, 197, 215
Mulvey, Laura, 178, 185n
Murder 154, 155-156, 157, 161, 174
Music, 150, 151-152, 157, 158, 159; Italian, marks, 152-153; language of, 154, 160; use of, as utopian symbol, 26
Mühlbauer-interview, 135, 136
Müller, Inge, 241, 242, 244, 260n, 261n; *"Beneath the Rubble I, II, III,"* 252-256; *"Rubble 45,"* 250-251, 252; biography of, 249, 250, 251; history in writing of, 245, 246, 247; memory and counter-memory in writing of, 248; theme of burial in writing of, 244; trauma and war in writing of, 244, 245, 246, 247, 248
Münster, Clemens, 3, 6n, 31n, 86n, 110n, 126n, 145n, 163n, 184n, 206n, 238n, 259n, 279n

Names, 97, 121
Naming, 43-44, 78-81, 116-117, 252; allegories of, 43, 44, 45
Narrative, 35, 116, 117-118, 119, 123, 132, 177, 226; national, 243
Narrator, 151, 152, 154, 157
National Socialism, 214, 221, 222, 224, 227, 246, 247
Nazi, 277; occupation, 2, 244, 246
Negative Remembrance, 268
Neo-Orientalist anxiety, 213

Neo-Positivists, 93, 96;
   approach of, 98;
   Bachmann's work and, 95;
   position of, 94
New Capitalism, 189, 190
Nietzsche, Friedrich, 83, 266, 279n
Nomadism, 192
Novalis, 210, 219n
Nuremberg Trials, 267
Nyman, Heikki, 112n, 114n

Ocularcentrism, 211
Oedipal triangle, 174
Oetrasch, Wilhelm, 142n
Ohl, Hubert, 146n-147n
Ohloff, Franke, 140n
Oppression, 256
Origin, 210, 250, 276
Other, 274
Otherness, 209
Overdetermination, 263, 264, 265, 274

Pain, 223
Pascal, Blaise, 103-104
Passage, Charles E., 125n
Past, 192, 193, 223, 224, 226, 242, 247, 248, 254, 268, 271, 276; personal and national, 4; and present, 5
Patriarchal discourse, 150, 153; order, 274
Patriarchy, 4, 5, 132, 175; critique of, 172
Pattillo-Hess, John, 142n, 167n
Peace, 245
Perloff, Marjorie, 22, 31n, 111n, 206n
Petrasch, Wilhelm, 167n
Phenomenology, 38
Philosophy, 210, 273; as critique of language, 97; Bachmann's critique of, 96, 100; logical turn of, 97; questions concerning the discipline of, 94, 97; therapeutic vision of, 94
Pichl, Robert, 3, 6n, 124n, 125n
Pietrass, Richard, 261n
Plath, Sylvia; *Bell Jar, The*, Bachmann's draft on, 3; "Lady Lazarus," 1
Plato, *Timaeus*, 175
Play of signifier, 49
Poe, Edgar Allan, 38, 42, 43
Poésie pure, la, 37
Poet, 45, 53, 54, 55, 57, 60, 62, 63, 64
Poetic, 253, 265, 268; traditional, conceptions, 222; effect, 115, 119; function, 225; language, 47, 48, 60, 263; speech, 226
Poetry, 19
Political, 263, 265
Positivism, logical, 96
Postcoloniality, 209
Postmodern, 42, 210, 277; man, 189; poets, 45
Poststructuralism, 128
Presence, 55
Present, 242, 248, 254
Presentation, 267, 270, 277
Pressure, cultural, on

women, 172
Pre-symbolic speech, 255
Primal scene, 210
Primitivism, 210
Probst, Gerhard R., 165n
Projection, 132
Protagonist, split female, 170, 171
Proust, Marcel, 146n
Psychoanalysis, 174, 227, 269
Psychoanalytic relation, 270

Race, 209, 269, 274
Reader, 123, 222, 223, 224, 274, 275
Reading, 68, 73, 272, 275, 278; fleeting moment of, 67; mode of, 68
Recollections, 243
Reed, Carol, 155, 157, 165n; *Third Man, The*, 155-157
Reich-Ranicki, Marcel, 118, 124n, 125n
Reification, 264
Remembering, 4, 5, 241, 250, 254
Remembrance, 221, 223, 224, 228, 229, 230, 231, 232, 233, 234, 235, 242, 247, 248, 255, 266; collective, 226, 227; subjective, 226, 227
Remmler, Karen, 6n, 261n, 266, 268, 270, 271, 281n, 282n, 283n; *Waking the Dead. Correspondences between Walter Benjamin's Concept of Remembrance and Ingeborg Bachmann's "Ways of Dying,"* 256
Repetition, 268
Representation, cinematic, 173
Repression, 243, 248, 263, 265
Resistance, 223, 225, 234, 237, 246, 266; cultural, 278
Rhees, R., 206n
Rilke, Rainer Maria, 38, 43; *Dinggedichte*, 43
Rituals, 246, 247
Rodais, Chantal, 182n
Roeder, Anke, 172, 174, 184n
Rohn-Waechter, Gudrun, 169n
Roloff, Hans-Gert, 124n
Romantic Movement, 133
Rosen, Phillip, 184n
Roth, Joseph, 215, 220n
Roudiez, Leon S., 88n, 206n
Röhnelt, Inge, 146n
Römhild, Dorothee, 182n
Ruin, 241, 250, 251, 277
Rupp, Heinz, 124n
Russell, Bertrand, 96-7, 98, 110n

Sappho, 42, 43
Sattmann, Peter, 125n
Sartre, Jean Paul, 269
Sauter, Josef-Hermann, 205n
Schizophrenia, 179, 195
Schmid-Bortenschlager, Sigrid, 142n, 148n
Schmidt, Christoph J., 260n
Schmidt, Tanja, 125n
Schneider, Jost, 164n, 189,

300 Index

205n
Schnitzler, Arthur, 197
Scholz, Rüdiger, 281n
Schönberg, Arnold, 153-154
Schöne, Albrecht, 122, 125n
Schroeter, Werner, 161, 168n, 170, 171, 172, 176, 177, 178, 179, 180, 183n, 184n; *Death of Maria Malibran, The*, 172, 183n; *Eika Katapa*, 183n; *Kingdom of Naples*, 183n; *Palermo or Wolfsburg*, 183n; *Queen, The*, 183n; *Two*, 184n
Schwarzer, Alice, 182n
Schweppenhäuser, Hermann, 259n
Scopophilia, 178, 181
Sebald, W. G., 253, 259n; *Natural History of Destruction, The*, 241
Sennett, Richard, 205n; *Corrosion of Character*, 189
Seeing, 122
Seem, Mark, 279n
Seiderer, Ute, 182n, 183n, 185n
Self, ideal, 174; pre-linguistic, 174; symbolic, 173, 174
Self-manifestation, theme of, in Wittgenstein, 100
Sexuality, 209
Sheppard, Richard, 164n
Sheridan, Alan, 185n
Shoah, 243, 246, 251, 256, 258, 265, 269, 271, 274, 275
Sieglohr, Ulrike, 179, 184n, 186n
Sign, 175
Signifier/Signified, 49, 173, 275
Silence, 150, 151, 173, 222, 243, 244, 245, 257, 258; articulation of, 4; as reaction to scientism, 104; importance and permanence of, 2; language of, 1; value of, 102
Skepticism, 95
Smock, Ann, 259n
Sollers, Philippe, 173, 184n
Speaking, 19, 121, 122
Spectacle, 177
Spectator, 170, 177
Speech, 19, 22
Speechlessness, 151, 157, 255, 256
Spiel, Hilde, 167n
Spiesecke, Hartmut, 164n
Steiner, George, 2, 187, 202, 206n
Stephan, Inge, 145n
Stevens, Wallace, 38, 43
Stillmark, Alexander, 124n
Stoll, Andrea, 6n, 164n, 167n, 238n
Strauss, Richard, 154, 158, 165n
Structural, 115; forms, 116
Structure, textual, 118
Struggle, 266
Stuby, Anna Maria, 145n
Subconscious, 120
Subject, 50, 58, 79, 190; diasporic, 193;

disembodied, 216;
dissolution of, 96;
feminine, 49; masculine,
178; multilingual, 189;
plural, 77, 82; poetic, 48,
49, 50, 80; speaking, 71,
173, 174, 175, 177
Subjectivity, 73, 122, 174,
223, 242, 247; and identity
of "I," 42; as difference,
171; female, 160;
gendered, 171
Sublimation, through
language, 107
Suez Crisis, 211
Suffering, 172, 215, 253, 269,
275
Suhrkamp Publishing House,
127
Summerfield, Ellen, 239n
Superposition, 58; effect of,
49
Swiderska, M., 114n
Symbolic, 175, 176, 177, 179
Syntax, cinematic, 170, 173

Testimony, 267
Thiem, Ulrich, 238n
Third Reich, 247
Third World, 211, 212
Thürmer-Rohr, Christina,
143n, 144n, 148n
Tiedemann, Rolf, 239n, 259n
Tiffin, H., 220n
Time, 36-37, 39; and history,
37, 39; event in, 62;
fragmented, 40
Torgovnick, Marianna, 212,
214, 219n; *Going Primitive*,
210; *Primitive Passions: Men,
Women, and the Quest for
Ecstasy*, 210
Tradition, poetic, 48
Transcendental ego, 173;
homelessness, 210
Translation, 193
Trauma, 232, 241, 242, 243,
244, 245, 246, 247, 248,
250, 251, 252, 253, 255,
256, 257, 258, 265
Treude, Andrea, 169n
Trezise, Thomas, 280n
Truth, 225
Tucker, William, 280n

Uncanny, the 195
Unconscious, 263, 275
Unspeakable, the, 18, 27, 202
Utopia, 228; fragment of,
235; language of, 204

Verfremdungseffekt, 180
Victim, 121, 243, 246, 247,
256, 258, 268, 274, 275
Victimization, 269
Vienna Circle, 93, 95, 96
Viennese modernity, 108;
society, 275
Vietnam War, 211
Violence, 170, 173, 174
Voice, 39, 45

Waldheim-Affair, 246, 247
Wallner, Friedrich, 125n
War, 253, 254, 256, 258;
concept of, in Bachmann's
poetry and prose, 26
Weber, Dietrich, 31n

Webster, Mary, 182n
Weidenbaum, Inge von, 3, 6n, 31n, 86n, 110n, 125n, 126n, 140n, 145n, 163n, 167n, 184n, 206n, 219n, 238n, 239n, 259n, 260n, 279n, 283n
Weigel, Sigrid, 135, 142n, 143n, 145n, 146n, 148n, 264, 265, 266, 267, 268, 271, 280n, 281n, 282n, 283n
Weimar, 277
Westermann, Klaus, 220n
Whiteread, Rachel, *Holocaust-Denkmal*, 277
Winch, P., 112n
Witness, 243, 251, 255, 256, 258, 267
Witte, Karsten, 182n
Wittgenstein, Ludwig, 6n, 29, 93, 94, 95, 96, 98, 99, 101, 103, 107, 108, 110n, 111n, 112n, 113n, 114n, 119, 120, 157, 159, 187, 204, 206n, 271; *Blue Book, The*, 94; *Notebooks*, 102; *Philosophical Investigations*, 93, 94, 95, 96, 97, 100, 105, 106, 202-203; *Tractatus Logico-Philosophicus*, 4, 93, 94, 95, 96, 97, 98, 99, 100, 102, 104, 105, 106, 107, 202
Wolf, Christa, 161, 165n, 168n; *Kindheitsmuster*, 247
World War II., 265, 268
Wright, Georg H. von, 112n, 113n
Writer, 177
Writing, 173, 231, 237, 243, 248, 271, 273, 274, 275, 277
Wuchterl, Kurt, 113n

Yegenoglu, Meyda, 212, 220n

Zadow, Ingeborg von, 184n
Zanger, Abby, 90n
Zantop, Susanne, 183n, 280n
Zisselsberger, Markus, 182n
Zohn, Harry, 282n

Compiled by Julia Friday